The Man, The Record

The Life and Times of Clifford J. Dickman

The Man, The Record

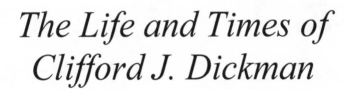

The Life and Times of Clifford J. Dickman

Henry J. Dickman

To Grandma and Grandpa

CONTENTS

INTRODUCTION

The inspiration for this book came, fittingly enough, from another book: *American Priest*, which chronicles the life of the longtime Notre Dame president Fr. Theodore Hesburgh, C.S.C. [1] The biography introduces the Hesburgh of national renown—friend of presidents and chairman of the U.S. Civil Rights Commission. So too does it study Hesburgh the professor and priest—who dedicated his entire life to the institution that was his home and to the religious order that was his family. By the end of the story, the significance of the biography's title is evident. Fr. Hesburgh epitomized a distinctly *American* brand of Catholicism: pragmatic in application, engaged with secular politics and culture, and practiced at both the local and national levels.

The idea for this book may have been stoked by reading the full account of Fr. Hesburgh's years, but the spark behind it was *American Priest*'s introduction, in which the author explained the process of interviewing his subject. Hesburgh and his biographer spent several days at Notre Dame's Land o' Lakes property in Wisconsin, fishing by day and looking back on a life of complexity and consequence by night. For me, the prospect of interviewing such an all-American figure, sharing his story, and using it to convey a larger narrative about both a local community and our nation as a whole was positively intriguing. But whose life, I wondered to myself, is so rich with these kinds of experiences that it could be the subject of this kind of book? The question virtually answered itself: the life of my own grandfather, Clifford Dickman.

If you had to sum up Cliff Dickman's life in a phrase, it would be "the American dream." From being raised on an Indiana farm, earning his way into college on athletic talent, serving in the United States Army, raising a family of eight children with his wife of more than 65 years, growing a local business, engaging in a lifetime of service to his home community and church, and leading a city government as mayor, Dickman is one of the classic cases of an all-American life.

What is it that makes these life stories "all-American"? Why do we so value a gritty upbringing, military service, feats of athleticism, bold entrepreneurship, and community engagement? It is because these experiences—which are so often fraught with hardship and risk—form the bedrock of a life well lived in the United States. Hard times in the cornfields and on the battlefields teach us industriousness. When we miss the game-winning free throws or our enterprises turn upside-down, we gain resilience. In transacting business or engaging in politics, we learn to show fairness toward our fellow citizens. And throughout it all, we express charity toward our neighbors, by which we make our common home a better place for all to live. These virtues—hard work, resilience, fairness, and charity—lie at the foundation of all that is good in our country.

The all-American life is not only defined by these virtues; it is a product of the way we acquire them. In the Old World from which we broke away in 1776, a "great life" meant being born into an aristocratic family, assuming a high military rank, or succeeding to a position of nobility removed from the masses. But this was not so in the New World. The great American life is a product of experience, not inheritance. It is lived by someone who makes something out of nothing, who rises from the low ranks to the heights. It is not an easy path. As Theodore Roosevelt once said: "[I]t is only through strife, through hard and dangerous endeavor, that we shall ultimately win the goal of true national greatness." [2] Yet importantly, these hardy, character-forming experiences are open to anyone, and that's why the all-American life has been lived by such an eclectic group of citizens—from a Notre Dame priest, to immigrants born in faraway lands, to a farm boy from eastern Indiana.

My goal for this book is to tell the story of an American life well lived, and through the lens of that life, to renew respect for our national virtues and the experiences that produce them. Clifford Dickman has undeniably lived a good life: he has bounced back from hard times, exercised a sunup-to-sundown work ethic, held unwavering respect for all people, and dedicated himself to the betterment of his homeland. But we would be remiss to attribute his life story to accident, or to simply think of him as a "good egg." Rather, Dickman's opportunities and teachers—and even more so, his trials and opponents—cultivated a man of character, and that character proves worthy of our study.

Dickman's story presents us with a few issues to ponder, and as our subject himself would do, I'll address them directly. First is the role of good fortune in Dickman's life. While the positive moments he enjoyed were undeniably attributable to his efforts, so too did they often grow out of circumstances beyond his control—sometimes by providence, other times by luck. From his earliest days, he earned the nickname "Cooley Boy" because the family's landlords, the Cooleys, doted on Cliff over and above his siblings. The "Cooley Boy" would enjoy strokes of good fortune throughout his life, such as his unique service in the Army and the gift of good health for himself and his family. Does that diminish the moral force of his accomplishments? Or does it make him less worthy of our study, since we have no agency in replicating his luck in our own lives?

No to both, in my view. First, we must credit Dickman for recognizing that he has enjoyed a life of many blessings. Successful people can easily fall into the trap of believing in total self-sufficiency, when in fact we all are highly dependent on God and one another. We can steer our destiny, but we are not its master. Dickman will be the first to tell you that. Second, we must credit him again because he didn't let life's opportunities pass him by. He seized those chances and built on them, even when they came with hardship. For example, while there's no doubt that Dickman was born with more physical talent than most, he became a great athlete only because of the tireless effort he poured into practice. Third and finally, we must also bear in mind that Dickman absorbed plenty of misfortune in his day too—family heartbreak, political collapse, and business stagnation. When luck ran out, he persisted. That is the true test of character.

Allow me to address another theme raised by this book. As the book's title suggests, Clifford Dickman is a certain type of man that is in short supply these days: he is a manly man. Manliness is a trait that has become much maligned in modern America, but this is either because manliness is misunderstood or because it has been distorted into some other pernicious thing by poor examples. But properly understood, manliness is a collection of virtues—specifically, those which tend to be more prominent in men. All virtues lie at the midpoint between two extremes, and the manly virtues are no different.[3] Manliness is neither belligerent nor timid; it is assertive. It is neither reckless nor lethargic; it is spirited. And it is neither overbearing nor selfish; it is chivalrous.

Dickman's virtuous manliness is on display throughout this book. Trained to milk cows as a small boy, he spent his entire life working with his hands. A product of contact sports, he made his way through the world by outhustling competition and staying tough through thick and thin. Attuned to measured risk-taking after purchasing a business at 28 years old, he later staked his own finances and reputation on vying for elected office. And inspired by the example of his father-figure older brother, he was a determined protector and provider for his own family. In observing the life of someone who displayed true, virtuous manliness, perhaps we might respect its inescapable and positive influence in the lives of men and women today.

Finally, this book pays tribute to Clifford Dickman's home, which is my own home too: Richmond, Indiana. Richmond has a venerable history that few appreciate—I certainly didn't during my younger years. Chapter 2 explains the development of the city up to 1930, when our protagonist was born. Later chapters offer vignettes of Richmond's continued change over the twentieth century through the lens of Dickman and his family.

But just as I hope this book evokes themes that extend beyond the life of one man, so too do I hope its ramifications transcend one town. During the forty or so years that are the primary focus of this book (approx. 1955–1995), Richmond was emblematic of many Rust Belt communities of the day. The city, which had historically been a manufacturing powerhouse, was coping with the pain of heavy job losses and a contracting population from its peak of about 40,000. But throughout all this time, Richmond was a paradigm of strong local society whose citizens knew, trusted, and depended on each other. Whether as a businessman, a politician, or simply an engaged citizen, Clifford Dickman was a leader in stitching that community together.

Earlier, I stated that charity toward others in one's community is a core American virtue. This may surprise some. Aren't we the nation of individualism, of pulling yourself up by the bootstraps? Indeed, we are an individualistic nation in that we generally assume responsibility for our own needs, rather than relying on the state. But we are not fully autonomous units without any duties or obligations to each other. Clifford Dickman and his Richmond contemporaries wouldn't have recognized such a lonely, self-centered society. They expected their fellow citizens to embrace personal accountability, but when an honest neighbor was in need, they didn't hesitate to lend a hand.

Perhaps the best display of the dichotomy between these two visions of America—hyper-individualism versus a society of good neighbors—is Frank Capra's classic *It's a Wonderful Life*, the greatest film our country has ever produced. The movie's villain, Mr. Potter, is a greedy banker who cares only about money and power—foreclosing on his clients without mercy and herding his fellow Bedford Falls citizens into slums to keep them under his thumb. At the end of the movie, we see a counterfactual Bedford Falls that is completely under Potter's control, and it's a depressed, spiritually bankrupt place: old men are alcoholics, bar fights routinely break out on the streets, and the downtown is dotted with strip clubs. But in the real-world Bedford Falls, there's one institution that Potter doesn't control: the Building and Loan, which is run by the movie's hero, George Bailey. Because of George's trust in his fellow townsmen and his personal sacrifices for them in their hours of need, the people of Bedford Falls are able to escape Potter's slums and purchase their own homes. In other words, George's neighborly attitude enables his fellow citizens to take control of their own lives, and the entire community flourishes as a result.

Richmond embraced the Bailey view of American society. Clifford Dickman and his contemporaries were remarkably involved in building up their home community—not only for themselves, but for their neighbors. They responded to each other's needs in times of emergency, and they sacrificed their limited time to all manner of community associations: lunchtime clubs, trade groups, political parties, men's and women's clubs, youth athletic contests, fundraising initiatives, and advisory committees, to name a few. Their work through these associations bore much fruit: they raised millions of dollars for community causes, built houses of worship, cheered on their high school sports teams, hosted grand parades, and improved social services.

Dickman brought his good-neighbor philosophy to government when he eventually became Richmond's mayor. He rejected the accumulation of power in the federal government, but he didn't believe in dismantling all order and authority. Rather, he led the charge to bring government closer to home. He disapproved of Richmond's reliance on the federal and state governments for revenue, so he repeatedly called for municipalities to have their own authority to collect taxes. Even within the city itself, Dickman tried to localize problem solving, calling on citizens to form associations to care for their own neighborhoods, rather than relying on city employees to do all the work for them. He understood that for communities to thrive, people can't simply expect others to solve their problems for them. They have to be responsible for finding the solutions—often by banding together with those close to them.

This book raises the same inquiry that lights up our movie screens every Christmas season: how can we build our homes into strong, vibrant communities like Bedford Falls? My hope is that through studying the dedicated civic leadership of Dickman and his Richmond contemporaries, we might glean some answers.

For all my aspirations about the larger themes and theories that animate this work, my primary aim is to record the story of Clifford Dickman. His life and times are representative of much, but far more importantly, he is concretely responsible for shaping *one* family, *one* church, *one* business, and *one* city. Those entities deserve to know his story, which is their story too. And rest assured, it's an entertaining one. When Dickman regales someone with the tales of his life, the listener can't help but laugh, shed a tear, shake his head in disbelief, and wonder. It's a heavy burden to tell the story of a storyteller, and I hope to have done him justice.

This book is also a profile of Cliff's wife and my grandmother, Martha Jane, who has likewise lived a great American life. Like Cliff, she developed proven character through a strict, though warm, upbringing. She experienced tremendous blessing in her lifetime, but she also knew heart-wrenching loss. Throughout it all, she devoted every fiber of her being to family and community.

Martha Jane and her husband were a team. Cliff was the family's public face, and this was possible only because of Martha Jane's work and sacrifice—for it was she who financed the young couple in their early days, she who was instrumental in generating respect for the family in the community, and she who ran their house: the foundation of their entire lives. If Clifford Dickman showed the breadth of the family's attitude of service through his community involvement, then Martha Jane showed its depth by intensely ministering to those living under their roof. The latter made the former possible.

Allow me to close with a roadmap and a promise for the pages that lie ahead. While the book generally proceeds in a chronological fashion, its organization is by theme. That means a chapter covering one topic might end in 2000, while the next begins back in 1976. This is intentional. Many biographies are about people who've achieved one great thing, so it makes sense for the book to strictly track the timeline of that one thing and, along the way, fill in the gaps about other aspects of the subject's life. That's not the type of subject we have here. The fine achievements and amusing stories of Clifford Dickman's life arose from many domains. Accordingly, it makes the most sense to consider these domains distinctly, even if there is some temporal whiplash (my apologies).

And now for my promise to you, the reader. Though this is the work of a grandson writing about his grandfather, I have not embellished Clifford's story or biased my commentary in his favor. I have given him a fair shake, and he wouldn't expect anything different. But while a reputable, honest biography must treat its subject even-handedly, a biographer undoubtedly reaches a final verdict on the subject's life. I'll reveal my own verdict up-front: I admire my grandfather, much more so after researching and writing this book. I suspect that by the time you reach the end of the story, you will too.

1

THE FARM

In the heart of America, the east and west forks of the Whitewater River converge and wind south to the Ohio River. At their juncture in rural Franklin County, Indiana lies the town of Brookville. It was there on January 10, 1930, that Joseph and Anna Dickman welcomed their seventh child, Clifford John Dickman, into their family.

Joseph and Anna Dickman were not natives of Brookville; they had moved there in the late 1920s from their shared birthplace of Oldenburg, Indiana. Only about 15 miles away from Brookville, Oldenburg had been founded by immigrants from Oldenburg, Germany in the mid-nineteenth century. The German Oldenburg, located in the northwest corner of the country, remained predominantly Catholic even after the Protestant Reformation.[1] That identity became one of the defining features of the Hoosier Oldenburg. Its numerous Gothic-style Catholic churches with tall steeples earned it the nickname "the Village of Spires," and today, a plaque in the town commemorates a Catholic priest as the founder of Oldenburg.[2]

Like many who were born in Oldenburg, Joseph Henry Dickman descended from German immigrants. All

1

four of Joseph's grandparents were born in northwest Germany, immigrated to Oldenburg, farmed the land there, and had children. Clemens Dickman and Louise Weber—Joseph's father and mother—were born in the Village of Spires in the 1850s.[3] Their son Joseph, born October 13, 1893, grew up with four siblings in a farming family, and after completing eighth grade, he left school behind and took up the family business of farming.

Joseph Dickman's wife, Anna Tebbe, likewise came of German stock. Her grandfather, William Tebbe, Sr., immigrated to Indiana from Germany as a young man and married 15-year-old Josephina Ferkenhoff, the daughter of fellow German immigrants living in Oldenburg. William Sr. and Josephina carried on the family's farming tradition, acquiring 120 acres of their own outside the village. Their son William Tebbe, Jr., married Anna Marie Gruenker, and on January 3, 1897, William Jr. and Anna Marie became parents to Anna Elizabeth Tebbe.[4] She, like her future husband, gave up school after eighth grade to commit herself full-time to the needs of her family.

As lifelong residents of the same small town, Joseph Dickman and Anna Tebbe surely knew each other for most of childhood and adolescence. They were wed at Holy Family Catholic Church in Oldenburg on November 20, 1918. Their first married adventure was shared employment on a local farm outside the Village of Spires, and children soon arrived. Their first, Kathleen, was born in January 1920, and eight more followed: Dolores, Floyd, Bernadine, Joann, Jerome, Clifford, Susann, and Corrine.

In the mid-1920s, the young Dickmans left Oldenburg behind forever and headed to Brookville. After a brief stint at the Masters family farm, they settled on the farm of Charles and Ella Cooley. Not having enough money to buy land of their own, Joseph and Anna worked as tenant farmers. In exchange for their farming work, the Cooleys paid the Dickmans and allowed them to board in their house. It was a sensible arrangement considering that Charles and Ella had no children of their own. It was in the Cooley house that Cliff was born in early 1930.

Clifford entered the world at a bleak time in American history. The stock market had suffered an unprecedented collapse just a few months earlier, instigating the Great Depression. While all Americans felt its toll, farming families in the Midwest lived more securely than most. Demand and prices for farm products were low, but a farmer could at least guarantee food for his family—something that urbanites couldn't take for granted. And the tragic Dust Bowl storms that eviscerated so many other American farms left eastern Indiana untouched. The Dickmans and the Cooleys weathered the Depression well.

Joseph and Anna had their hands full. They raised nine children in a family that toiled all day, six days a week. Fortunately, they had willing helpers in Charles and Ella Cooley. The couple took on significant responsibility in babysitting and caring for Cliff in his early years, which sealed the bond between the three of them for good: Cliff was the closest thing they ever had to a son. As Cliff grew up, even long after his family had moved away from Brookville, he was known as the "Cooley Boy" thanks to the spoiling he got from Charles and Ella. Most notably, Cliff was the first member of his family to have a bicycle, courtesy of the Cooleys. It was a used bike, but that shortcoming was eventually remedied when Charles and Ella bought him a brand-new bike from Sears. After the Dickmans moved away, Cliff returned to Brookville every summer and spent six weeks with the Cooleys. He remained like a member of the family until 1953, when the

3

already-widowed Charles Cooley passed away. Of the $12,000 Cooley estate, about $1,000 was bequeathed to other family and friends, and the remainder was left to Dickman.[5]

In 1935, when Cliff was five years old, opportunity came calling for the Dickmans again—this time, in Webster, Indiana, about 35 miles north of Brookville in Wayne County. Webster, originally named Dover, had been lightly settled for about sixty years before it was finally established as a township in 1870. At the time the Dickmans moved to Webster, the township was home to fewer than 600 people.[6]

Joseph and Anna purchased their new, 154-acre plot of farmland for $10,000. The seller was John Flatley, a Webster resident who had fallen into bankruptcy and was forced to give up his land. To cover the down payment, Joseph had to borrow $500 from his father and another $500 from an aunt; the remainder was borrowed from the Bank of Louisville. It was the first time the Dickmans owned, rather than rented, their home.

The farm, located at 5713 Flatley Road, was in state-of-the-art condition for its time. John Flatley had constructed several barns on the property for storing tractors and other farming equipment. The house itself was also ahead of its time for 1935 rural Indiana: it had running water. The well's pump was attached to a windmill, and when the wind blew, the windmill turned and pumped water into a tank in the attic of the house. From there, the water would flow down when the faucet was turned on. It was a marvel for its day.

The Dickmans' lives had taken a turn for the better, but they certainly weren't living in luxury. For the first couple years, there was no electricity in the house or the out-buildings. That meant at night, their work was guided by lanterns, a serious fire hazard that fortunately never materialized. The windmill usually pumped water for them, but when there was no breeze, the entire family had to take turns manually pumping water from the well and carrying buckets into the house. And of course, as was common at the time, the house did not have an indoor toilet until 1945, when Cliff was 15. Instead, they started with a "three-holer": a homemade, outdoor toilet with three holes (one was situated lower for the kids). A couple years later, they got a "government toilet"—an improved latrine that, mercifully, had only one hole.

Squeezing a family of 11 into a three-bedroom home was no mean feat either, albeit not a novel challenge. At both the Cooley and Dickman farms, the three rooms were divided among the three boys, the six girls, and the parents. Floyd, being the oldest, had the privilege of his own bed; Cliff and his older brother Jerome shared. The children had their bedrooms upstairs, while the parents took the downstairs room.

The Dickmans were hog and dairy farmers. They planted corn, wheat, and clover hay, which in turn fed the 40 hogs that they sold annually. By the time the hogs were fattened up to about 225 pounds, Joseph sold them to a butcher, usually in Cincinnati. As a special treat, the family slaughtered one hog for themselves every year, which would be canned for gradual consumption over the winter. They also had 15 dairy cows and sold about 35 gallons of milk per day to Wayne Dairy in nearby Richmond. Chickens played a role in the farm's operations too. Each spring, the family purchased 100 chicks. While many didn't make it, the survivors provided the family with eggs. When the roosters were fully-grown, Anna butchered, skinned, and fried them for supper—one of the best items on the Dickman menu. The family also owned two horses, which pulled plows and spreaders in the field.

Life on a farm might sound idyllic, but the testy animals and heavy farming machinery gave rise to many freak accidents. Clifford had his closest call at only five years old. He and his brother Floyd, then 12, were driving their horses back to the barn after spreading manure in the field. Without warning, their horse-drawn cart ran roughly over a concrete drain, bouncing Cliff off the cart and face-down into fresh manure. The oblivious horses carried on, and before Cliff could react, the front wheel of the manure spreader rolled onto his back. Pinned down in the thick manure and unable to breathe, Cliff flailed to no avail until Floyd heroically halted the horses, muscled the spreader off his brother, and yanked him out of the manure. He'd been suffocating for about 20 seconds—dangerously long for the lungs of a 5-year-old. Cliff was spared that day; he suffered nothing more than the lingering stench of manure. But unforeseeable calamity would strike the Dickmans again, and the next victim would not be so lucky.

The Dickmans lived and prospered by the sweat of their brow, and their work was brutal, exhausting, and interminable. Mondays through Fridays took the same schedule. The children would rise at 6:00 a.m. for the first task: milking the cows. Cliff learned to milk a cow when he was nine years old. As soon as he mastered his first cow, he was responsible for two. And as soon as he got two down, he took on a third. He, his father, Floyd, Jerome, and Bernadine shared the responsibility of milking the family's 15 cows in the morning and the evening. The milk was collected into 10-gallon cans, which were picked up daily and taken to Richmond. After the milking, the kids came in, cleaned up, and ate the breakfast prepared by their mother.

6

With morning chores finished and breakfast eaten, the kids caught the school bus at the end of their driveway, which took them to Webster High School. It was a single school building for children in grades 1–12. Each class had about 15 kids, too few for a single teacher, so the grades were consolidated. In one room, a single teacher was responsible for first, second, and third graders. She rotated her attention among the classes, teaching each grade for an hour at a time while the other two grades completed their homework. The fourth, fifth, and sixth graders were similarly grouped together, as were the seventh and eighth graders. The high school classes, which were considerably smaller given the number of dropouts, were all educated together in a single auditorium.

Many of Cliff's classmates and siblings were eager to escape the classroom. They came from farming families, and they were ready to get to the business of farming like their parents. But Cliff always enjoyed being a student. It was a chance to rest from the otherwise nonstop schedule of manual labor. And he had a natural curiosity that made him enjoy learning for its own sake. Indeed, he often tuned in to the lectures his teachers gave the older students in the room, which he thought gave him an edge when he reached those grades. "He was always energetic and always at his books," his teacher Agnes King later remembered.[7] Another, Flo Pilgrim, remarked that "[h]e wasn't an 'A' student, but he was an ideal student, very conscientious, very personable, easy to work with. He liked to get into things and be a part of them, be involved."[8] Those descriptions not only fit the Clifford Dickman of school days, but well beyond. There was, however, one trait that he would grow out of: shyness. While he was quite the socialite around friends (indeed, he'd be president of his graduating class), Mrs. King recalled that he

7

was "scared to death when he had to give a talk" to the full class.[9]

When the school day was complete, it was back to work at home. Afternoon chores involved a miscellaneous collection of tasks, which went on until supper was ready. The younger kids took on menial tasks, like collecting oil or wood for the stove, shucking corn by hand, or feeding the cattle. The responsibilities grew weightier as they grew older, such as planting and harvesting.

If the boys were outside, they typically were helping their father. Having spent his whole life in agriculture, Joseph was a successful farmer and trained his children well. He had extraordinary physical strength, so much that he would show off for his friends by bench pressing the front end of a tractor. He had something of a mean streak in his character too. He'd gather local farmers in his barns at night, where they'd fight each other with their bare hands. He had a rough-and-tumble way of playing with his kids too. For instance, he liked to grip a spark plug on a tractor with one hand, grab one of his kids with the other hand, and acting as an electric conduit, give them a mild jolt of electricity. It wasn't painful for the kid on the receiving end, but it wasn't comfortable either. On occasion, though rarely, Joseph's rough nature resulted in brutal discipline for his sons. One day, Clifford and Jerome were riding on a horse-pulled wagon with their father and approached a closed gate. The boys usually alternated responsibility for hopping off the wagon and opening the gate, but this time, the two bickered back and forth about whose turn it was. Joseph lost his patience. He ordered both boys off the wagon, and taking a rope, he whipped them across the back. Joseph was a devoted family man who was loved by his children, but he dispensed justice and enforced order harshly.

Though Clifford's life would likewise be marked by toughness and discipline, he drew his personality (not to mention his looks) from his mother Anna, who possessed the same hardiness as her husband but displayed it more gently and forgivingly. Anna was a remarkably hard worker, toiling away from sunup to sundown without a word of complaint. She was typically the first to rise in the morning, lighting the flame in the family's multi-function stove. The fire in the stove's center heated an oven underneath, iron plates on top (like modern stove plates), and a water tank on the side. Anna baked 18 loaves of bread from scratch every week, and her nightly suppers were sumptuous; no one in the Dickman family went hungry. She was famous for her pies, and she made all varieties: lemon, minced meat, and custard were chief among them. Cliff had about a quarter of a pie every day. Indeed, word of the pies even circulated around Richmond. In later years, one of the local priests, Father Robert Minton, would cruise down Flatley Road with the hope of finding Anna's pies cooling on the windowsill; if they were there, he'd pull right up the driveway, knowing that she couldn't deny the cleric some homemade treats.

Once Joseph decided that the afternoon's work was complete and Anna finished preparing supper, the family gathered for a feasting on bread, meat, and pie. But the day was not yet done for the Dickmans. The cows had to be milked a second time before turning in, and then, the kids had to wrap up any leftover homework from school. Finally, by 9:00 p.m., the lights were off, and having stretched the limits of their minds and muscles, the kids immediately fell asleep.

Saturdays for the family involved more work, not less. The milking went on, and the kids did all they could to help their dad keep the operations of the farm running smoothly. The Dickmans had a reputation in Webster for being one of the hardest-working families, so the boys were often sought out for help with farm work. For one day's work of baling a neighbor's hay, they'd each earn a dollar, but because all money belonged to the family, they promptly handed over their hard-earned cash to their parents. Indeed, even after Kathleen had dropped out of school and gone to work as a live-in housekeeper in Richmond, her $3 weekly salary was turned over to her parents when she saw them at church on Sundays.

Anna's burdensome workload carried on through the weekends. She was responsible for all the shopping, a task which usually involved bartering farm products for dry staples. She also took charge of keeping everyone clothed and cleaned. While the family always wore store-bought pants and overalls, their shirts were homemade. Anna, not one to let anything go to waste, bought flour for the family in 100 lb. cloth bags, and she saved that cloth to make shirts for the kids. Weekends were an opportunity to sew those shirts and clean them. As was standard practice for the time, she washed the clothes manually over a rack with soap and water and hung them up on the clothesline to dry.

The kids got one special Saturday treat: their once-a-week chance to take a bath and put on fresh clothes. The bathing process involved filling up an oversized pan of water, heating it on the stove, and carrying it up to a tub in the bedroom for cleansing.

Sunday was a well-deserved day of rest, save the twice-a-day milking chore, which could never be shirked. The family traveled down to St. Andrew's Catholic Church in Richmond for Sunday morning Mass. At the time, there were two Catholic churches in Richmond: St. Andrew's and St. Mary's. Although only a few blocks apart, their parishioners were starkly divided: St. Andrew's was the German church, while St. Mary's was the Italian church. The Dickmans had a rich faith. They never missed Sunday Mass, and they went to confession as a family twice a month. They prayed at every meal, and during Lent, the family had a tradition of saying the Rosary each night, which Joseph led.

After the religious obligations were observed, the family went home to Webster, where the kids at last had an afternoon of freedom for sports, games, or time with friends. Indeed, it was on these Sunday afternoons that Cliff was first able to practice and refine his athleticism, the most important skill he'd ever have.

It was a life that revolved around work and yet was not defined by it. Whether it was making flour-bag shirts, pumping 35 gallons of milk every day, or dishing up oversized supper pies, the Dickmans' daily rituals had a unifying theme: they were in service to the betterment of the family. Joseph and Anna, like their parents before them, aimed for their family to have a standard of living that steadily improved, and everyone was expected to contribute. And indeed, as the years went on, the Dickman family prospered, and they lived quite happily through it all.

★   ★   ★

America was sent reeling on December 7, 1941, when the Imperial Japanese Navy launched a surprise attack on Pearl Harbor and killed thousands of U.S. sailors. At President Franklin D. Roosevelt's urging, Congress passed a declaration bringing the United States into the Second World War.

The war did not affect the Dickmans particularly harshly. If anything, because the prices of milk, grain, corn, and hogs increased, the war gave the family a small financial boon. The biggest fear, of course, was that Floyd

11

would be drafted. He was 18 and therefore eligible for the draft when America entered the war, and this naturally caused his parents, especially Joseph, a great deal of consternation. Yet due to his critical leadership on the farm, Floyd's draft number was never called.

But while the war might have spared the Dickmans, tragedy would nonetheless strike them in a terrible way. On Friday, September 4, 1942, Joseph drove a trailer to the Glen Miller Stockyards in Richmond for the weekly livestock trade. At 5:30 in the evening, driving west on Webster Road and only about a mile away from home, Joseph was struck by a train running at 90 miles per hour as he was crossing the railroad tracks. The crossing was blind: a house blocked Joseph's view of the train barreling down the tracks until it was too late. Joseph was pronounced dead on site.[10]

The rest of the family was at home. Cliff and Jerome had just finished school and were tossing a ball in the yard. Sheldon Moore, a neighbor who was about 18 years old, rode up to the house on his motorcycle, and he let the boys know that their father had been hit by a train. Moore told them that Joseph had been hurt but didn't know any more than that. Cliff and Jerome immediately hopped on their bicycles—the ones that Charles and Ella Cooley had given Cliff—and rode down to the tracks. But before they could get there, they were stopped and told the terrible news: Joseph had not survived. The Webster townsmen, pitying the boys, did not let them go any nearer. Cliff and Jerome turned back to the house, where they found their mother standing on the porch, waiting to hear Joseph's fate. And there, Cliff and Jerome, at 12 and 14 years old, told their grief-stricken mother that her husband had been killed.[11]

It was unimaginably devastating. Their father, though a tough disciplinarian, had been a dedicated family man and example of hard work and piety. He had loved them all deeply, fretted over them, and raised them to be sturdy and diligent citizens of the world. And they had loved him. On the night that Joseph passed, Cliff and his siblings, who still had to complete their milking chores, simply sat there between the hind flanks of the cattle, softly crying. Eighty years later, he still wilts with sadness as he recalls his father's death.

Anna was completely rocked by the loss of her husband, and her grief was only compounded three months later when her mother passed away. She'd known Joseph most of her life, married him at age 21, had been his partner in life for 24 years, and raised nine kids with him—and without any warning, he was gone forever. Though she went on to outlive her husband by 42 years, she never really overcame her loss on that terrible September Friday.

But while the family was emotionally and spiritually shattered, the work of the farm miraculously went on without a hitch. That was to the great credit of the family's third child and eldest son: Floyd. At 19 years old, Floyd immediately picked up the mantle as the leader of the family's farming operation, and the unrelenting spirit of hard work that his father instilled in him came to full fruition. He was simply extraordinary. He butchered and castrated the hogs, traded the cattle, marketed the hog meat, took over the planting and harvesting, and sold the milk. And Floyd became more than a brother to Cliff. He became a father figure, a role that never really faded for the rest of their lives.

And so, against seemingly insurmountable odds, the Dickmans carried on, and they carried on well.

13

While Cliff's brother Jerome dropped out of school at age 16 to join his brother full-time on the farm, Cliff stayed the course, and he ultimately became the only boy in his family to graduate from high school (Dolores, Joann, Susann, and Corrine also graduated from high school). He fared well with academics, but more than anything, his high school years would be marked by athletics.

Cliff hadn't had much opportunity to play sports growing up, unlike his fellow classmates and his peers in Richmond. Life on the farm, especially the bustling Dickman farm, was simply too time-consuming and physically demanding to allow for athletics. But they got a lucky break: their neighbor gifted the Dickmans a basketball goal, which they set up in one of their barns. Cliff played with his brothers and, on Sunday afternoons when the family rested, they invited other friends to come over for games. Cliff quickly proved himself an able athlete. This sometimes caused some tension, as Jerome didn't always take well to being outplayed by his younger brother. But they were good sports, and they made each other better players.

The boys also played outdoor basketball at school. There, Cliff began to exhibit what would become his signature style of play: scrappy, physical ball in the paint. He was never one to launch low-percentage perimeter shots; instead, he scored on underhanded put-ups, tip-ins, and a deadly hook shot. He even managed to perform well when going up against bigger and older kids, a toughness that earned him the nickname "Scrub" and made him a formidable presence on the court for years to come.

It wasn't until seventh grade that Cliff Dickman finally played in an official basketball game for Webster.

The school team, which put up only two points, lost the game. By eighth grade, Webster doubled their schedule to two games. It wasn't much, but it was enough to make clear that Dickman was a team leader and high scorer. In one of the two games, a 28–16 loss to Fountain City, he scored 12 of Webster's points.

In high school, Dickman donned the uniform of the Webster Pirates. Their operations were quite primitive compared to others in the county. The Pirates' outdoor court was a patch of dirt with goals on either end, and while the middle school kids didn't mind playing on a muddy or snowy court during recess, that wouldn't suffice for the high school team. Instead, the team traveled to practice at Highland School, a few miles south of Webster on the north side of Richmond, or Dennis Middle School, on Richmond's west side. They played their home games at Centerville, Boston, or Fountain City High Schools when those teams didn't have games of their own scheduled. For all this, the county referred to the Pirates as "the gymless crew."[12]

Dickman quickly established himself as the team's top player. Starting in his sophomore year, the newspaper's summaries of Webster basketball performances regularly described Dickman as "pacing the attack."[13] At 6'2" and weighing in at 185 lbs., he was a dominant force in the paint, playing the gritty style of ball that he'd picked up at recess in his younger days. He constantly strived to improve. He kept meticulous handwritten records of his statistics, which showed his scoring average doubling from his freshman to senior year.

By Dickman's junior year, the Pirates improved from finishing at the bottom of the conference to the middle of it. That was in large part thanks to Bob Martin, the team's new head coach. Martin was a Richmond native whose outstanding skill in baseball landed him a contract with the Pittsburgh Pirates triple-A baseball team. But the low minor-league salary forced Martin to give up his major-league dreams, so he came home to Indiana, earned a teaching degree at Ball State, and then took up coaching at Webster High.[14]

Martin's youth and bright ideas were integral to spurring Webster basketball on, and so was the continued improvement of his star player. "The Pirates have an outstanding scorer in young Cliff Dickman," the newspaper reported, and he finished the season with the second-highest scoring average in the conference (17 points per game).[15] He continued to refine his signature hook shot, inspiring Coach Martin's young son Mike to spend hours in the driveway working on his own hook.*[16]

Dickman's performance peaked during his senior year. Even when opposing defenses strategized to keep the ball away from him, he still managed to net a sizable chunk of the Pirates' points.[17] He was the highest scorer in that season's Wayne County Conference tournament, with 58 points in three games.±[18] The Pirates easily won the conference consolation game against Milton High to take third place in the county, and Dickman shone. With 34 points, Dickman set the Richmond Civic Hall single-

---

* Young Mike Martin's imitation of Cliff Dickman's shooting was time well-spent, as he went on to become a star basketball player for Richmond High School and Earlham College. In later years, Del Harris, a former Earlham coach then serving as an assistant coach for the Los Angeles Lakers, described Mike Martin as "one of the best pure shooters I ever coached."

± Webster usually faced off against other Wayne County teams: Boston, Cambridge City, Centerville, Economy, Fountain City, Greens Fork, Hagerstown, Milton, Richmond's "B" Team, Whitewater, and Williamsburg.

game scoring record and was only one point shy of out-scoring Milton's entire team.[19] He finished the season averaging a conference-high 18.4 points per game.[20] His final matchup, a 53–47 sectional loss to Williamsburg, ended with a strong rally by Dickman until foul trouble turned him and three other key players out of the game.[21] It was the best year that Webster basketball had ever seen. After four seasons, Dickman had netted 1,057 points for the Pirates.

He also forayed into two other sports during his high school years—baseball and track. Unlike other kids (especially in Richmond), Dickman had never played sandlot baseball, but he got his chance to learn the game in high school as third baseman for the Webster Pirates. They had reasonable success on the diamond, topping out as runner-up in the Wayne County Championship. In track, Dickman signed up for an event in which he would continue to compete for 65 years: the shot put. He also participated in the javelin, long-jump, and high-jump events, collecting ribbons from tournaments all around Wayne County.

For many young athletes, sports are a form of exercise, a fun pastime, and a source of childhood memories. But for Cliff Dickman, sports would be the launching pad for his entire future—in college, business, and politics. He never quit living the life of an athlete. In high school, he had proven himself to be a physical, scrappy teammate, and his reputation across Wayne County as an outstanding competitor was solidified. In the words of Jim Cox, a Webster native who has written a fine historical account of his hometown: "There's little doubt that Cliff Dickman is the best all-around athlete ever to graduate from Webster High School."[22]

17

In the spring of 1948, as Dickman's high school graduation approached, he found himself at a crossroads. With Floyd and Jerome at the helm of the farm's operations, and new agricultural technologies reducing the need for additional manpower, Cliff knew that there simply wasn't room for him to keep working on the farm. College didn't seem like an attractive option either. Instead, he took a new job at Johns-Manville, starting in his final semester of high school after basketball season finished. The company manufactured insulation on the west side of Richmond, and Dickman worked the third shift—10:48 p.m. to 6:48 a.m. He needed the money, for he'd recently borrowed $2,100 from his mother to buy his first car: a Pontiac convertible. Dickman started at Johns-Manville working in the "granulator room" before being quickly promoted to an inspection position. It was a plum job which mostly involved checking the output of the insulation-producing machines to ensure that they met the proper specifications. But Dickman knew he wouldn't make a career at Johns-Manville, and doubts about the longer-term future lingered. A year would pass before he was presented with his next big opportunity in life.

But there was one significant change in Dickman's life by May 1948. When he graduated from Webster High alongside his eight classmates, Dickman had a special guest in attendance at the ceremony: his new girlfriend. She was a Luerman girl from Richmond, and her name was Martha Jane.

2

RICHMOND

Before turning to Clifford's new belle and her family, permit a detour to the story of her hometown: Richmond, Indiana. Martha Jane and eventually Cliff would come to witness and even shape a great deal of Richmond history in the second half of the twentieth century. We cannot understand them if we fail to understand the land they inherited and inhabited.

Richmond lies directly east of Indianapolis on the Indiana–Ohio border. It was founded at the turn of the nineteenth century by Quaker migrants from North Carolina. The exhausted farmland in the Tar Heel State had dried up agricultural opportunity for the Quaker farmers, and they desperately sought to escape the culture of slavery so deeply engrained into southern society. They found their refuge in western Ohio and eastern Indiana.[1]

Two Quakers figured prominently in the establishment of Richmond: John Smith and Jeremiah Cox. At the time they arrived in the area, the division of land between American citizens and Indian tribes was governed by the Treaty of Greenville, signed in nearby Greenville, Ohio in 1795. The treaty drew an imaginary line: the east side was for American settlement, while the west side belonged to the tribes. Only a tiny sliver of modern-day Indiana fell on the east side of this line, so this is where Smith and Cox acquired land in 1806—the land that would one day become Richmond.

Of course, treaty lines would not inhibit Indiana's development for long. In 1809, Territorial Governor (and future U.S. President) William Henry Harrison signed the Treaty of Fort Wayne, which pushed the boundary line for American settlement about 15 miles further west of Richmond, into modern-day Cambridge City. More treaties and battles between the federal government and the tribes soon followed, driving the Indiana Territory's boundaries further west.[2]

John Smith and Jeremiah Cox were concerned less with tribal conflicts and more with improving their new Indiana home. In the coming decade, they developed the area into a tiny village, which helped to support more Quakers still pouring into the surrounding farmland.[3] Cox, notably, served as a delegate to Indiana's constitutional convention, which ultimately paved the way for the state's admission into the Union at the end of 1816.[4] Two years later, on September 1, 1818, the 24 qualified voters living in Smith and Cox's settlement voted to incorporate as a town, and they named it Richmond.[5]

The city quickly prospered. First came the National Road, America's inaugural national highway that promised to connect western Maryland with the growing Midwest. Richmond had two advantages which led it to capture a segment of the road. First, Congress decided that the National Road should connect Ohio's capital in Columbus and Indiana's new capital in Indianapolis, and Richmond lay halfway between the two. Second, Wayne County remained Indiana's most populous until the

RICHMOND

1850s, and Richmond was the county's fastest-growing city. As one of the earliest harbingers of Indiana's promise, it was only natural that the great link to the Midwest would serve this town.[6]

The road worked wonders for Richmond. Even before construction was completed, the city saw more westbound pioneers passing through in one month than the city's total population. Tavern owners, the farmers who supplied them, and innkeepers all benefited from this traffic. And the construction brought Richmond a critical piece of infrastructure: a bridge crossing the Whitewater River Gorge, the deep ravine which splits the town in two.[7] This early windfall cemented Richmond's status as a transportation hub, suitable for belonging to a state whose moniker is "the Crossroads of America."

Richmond soon became a railroad capital. Amidst fears that a Cincinnati–St. Louis railroad line across southern Indiana would undermine Richmond's transportation dominance, the Terre Haute and Richmond Railroad Company was chartered in 1847. The new company's line spanned the state in the center rather than in the south: Terre Haute and Richmond were the western and eastern boundaries, respectively, and Indianapolis was the central hub in the middle.[8] Only a few years later, Richmond was connected by rail directly to Dayton and Cincinnati. These links enabled Richmond to welcome trains from great eastern cities, including Philadelphia, Pittsburgh, Baltimore, and Cleveland, and send them off to great western cities, like Chicago and St. Louis.

Richmond's access to a national network made it an exceedingly attractive location to set up industrial plants and warehouses, and entrepreneurs quickly seized the opportunity.[9] One of the town's earliest operations was the Richmond Foundry, which manufactured plows.[10]

21

The Foundry foreshadowed the defining feature of the city's economic future: the production of agricultural machinery. Richmond's most prominent manufacturer, the Gaar-Scott Company, set up shop not long after. The industrial titan went on to become the world's leading manufacturer of both steam traction engines and threshing machines—a piece of farm equipment that removes grain seeds from their stalks.[11]

A string of manufacturing plants popped up in the 1870s. After a local pair of entrepreneurs secured a patent for a new type of lawn mower, Richmond became a production hub for these nifty machines. Before long, ten local companies were creating two-thirds of the world's reel mowers, making Richmond the "Lawn Mower Capital of the World."[12] Later in the decade, Wayne Works started to build farming implements and carriages,[13] and the Hoosier Drill Company started to produce seeding machines, which helped farmers efficiently plant grain, corn, and beans.[14]

The woodworking industry took off too. Richmond companies acquired wood by rail from Michigan forests, and they converted the lumber into school desks, church pews, doors, and blinds before distributing the finished products around the nation. The local leader in the woodworking industry was the J.M. Hutton Company, which produced coffins and caskets.[15] Yet another lumber-dependent enterprise that galvanized Richmond's economic growth was the Starr Piano Company. Established in 1872, the piano factory was situated in the gorge, harnessing the flow of the Whitewater River to power its operations. The company crafted thousands of pianos annually and built a reputation as one of America's finest piano makers.[16]

Richmond transformed dramatically over the nineteenth century from a tiny Quaker hamlet into a manufacturing powerhouse. But despite the upheaval, the city maintained its connection to its founding Quaker roots, most notably through its local liberal-arts school, Earlham College. Quakers had continued to flood into Richmond and its surroundings throughout the 1800s. According to historian of Quakerism Thomas Hamm, "Indiana would equal Pennsylvania in its Quaker population, and Richmond would rival Philadelphia as a spiritual and intellectual center of the Society of Friends" by 1860. It was only fitting, therefore, that Richmond was home to a school committed to the tenets of Quakerism.[17]

Originally founded as Friends Boarding School in 1847, the school officially became Earlham College twelve years later. The school was named after Earlham Hall, the English estate of an influential nineteenth-century Quaker named Joseph John Gurney. Gurney had visited Indiana in the 1830s, and his forceful personality made him an unforgettable figure to the men who later founded the school, so they named it after his estate. The school was ahead of its time in many ways. For one, Earlham was co-educational from the start. Oberlin College, America's first co-ed institution of higher education, had been founded only 20 years earlier, and Indiana's state universities had yet to admit women. Moreover, while Quakerism would always exercise a strong influence over student life at Earlham, the school quickly abandoned its requirement that its students be Quakers. Over the years, Earlham developed a progressive streak that sometimes led to tension with its conservative Richmond neighbors. But undoubtedly, Earlham's status as a premier liberal-arts school in the Midwest attracted intellectual talent and financial investment to Richmond, important resources that fueled the town's growth.[18]

One passionate Quaker couple was especially significant in Wayne County history: Levi and Catharine Coffin, who were North Carolina expats living a few miles north of Richmond. They were staunch abolitionists, and soon after arriving in Indiana, their home became a waystation on the Underground Railroad. Levi even earned the nickname "President of the Underground Railroad" for assisting thousands of runaway slaves escaping the South.[19] Though many of the slaves migrated to Canada to evade the reach of the Fugitive Slave Act, a sizable number made their homes in Wayne County, as they were treated equally and respectfully by their Quaker brethren. That sowed the seeds for another religious denomination to take root and gain influence in Wayne County: the African Methodist Episcopal Church, which grew under the direction of AME Bishop William Paul Quinn.[20]

As the nineteenth century ebbed on, the Quaker and AME congregations were outpaced by Catholic and Lutheran denominations, powered by the steady stream of German immigrants into Richmond. By 1870, 40% of Richmond's population was foreign-born, three-quarters being German and most of the remainder being Irish or Italian. That meant more than half of Richmond's churchgoers were either Catholic or Lutheran; only a sixth were Quaker and another sixth Methodist.[21]

The immigration wave from Europe also caused the city's political dynamics to shift. The Quakers and former slaves had overwhelmingly been Whigs and later Republicans because of the parties' anti-slavery positions. But the poor immigrants from Germany and Ireland often tilted toward the Democrats. Republican city-council members in Richmond tried to gerrymander away the Germans' political influence, with only limited success.[22]

Richmond's political swing, coupled with a few other factors, transformed the town into a regional hub for political activity. For one, Richmond was growing fast as a population center and source of votes, which led it to displace nearby Centerville as county seat in 1873.[23] For another, one of Indiana's great political leaders, Oliver P. Morton, hailed from Salisbury, halfway between Richmond and Centerville (it no longer exists). Morton served as Indiana's governor during the Civil War, and he was one of the Union Army's most energetic supporters. Any time President Lincoln called on the states for more troops, Morton responded boldly, and at one point, when the state legislature failed to provide salaries for the soldiers, Morton personally raised $500,000 in just a few days.[24] With his support, six regiments were organized and trained in Wayne County, each comprised of about 1,000 men. Morton later went on to serve as a U.S. Senator and was instrumental in passing the constitutional amendments and civil-rights legislation of the Reconstruction Era.[25]

The combination of changing demographics, a growing population and money center, Morton's nationwide recognition, and easy rail access enabled Richmond to play host to a number of U.S. presidents in the postwar era. These visits were usually part of a whistle-stop tour to drum up electoral support. Ulysses Grant, William Howard Taft, Woodrow Wilson, Franklin Roosevelt, Harry Truman, and Dwight Eisenhower made train stops at Richmond's Pennsylvania Depot on their way west, where they were greeted by throngs of citizens.[26] Benjamin Harrison, America's Hoosier president, visited the city many times. Indeed, after leaving the White House and resuming his law practice, he litigated the famous "Morrisson Will" case in Richmond, which ended up being America's longest jury trial in the nineteenth century.[27] Theodore Roosevelt was also a frequent visitor to Richmond before, during, and after his presidency. He is most remembered for delivering an impassioned speech at the bottom of a hill that now bears his name in Glen Miller Park.[28]

The most memorable of these presidential visits was also the most somber. Abraham Lincoln's funeral train, en route from Washington to his home in Springfield, Illinois, made a stop in Richmond at 3:15 a.m., where an estimated 12,000 citizens (double the city's population) came out to pay their respects to the sounds of tolling church bells.[29] On another sad trip, President Rutherford B. Hayes paid a visit to say goodbye to his dear friend Senator Morton, who lay dying in Richmond.[30]

It wasn't just presidents that focused the political limelight on Richmond. Former Speaker of the House Henry Clay visited Richmond during one of his many bids for the White House.* The Great Compromiser was not received warmly by the abolitionist Quakers, for Clay personally held slaves on his Kentucky farm. After an ugly confrontation with the Quaker audience, who demanded that he free his slaves, Clay's political fortunes took a dip, contributing to yet another failed run for the presidency.[31] But the abolitionists weren't necessarily treated better. Frederick Douglass's first visit in 1843 ended badly; while speaking to an abolitionist meeting, imposters pelted him with eggs. But when Douglass returned 37 years later, he forgave the city and expressed

---

* The site of Clay's rally is marked with a stone at the corner of Seventh and South A Streets, near St. Mary's Catholic Church.

his joy that the faces of the crowd were "beaming with that happiness only vouchsafed to the free."[32] Around that time, Susan B. Anthony also visited and addressed the people of Richmond, with whom she had a kinship arising from her own Quaker roots.[33]

By the turn of the twentieth century, Richmond was completely unrecognizable from the Quaker hamlet founded by John Smith and Jeremiah Cox. The Gilded Age—which so often conjures up visions of New York City and its glittery ballrooms, high-rise tenements, and industrial innovations—unfolded in Richmond too, albeit on a smaller scale. The city's manufacturers, old and new, prospered like never before; indeed, Richmond was a Midwestern leader as it boomed with opportunity and developed new technologies at an unprecedented rate. By 1905, it ranked eighth among American cities for the manufacture of farming machinery.[34] The lawn-mower companies began adding motors to their cutting machines.[35] Wayne Works expanded from the production of carriages to automobiles and buses, and by World War I, it was supplying the military with ambulances and troop-carrier vehicles.[36] Hoosier Drill joined the American Seeding Company* and doubled the size of its Richmond operations.[37] The Gaar-Scott Company had been sold in 1911 and vacated Richmond, but its former complex was soon occupied by the new Richmond Baking Company, which produced crackers, cookies, and breads for sale in supermarkets around the country.[38]

Like the Gilded Age industrialists of New York and Chicago, Richmond's local business leaders were eager to

---

* American Seeding later merged with the well-known company International Harvester, which continued operations in Richmond for decades.

27

show off their newfound opulence. In the 1890s, Richmond was home to 47 millionaires, a sizable number given that the entire country had only about 4,000 millionaire households at the time.[39] These captains of industry built stately mansions along Main Street, which acquired the nickname "Millionaire's Row." To their credit, the wealthy families practiced *noblesse oblige* and invested back into Richmond. They formed service clubs, like the Commercial, Rotary, Kiwanis, and Lions Clubs.[40] They poured money into building the beautiful churches that dot the downtown and funded the construction of Reid Memorial Hospital.[41]

A hotter economy demanded more workers, and newcomers came to Richmond in droves. The city's population tripled from 6,600 during the Civil War to 18,200 by the year 1900.[42] And this trend barreled onward through the 1920s, with Richmond crossing the 30,000-person mark and expanding in area to about 25 square miles, nearly the same as its current size.[43]

Amidst the economic and demographic transformations, the twentieth century inaugurated one of the darker moments in Richmond history: the rise of the Ku Klux Klan. Led by Grand Dragon D.C. Stephenson, Indiana's Klan became the most prominent in America during the early 1900s. Richmond is a part of that story. Between 1922 and 1926, 40–50% of eligible Richmond men joined the Klan, about 3,000 people. It's at least some solace that the Richmond Klan was "subdued" relative to organizations in other Indiana cities, and as far as we know, the local chapter did not provoke violence. Nonetheless, the sight of hooded figures and cross-burning rituals stirred feelings of fear among those whom the Klan tried to intimidate.[44]

Yet one development in the city defied the turn toward prejudice, and delightfully, it emanated from America's newest trend: jazz music. The Starr Piano Company, like the city's other manufactures, was booming like never before. By 1920, building pianos at a rate of 15,000 per year, Starr Piano made a bold choice that forever etched its place in musical history: it founded the Gennett Records Division, which produced disc records and the phonographs that played them. Gennett was a pioneer in its field. America's leading jazz, blues, and country artists traveled to Richmond, and notably for an area where the Klan was active, white and black musicians alike were invited to record in Richmond. A sampling of the stars that recorded in the Whitewater Gorge includes Louis Armstrong, Jelly Roll Morton, Hoagy Carmichael, Duke Ellington, Lawrence Welk, King Oliver, Fats Waller, Bix Beiderbecke, and Gene Autry.[45] Hoagy Carmichael was an especially frequent visitor, and he even recorded his famous tune "Stardust" at Gennett. He summed up the serendipity of the Jazz Age converging on Richmond in this way:

> In the farmland among the Indiana corn—and from the 'cow pasture universities'—there sprouted a beardless priesthood of jazz players and jazz composers. Instead of buttermilk, we were nurtured on bathtub gin and rhythm. It 'just happened'—like a thundercloud.[46]

The success of Gennett Records was readily apparent. Within five years of launching, it was producing 3 million records a year, and thanks to Richmond's solidified place in the nation's rail network, its products were distributed around the United States and the world.[47] The company even welcomed William Jennings Bryan, one of the greatest orators in American history. Having delivered his famed "Cross of Gold" speech hundreds of times around the country, Bryan recorded the speech for posterity in Richmond with Gennett.[48]

One more entrepreneurial success story of the Gilded Age bears mention, for no chronicling of Richmond is complete without mention of its nickname, "the City of Roses." The city owes that title to Edward Gurney Hill, an English immigrant with a special flair for growing and selling roses. Upon settling in Richmond, he founded the Hill Floral Company, which grew and sold millions of flower arrangements every year. The roses were grown in a massive greenhouse on the west side of Richmond, which at the company's peak covered more than 1,000 acres.[49] The city's floral heritage remained an important part of Richmond's identity well into the late twentieth century.

Even at Richmond's peak affluence and prominence, its average citizens, of course, were not leading lives of luxury; their employers on Millionaire's Row may as well have lived on a different planet. They lived, in today's parlance, paycheck to paycheck. The 1910 and 1920 censuses revealed that 57% of homes in Richmond were rented, a high figure for a town with relatively low property values. Modern workplace-safety standards and the social safety net did not yet exist, making life brutal for the blue-collar workers who were injured on the job or became ill.

But for daily wage earners, there was one unmistakably important characteristic of Richmond's economy: jobs were plentiful for those willing and able to work. And though wages were low, the hardy people of this time were more than capable of living happily on modest means.[50] It was this basic assurance of steady employment, not to be taken for granted in other parts of the world, that had attracted a multitude of immigrants to the city over the years. And in 1925, it beckoned a young couple from northwest Germany—Martha Jane Luerman's parents.

3

Martha Jane

Henry Luerman and Hedwig Seegers arrived in Richmond, Indiana at the peak of its Roaring Twenties glory. They came with almost nothing to their name, but like so many of their immigrant forebearers, they were eager to call the United States their own country and to make the City of Roses their new home.

Henry John Luerman—"Heinrich Luermann" at birth—was born in the city of Münster on June 18, 1900. Münster, like Oldenburg, is in the northwest corner of modern-day Germany (they are about 100 miles apart), and it was home to about 80,000 during Henry's childhood.[1] The city thrived throughout most of the second millennium as an intellectual capital, economic giant, and center of religious architecture. But history remembers Münster most for playing host to a watershed event in Western diploacy: the Peace of Westphalia. Signed in 1648, this series of treaties concluded the Thirty Years' War and recognized, for the first time, the principle of peaceful co-existence among independent, sovereign nations. Some of those treaties were signed in Münster. One consequence of the Peace was that Westphalian territory, including Münster, remained under the domain of Catholic clergy—much like Oldenburg, Germany 100 miles to the north.

Münster's old splendor was not reflected in the life of young Henry Luerman. He grew up under incredibly hard circumstances. His father, Theodore, died when he was only three years old, leaving his mother, Antonia, to provide for the family of three boys. Antonia took on a series of odd jobs to keep food on the table, all while juggling the child-rearing herself. Even by the standards of Germany in 1900, they were very poor. Eventually, the Luermans moved 20 miles to the village of Borghorst, where Henry met his wife to-be.

Hedwig Florence Seegers was born in Borghorst on September 1, 1902. She grew up alongside three brothers and two sisters, and though her life had challenges, her fortunes were well ahead of Henry's. Her parents, Heinrich and Mary Elizabeth Seegers, owned and operated a ratskeller, a German bar and restaurant, and it easily met the family's needs. Hedwig's sisters eventually took over and ran the ratskeller themselves.

When Henry was 14 years old and Hedwig 11, Germany joined Austria-Hungary in declaring war on the Allied Powers of Great Britain, France, and Russia. World War I was underway. We don't know what kind of experiences the Luerman and Seegers families had in the war, but life must have been extraordinarily difficult. All national resources—food, fuel, clothing—were poured into the war effort, leaving little behind for ordinary families. All the while, the Allies kept up a naval blockade against Germany to prevent their enemy from receiving crucial supplies. The tactic worked from a military perspective, though it led to widespread starvation throughout Germany and undoubtedly affected the Luerman and Seegers families. Young Henry and Hedwig were mercifully spared from witnessing the grotesque combat that defined the Great War. The closest foreign land to Münster and Borghorst was the Netherlands, which remained neutral during the conflict. Nonetheless, the two teenagers likely witnessed a great deal of troop and equipment movement heading south to Belgium and France, and they surely lost a number of family members and friends to the war.

Post-war Germany treated them hardly any better. The Treaty of Versailles required Germany to make exorbitant reparations to the Allies and forced the proud nation to give up its resource-rich territory. Predictably, the economy foundered. Germany's new government, the incompetent Weimar Republic, responded by printing money in excess. The result was a severe hyperinflation that quickly rendered a family's entire life savings worthless. Germany was in shambles. It's hard to imagine how eager young Germans would have been for a chance at a new life.

One such German, Henry's brother Anton ("Tony"), jumped at the chance to move to the United States and made the crossing in July 1923. The boys had an aunt and uncle, Josef and Pauline Jessing, who lived in the growing manufacturing town of Richmond, Indiana. After Tony landed at Ellis Island, he moved to Richmond to join his Uncle Josef and Aunt Pauline.

Henry didn't need much persuasion to join his brother. His U.S. immigration record states that he had been a "weaver" in Germany, and as with most other professions, there were few opportunities for work.[2] Hedwig, now his fiancée, was eager to make the move to America, as well. Her mother had passed away, and her father remarried shortly afterwards. Hedwig didn't have a warm

35

relationship with her stepmother, which may have eased the fear of emigration.

Henry and Hedwig planned to marry in Germany before they set sail, but their visa applications to the United States were approved earlier than expected. Their once-in-a-lifetime chance had come, and there could be no delay—not even for a wedding. On New Year's Eve 1924, only two weeks after their visas had been issued, Henry and Hedwig boarded the SS *Mongolia* at the port of Hamburg. Saying goodbye to their heartbroken families and devastated homeland, they looked ahead to building their own family, and a brighter future, in America.[3]

The *Mongolia* arrived at Ellis Island on January 12, 1925. Henry and Hedwig's first sight of the United States, as for so many other immigrants in this nation's history, would have been the Statue of Liberty set against the New York skyline. They were admitted into the country after the immigration officer chopped the second "n" off Henry's German surname. Like Tony, Henry and Hedwig set off to join Josef and Pauline Jessing at 114 South 3rd Street in Richmond. Fortunately, they had not made the Atlantic crossing alone. They were joined by Henry's mother Antonia, who was not immigrating but only visiting her older son Tony in Richmond.

Opportunity like none they had known before awaited them in Richmond, but success would not come easy. Neither Henry nor Hedwig spoke a word of English, and they both attended night school to begin learning the language. The process of officially becoming American citizens was lengthy, and they were not granted the privilege until September 24, 1931—almost seven years after they had arrived.[4]

Upon settling in Richmond, Henry quickly landed his first job in the booming factory of the Starr Piano Company. He worked as a "finisher," putting all the final polishes and varnishes on freshly manufactured pianos, and in exchange, he earned $2 a day. Henry and Hedwig never learned to drive a car; throughout their lives, they walked everywhere, including to and from work.

Four months after arriving, Henry and Hedwig were able to marry on May 8, 1925 at St. Andrew's Catholic Church, Richmond's German parish. The newlyweds moved into their first home, a duplex located at the corner of South E and 9th Streets. They rented the house for $22.50 per month—a shockingly low figure in today's terms, but a price that would have taken Henry 11 working days to earn on his Starr Piano salary.[5] Children soon followed: Mary was born in March 1926, followed by Carl, Hilda, Henry Jr. (who went by John, or "Junie"), Martha Jane, and Bob.

Martha Jane joined the Luerman family on April 21, 1932. She had the blessing of being born into a very warm, happy home. The Luerman parents never argued in front of their children; to the contrary, the kids saw nothing but deep affection between their parents. Martha Jane and her siblings got along splendidly—playing well together, supporting each other's dreams, caring for their parents. Her brother Carl modeled the family's closeness. As a teenager, he ran an ice-cream route, pulling a cooler behind his bicycle and selling the cold treats to neighbors. When Carl had finally saved enough money, he used it to buy his family a new refrigerator. Eventually, he bought a car, and because his parents couldn't drive, he willingly became the family's chauffeur.

Just before Martha Jane was born, the Luermans had purchased a house at 831 South 7th Street. The house brought a mix of good and bad luck. During the Great Depression, their home insurer went insolvent, leaving the Luermans with no coverage. Henry swore off insurance and refused to buy it ever again; providentially, he never needed it. The house was also centrally located, which made Henry and Hedwig's sole mode of transportation—walking—much easier to manage. The proximity turned out to be invaluable for their health. Henry suffered from heart problems for most of his life and frequently had to rest during his walks. Hedwig endured sores on the bottom of her feet, and while never uttering a word of complaint, the constant walking must have been intolerable.

831 South 7th Street was a lively home filled with charming moments and memories. The house had three bedrooms upstairs, and like the Dickmans, one was for the parents, one for the boys, and one for the girls. They had dear friends as neighbors, including the Maurer family; the two families basically grew up together. One of the Maurer girls, Marilyn, was one of Martha Jane's lifelong best friends, and one of the boys, Charlie, eventually wedded Martha Jane's oldest sister, Mary. The neighborhood was safe, so the Luermans and Maurers played in the alley adjoining their streets by day or night without concern.

A Richmond neighborhood was quite a different place to grow up from a Webster farm, but there were some similarities. As in Webster, water had to be pumped into the house (although in Richmond, the pump was inside the house). The water then had to be manually heated on the stove, which was powered by the coal that Henry hauled inside early in the morning and Hedwig stoked throughout the day. As was also true in Webster, clothes had to be washed by hand. And in the early years, there was no indoor toilet, only an outhouse with a two-hole toilet. When Martha Jane was eight years old, she broke her parents' orders and brought her beloved Shirley Temple doll to the outhouse, where it was forever lost to the toilet's second hole. Henry was a generous father, but even he refused to retrieve it for her.

The Luerman children attended kindergarten at Hibberd School, then moved to St. Andrew's Catholic School for first through eighth grade, and then returned to Hibberd for ninth grade. They finished tenth through twelfth grade at the newly constructed Richmond High School, each graduating with a class of about 300 (as compared to Webster's class of nine in 1948). The one exception to this track was Martha Jane's brother Junie, who entered St. Meinrad Seminary in southern Indiana after eighth grade to begin his formation for the priesthood. The Luerman kids walked the roundtrip to and from school twice a day, making a midday jaunt home for lunch. Fortunately, because they lived in the center of town, school was never more than 10 blocks away.

Martha Jane always enjoyed being a student. While in high school, she settled on her goal of working in an office after graduation. She took all the stenography, typing, shorthand, and bookkeeping classes that Richmond High had to offer, and she excelled at them, earning more than her fair share of perfect exam scores.

When the school day was over, the children had chores waiting at home, mostly in Henry's garden. The kids were in charge of gathering grapes and berries off the bushes, picking cherries off the trees, and tending to the tomatoes, green beans, and strawberries. They also owned chickens and rabbits, and the children were responsible for picking up the eggs and cleaning out the cages.

As the Luerman children got older, they took on part-time jobs. The boys ran newspaper and ice-cream routes to earn spare money. Martha Jane got her first job at age 14 at Wayne Dairy where she collected orders, scooped ice cream, and served up barbecue sandwiches. She'd work until 10:30 p.m. and then walk home, often by herself without any need for worry. Two years later, she took a part-time job at McClellan's in downtown Richmond, a "dime-and-dollar" general store.

While the kids completed their schooling and attended to chores and jobs, Hedwig was hard at work in the house. She kept the water warmed, the house heated, and the clothes washed. She canned the fruits from the garden and used them to make jellies and bake pies—except for strawberry sweets, which were always to be saved for the summer when Junie came home from St. Meinrad. Every weekend, Hedwig whipped up two big cakes for the family and served a round steak with mashed potatoes and gravy for Sunday dinner.

In the early years, Henry spent the day at work in the piano factory. Later, he went to night school to become a tool-and-die maker and was eventually hired by Perfect Circle, a local manufacturer of piston rings for cars, trucks, and locomotive engines.[6] Because the factory was outside walking distance, he carpooled with colleagues to get to work. Though the workdays on the factory floor were exhausting, Henry stayed active when he got home. He checked in on his garden and inspected the children's daily pickings. Henry also knew some carpentry, and he put that skill to use in his spare time by fashioning cabinets from scratch for the kitchen. He made his own grape wine too, which he would serve when their close friends, fellow German immigrants, came to the house to visit.

The Luermans also made regular visits to their only family in town, Henry's brother Tony. He and his wife, Hilda, had five daughters who always got along well with Henry and Hedwig's children. Henry's mother Antonia, or "Oma" as the kids called her (German for "grandmother"), also crossed the Atlantic on occasion to visit her boys. Antonia was the only grandparent whom the Luerman kids ever met. She was strict with her grandchildren, never caving to their requests for even a small treat. And of course, Oma's thick German was completely impenetrable to the young Americans.

For their part, Henry and Hedwig gained proficiency in English, especially Henry since he interacted with fluent English speakers at work. But German would always remain their primary language. The couple spoke in German to each other, and the kids, though never becoming fluent in German themselves, learned to understand what their parents were saying. The parents spoke in "low German," but because their friends spoke in "high German," the children could never understand anything the visitors said. The kids' native English fluency was a huge help to Henry and Hedwig. They taught their parents how to write in English, and for many years after, Hedwig asked the kids to proofread her English letters for grammatical errors.

The Luerman parents were strict with their children, but they were fair. Like the Dickmans, the Luermans did not spoil their kids. Indeed, Martha Jane didn't receive a bicycle until eighth grade, and she paid for it herself. This was probably a reflection of the fact that Henry and Hedwig always lived simply themselves, subsisting on a modest salary for all their years. Indeed, they couldn't even make the trip home to Germany until 40 years after they had immigrated. After they both passed away, their children found gifts that the couple had received which they had never used—a testament to the fact that they didn't need new things to be satisfied. And Henry, seeing his grandchildren's relative abundance of material goods, worried that they would be forced to earn a lot of money in order to be happy.

They lived simply, so they lived well. Henry's steady income and Hedwig's diligent labor kept the pantry stocked and the dinner plates full. And they were truly loving parents to their children, always demonstrating a positive, joyful attitude. A telling example: Mary had applied for a position with Fireproof Door after she graduated from high school. The interview had gone well, but she fretted because the company had asked for a telephone number to reach her, which she couldn't provide because the family didn't have their own landline. Henry encouraged Mary, telling her that if she was the right person for the job, they'd find a way to contact her. He was right; Fireproof mailed her a job offer not long after the interview.

Though the Luerman parents were not extravagant in their gift-giving, they used their craftiness to provide their kids with a wonderful Christmas every year. Their neighbors, knowing that the Luermans had limited financial means, gave them old dolls, clothes, and toys. Henry and Hedwig fixed the hand-me-downs up so that by Christmas Day, they were in mint condition for the overjoyed children.

Henry also made a noteworthy exception to their modest gift-giving practice when Martha Jane was a young girl. The next-door occupant of the duplex they had first lived in was a blind woman who sold religious items. Martha Jane, who saw these treasures in the window, yearned to have one for her dresser. Her father agreed, and he took her down to the store one day and let her pick any item she wanted. Money, for once, would not be a hindrance. She selected a beautiful statue of the Virgin Mary. That statue remains her most cherished possession—not because it had high material value, but because her father had given it to her even though he couldn't afford to.

Henry's generosity on this score was symptomatic of the family's deep faith. The Luermans instilled in their children the Westphalian Catholicism that they had grown up with in Germany—so much so that Junie went on to give his life in service to the Church as a priest. They practiced prayer habits at home, always giving thanks before their meals. The family made a special habit of attending weeknight prayer services during Lent. Where they could, they were generous with their resources: Henry had a special concern for lepers, and in later years, he sent whatever spare money he could to Mother Teresa of Calcutta. And of course, the Luermans were Sunday morning regulars at St. Andrew's Church, praying on the opposite side of the nave as the Dickmans for years.

One Sunday morning at church, Jerome Dickman pointed Martha Jane out to Cliff. Jerome had been seeing Martha Jane's older sister Hilda for about six months, so he knew the Luerman family. Cliff first plucked up the courage to talk to Martha Jane in February 1948 when she was on a shift at Wayne Dairy. He asked her out, but she was a few months shy of 16, the age that her parents would allow her to date. She turned him down.

But not even two weeks after her sixteenth birthday, Cliff got his date. At his invitation, she came to his baccalaureate Mass on May 2, 1948, and afterward, they went out to Maid-Rite for a tenderloin sandwich and a root beer (a food tradition that they kept up as an anniversary). The next weekend was their second date—Cliff's graduation from Webster High School on May 9. Raised in a family of walkers, the trip to Webster was one of Martha Jane's first travels outside of Richmond's city limits. After the ceremony, Cliff's mother and siblings hosted a party for him out on the Dickman farm, and Martha Jane had her first chance to see Cliff's home and meet his large family. When the party finished, he drove her back to Richmond in his new Pontiac convertible. The first two dates had gone well, and both were sure that there would be many more.

The rest, as they say, is history.

4

EARLHAM

Clifford Dickman's baccalaureate and graduation marked the beginning of many dates with Martha Jane. Usually, he picked her up at her house in Richmond, and the pair had an outing at the ballpark, a restaurant, or the movie theater. Though he wasn't a Webster Pirate anymore, Cliff kept up his athletic passion by playing on farm baseball teams, and whenever his girlfriend was available, Dickman was proud to have her in attendance as his fan.

Dickman kept up his third-shift position at the Johns-Manville plant, but after a year on the job, he turned in his notice. He simply didn't see a long-term future with the company— though admittedly, he didn't have any alternatives in mind. He spent the summer of 1949 helping out on the family farm, pondering what other opportunities might be in store for him. His uncertainties were resolved in July, when two men from Richmond drove out to Webster to pay Dickman a visit. Nothing would ever be the same.

The two men were Howie Helfrich and Don Cumley, the head basketball and football coaches, respectively, at Richmond's Earlham College. Dickman and his brother

45

Floyd were hauling manure when they arrived. Helfrich and Cumley had heard of Dickman's athletic talents, both from his Webster High days and from his time playing farm ball. They offered Dickman spots on the Earlham basketball and football teams and a partial scholarship to defray the cost of tuition.

Dickman had never considered college from an academic perspective before, although he was eager for the opportunity of four more years of sports. He had heard rumors that Union College in Kentucky was interested in having him play on some of their teams, but he never received an official offer. The Earlham opportunity came at the right time: a chance for an exciting future in athletics, and a four-year delay in figuring out exactly how he wanted to spend his life. He accepted the coaches' offer that day.

Earlham College was undergoing radical change when Dickman arrived on campus in September 1949. Like most colleges, World War II had shaken Earlham's foundations. At the height of the conflict, its enrollment had plummeted to 225 students.[1] Earlham also garnered deep resentment from its Richmond neighbors during the war. The college had admitted several Japanese-Americans as students to spare them from the internment camps. This led to sharp criticism from the local newspaper and many Richmond citizens.[2]

After the war, Earlham experienced an explosion in enrollment, thanks in large part to the G.I. Bill. By fall 1946, the student body had almost tripled to 600 students.[3] This new wave of students was a trend felt by universities throughout the nation, but Earlham's post-war development was notable in one way. While many

Protestant colleges weakened their denominational affiliation or abandoned it altogether during the post-war era,
Earlham strengthened its commitment to Quakerism.[4]

Earlham's growth was shepherded by its new president, Tom Jones, who took over in 1946 and led the university through Cliff Dickman's years. His presidency
was "a success by almost any standard."[5] By the time his
term concluded in 1958, enrollment had reached 1,000
students.[6] He doubled faculty salaries, and he increased
the university's operating budget from $250,000 to $1.5
million in his twelve years, all while refusing federal sub-
sidies (which he feared would lead to government control
of higher education).[7] Jones also instituted policies for
faculty tenure and academic freedom, bringing Earlham
into alignment with most other American universities at
the time.[8]

Tom Jones was an important character during Dickman's collegiate years, but no one at Earlham figured
more prominently than its professor of philosophy and
theology, D. Elton Trueblood. [9] Himself a Quaker,
Trueblood studied at Harvard and Johns Hopkins before
accepting a position at Stanford University as university
chaplain and professor of philosophy. But he soon became
discontented at Stanford. [10] In his autobiography,
Trueblood said that he sought "an institution of manageable dimensions in which an individual can make a real
difference," and one with an "unapologetically Christian
commitment."[11] And so, leaving behind the prestige of
Stanford and the glamour of California, Trueblood settled
in Richmond and took up teaching at Earlham.

Trueblood was an immensely popular teacher, both on
campus and beyond. He wrote numerous books on philosophy, theology, and politics, and he crisscrossed the country delivering well-attended lectures. He deeply believed

in the need for a more evangelical form of Christianity, one that occupied a more prominent place in national life. For Trueblood, theology and politics were deeply connected, and he became a staunch opponent of communism—the antithesis of a Christian worldview. He found his political home in the Republican Party, and given his national reputation, he became a prominent player in the political arena.[12] President Eisenhower appointed him as a religious advisor to the United States Information Agency, a 1950s-era public-relations effort aimed at improving the United States' standing in the eyes of foreign countries. Trueblood was friend to many other American presidents, as well. He delivered Herbert Hoover's eulogy, as Hoover was a fellow Quaker. And at the request of another Quaker president, Richard Nixon, Trueblood gave the invocation at the 1972 Republican National Convention.[13]

As a Quaker institution, Earlham tried to foster a peaceful campus environment, but the school experienced its share of controversy in the late 1940s and early 1950s. During World War II, certain conscientious objectors who refused to participate in the conflict were allowed to serve in the Civilian Public Service (CPS). They worked domestically, usually by serving in mental hospitals or laboring at public-works projects like the construction of new roads. After the war, President Tom Jones hired CPS alumni to teach at Earlham because their pacifist views were congruent with the tenets of Quakerism.[14] This upset Richmond residents, who viewed CPS objectors as cowards who had shrunk from the obligation to serve their country.

There was also some friction between the CPS professors and G.I. Bill students, who had just completed their harrowing military service. When the Korean War broke out in 1950, the tensions between veterans and CPS alumni were again heightened. President Jones tried to bridge the gap by arguing that the conflict in Korea was really a United Nations peacekeeping mission, and that hawks and doves alike should support the work of an international organization committed to peace. But ultimately, Jones came down on the side of the veterans by serving as chairman of the Wayne County division of the Crusade for Freedom, which rallied support for America's involvement in the war, much to the chagrin of pacifist professors.[15] Tensions were stoked yet again after the passage of the Selective Service Act of 1948, which required men aged 18 or older to register for military service. Several students, again claiming to be conscientious objectors, refused to comply with the law, leading to several FBI investigations on campus and further outcry from Richmond citizens.[16]

The scourge of McCarthyism also found its way into Earlham during the early 1950s. Given the college's pacifism, one might expect Earlham to have been a magnet for accusations of communist sympathies. Indeed, one Earlham professor, E. Merrill Root, wrote lengthy articles attacking fellow professors who evinced even the slightest Communist tendencies. Root was disliked by other professors at Earlham, even by the fervent enemy of communism Elton Trueblood.[17] Ironically, of all the faculty members to be suspected of communist sympathies, the most prominent accusation was against Trueblood himself. The attack was levied by a Texas newspaper after Trueblood made positive comments about the communal sharing of goods among the early Christians. It was a ridiculous claim, and it failed to gain traction. On the whole, Earlham fared better in the McCarthyite Age than one might expect, thanks largely to President Jones' firm and vocal commitment to never hire a communist faculty member.[18]

★ ★ ★

Thus, when Dickman commenced as a student at Earlham College in the fall of 1949, he arrived in the midst of tumultuous change both on campus and across the country. But Dickman's career at Earlham lay far away from these controversies. While he was both an engaged member of the Earlham student body and a distinguished alumnus, his success was primarily found on the basketball court, football gridiron, baseball diamond, and shot-put field.

Even before classwork began, Dickman had a rough start transitioning to his new life. He was the first member of his family to go to college, and at the time, college was not considered an accomplishment in a farming family. It was regarded as a playground for rich kids, not a place for real work.

Dickman's first day of football practice was Labor Day 1949.[19] When he came home at 6:00 p.m., he met an exhausted family that didn't want to talk to him. While he had been out playing football, his brothers and sisters had been baling hay. He was ignored throughout dinner, and Dickman felt ashamed for not having made any contribution while still eating and boarding in the house for free. For the first time in his life, he felt spoiled.

The guilt overcame him, and the next morning, he turned in his football equipment and quit school.[20] When he arrived back at home, he encountered his brother Floyd, who was surprised that he wasn't at football practice. Dickman told him that he had given up on college and was ready to resume farm work. Floyd gave his younger brother a hard look. "If that's what you want, then get the hell out," the older brother said, and he walked away.

The stern ultimatum rocked Cliff, for he had expected Floyd to welcome his retreat from college with open arms. Yet Floyd, who hadn't even completed high school and surely could have used the extra labor, refused to watch his younger brother pass up the opportunity to build a new, different life—a life that Floyd himself had not been called to. And Floyd was not a quitter. He couldn't quit when the responsibility of running a farm had been thrust upon him by his father's untimely death, and he wouldn't let another Dickman quit either.

After Dickman spent 15 minutes in the car thinking about Floyd's words, he made up his mind. He returned to Earlham, reported for practice, and never thought about quitting school again. Like most life-changing moments, Cliff didn't recognize at the time that Floyd had just sent his future on an entirely different trajectory, but it wouldn't be long before he came to this realization. Floyd was, yet again, a father figure for Cliff, and his act of selflessness evokes Dickman's abiding gratitude to this day.

College life may have seemed like an easy road to Cliff's siblings, but football practice was no picnic. Dickman had never played or even seen a football game. It was a baptism by fire. Coach Don Cumley had recruited Dickman for some of the game's roughest positions: offensive and defensive lineman. Dickman struggled to get acclimated to the game. The three-a-day practices were utterly exhausting. He found the abundance and complexity of the rules overwhelming, and it took him a while to figure out how to put all of the pads on. He also had trouble getting aggressive. He was nervous that a hard hit would knock his teeth out, a genuine risk given that the helmets didn't have facemasks.

Dickman didn't enjoy the physical aspect of the game until his junior year, when a new coach, Bob Meyne, and his assistant Walt Ney, took over from Cumley and adopted a new approach. Cumley had been a tough character. One letter, which he sent to his team before the beginning of a new season, exemplifies Cumley's coaching style:

> I am telling you for sure that we are out to win every game and no damn moral victories as last year. We are going to hit them before they hit us, and also no let ups as last year in the Taylor game.

In the margins, Cumley added a personalized touch for Dickman: "I will be looking forward to seeing you to just see how mean you have gotten this summer."[21]

Coach Meyne, on the other hand, was encouraging and upbeat, an attitude to which Dickman responded more enthusiastically. And in practice, Assistant Coach Ney started going up against Dickman in one-on-one blocking drills, which taught him how to hit—and hit hard. The Meyne–Ney combination taught Dickman to embrace, not just tolerate, physical contact.

For all the difficulties of learning the game, Dickman's natural athleticism and learned toughness from basketball enabled him to thrive from the start. In his freshman year, Richmond's newspaper, the *Palladium-Item*, reported that he had been "improving rapidly" during practice sessions, and he got to see playing time from the get-go.[22] Though the Quakers never won any conference championships, Dickman earned all-conference honors his last two years, and he was elected Most Valuable Player by his teammates his senior year, earning him a place of honor at a banquet in Indianapolis.[23] The newspaper summed up his college-football career well during

one of his last games: "Needless to say, Dickman performed well at [the tackle position]. He manages to shine
no matter where he plays."[24]

Dickman's success in football reflected something
more fundamental about his athleticism. While he undoubtedly had innate physical talent, the real source of
his success was his relentless effort. Quite simply, he outhustled all his competitors. He practiced more before
games, fought harder during games, and studied his performance more meticulously after games than anyone
else. He was determined to win. This was the attitude
that transformed him in four seasons from not even
knowing the rules of football to becoming the MVP of his
team.

Just after football season concluded, basketball was
underway. Dickman entered Earlham far more comfortable on the basketball court than on the football field; it
was where he had cut his athletic teeth, so to speak. The
head coach, Howie Helfrich, would become more than just
a basketball coach to Dickman, but also a lifelong friend.
Helfrich was only six years older than Dickman and had
been a star athlete at Oberlin College. His tenure at Earlham overlapped nearly perfectly with Dickman's:
Helfrich joined Earlham the year before Dickman arrived, and he left for a coaching job at Sacramento State
the same year Dickman graduated.

Helfrich had recruited Dickman to come to Earlham
in the first place, and he looked after him during his time
there. The coach and his wife invited Dickman over for
lunch in their home every day, as lunch food wasn't available on Earlham's campus. Helfrich also mentored Dickman on the football and baseball teams, for he served on
those coaching staffs, as well.

Dickman was present for one of the unforgettable moments in Helfrich's life. In his sophomore year, while at basketball practice, Helfrich was demonstrating a pivot move to his team, with Dickman defending the goal. Helfrich, a left-handed player, drove to the basket and, with the ball in his left hand, reached up to lay the ball in. But as the ball fell to the ground, so did something else: Helfrich's ring finger. The rim of the goal was connected to the backboard by a bolt, which protruded into the net. When Helfrich's left hand went up for the lay-up, the bolt snagged his wedding ring, and his finger was ripped off. [25] The finger was never re-attached, but Helfrich always bore it well. He was a banjo player, and he often referred to himself laughingly as the only three-fingered banjo player in the country.

Dickman attained fast success on the Earlham basketball team. When he arrived, a 6'7" star from Richmond High School was the starting center for Earlham. But in January 1950, Coach Helfrich called on Dickman to start the second half against Anderson College, and he put up a critical nine points. That same month, Dickman led Earlham's scoring in a road victory against Canterbury College.[26] From there on out, he was the starting center of the Earlham basketball team. Helfrich had given Dickman an opportunity, and he made the most of it.

Dickman was usually good for 12 points every game—his record high of 24 points came in a 53–52 victory over Hanover. [27] Even as a freshman, he regularly led the Quakers in scoring. The newspaper recognized Dickman as a "tower of strength under the baskets."[28] He stuck to the paint, preferring short, high-percentage shots that depended on muscle rather than finesse. In fact, in his entire college career, Dickman attempted only one shot that was further than halfway from the basket to the free-throw line. His nasty hook shot was tough to defend, and when those weren't hitting, he switched to an up-and-under shot. He led the Quakers in personal fouls committed, but he also got fouled himself quite a bit and scored a fair number of points as free throws.[29] He was a stronger rebounder and played tough defense, usually in the center of a 2-3 zone. Like in football, the Quaker basketball team was generally successful, although they didn't win any Hoosier Conference championships during Dickman's years. Though basketball MVP honors went to his friend and teammate Dudley Moore, Dickman was named an honorary team captain in his senior year.[30]

Cumley and Helfrich had only recruited Cliff Dickman to play football and basketball, but by the time spring rolled around, he was ready for the next adventure. He took on *two* spring-season sports: baseball and track. In baseball, Dickman played third base, as he had in high school. Though he did some pitching, he didn't have the wrist snap needed to be consistent (which he chalked up to years of milking cows). Third base was the perfect position for his strong, albeit less-accurate arm. On the hitting side, Dickman usually batted fourth or fifth in the order for Earlham. Under the direction of Coach George Van Dyke and, later, Howie Helfrich, Earlham's baseball team achieved reasonable success, winning about half of their 16–18 games each year. It was on the baseball team that Dickman earned his campus-wide nickname. Dickman's baseball glove was in ratty shape, so he borrowed the coach's glove to play third base. His teammates teased him for this and dubbed him "Glover." The nickname caught on across campus; even the Earlham student newspaper adopted the moniker.

All the while, Dickman was a member of the Earlham track team, participating in shot-put and javelin events. At his best, Dickman could send the shot more than 40 feet and the javelin over 170 feet.[31] The track team had more success than the football, basketball, or baseball squads. Earlham track frequently won conference titles, and Dickman's strong performance in shot put and javelin contributed crucial points that the team needed to win their meets.

It's hard to imagine playing two college sports at the same time. Usually, Dickman practiced shot put and javelin on his own time, squeezing it in around school and baseball practice. And fortunately for him, track meets and baseball games usually lined up well with each other. Whether at home or on the road, the Quakers typically had the track meet in the morning and baseball games in the afternoon, enabling Dickman to satisfy both obligations. There was only one significant conflict in four years: a baseball game at Hanover and the track conference meet at Rose-Poly in Terre Haute. The stakes were higher in the track meet, so baseball gave way that day.

When all was said and done, Dickman earned 16 varsity letters at Earlham College, which remains to this day the school's all-time record.[32] At the time, it was more common for college athletes to play multiple sports; Dickman played alongside several dual-sport athletes. But four sports in one year was virtually unthinkable. Dickman fittingly earned the award for outstanding athlete of the year after his final season.[33]

Sports at Earlham brought Dickman many new experiences. For one, he had the opportunity to travel like never before. He had games across Indiana and a few in Ohio—not bad for a farm boy who never went further than Richmond while growing up. Dickman also played alongside black teammates at Earlham, an experience he'd never had in Webster. The sports field, at least at Earlham, was a great place for whites and blacks to learn respect for one another and to grow in friendship. In the midst of a racially-charged period in national, no less Richmond, history, Earlham sports were integrated, and the teams were free of overt prejudice. But even still, the reality of racism wasn't altogether absent. Many Indiana restaurants were segregated at the time, and when the team traveled on the road, it was difficult to find places where the entire team could eat together. From their years of experience, they learned which restaurants served whites and blacks alike and chose to eat there on their road trips.

Earlham College itself was not free of prejudice either. In some respects, the college was ahead of its time: it admitted whites and blacks on equal terms, and on-campus housing was integrated. Nonetheless, the administration took a hard line against interracial dating.[34] When one of Dickman's black basketball teammates, Wilfred Doty, started dating a white student, the administration expelled both Doty and his girlfriend.

Undoubtedly and quite obviously, the promise of racial equality was far from fulfillment in the early 1950s, even at a Quaker college. But if nothing else, the great dream seemed closer to a reality on the sports fields at Earlham than most other places at the time.

★   ★   ★

Besides athletics, Dickman made another important commitment during his time at Earlham: Martha Jane. When he started college, she was in her senior year at Richmond High School. She frequently attended his ballgames and made friends with his teammates' spouses and girlfriends. After Dickman's family had gotten more adjusted to the idea of him going to college, they too started to attend the games with Martha Jane.

Shortly before graduating from Richmond High, Martha Jane started work as an office secretary at Hill's Floral Products, one of Richmond's most well-known companies. Thanks to Hill's worldwide distribution of flowers, their greenhouses covered more than 1,000 acres of top-quality farmland on the northwest side of Richmond, which required over 1.25 million square feet of glass.[35] It was a great place to work in all respects except its location: the office was outside walking distance from the Luerman household, so Martha Jane either had to ride the bus to work or count on a ride from her boyfriend.

After a year and a half at Hill's, Martha Jane transitioned to Jenkins Properties. The Jenkins family owned a large number of properties in Richmond—gas stations, an apartment building, a bowling alley, the Medical Arts building, and several other locations—and their company rented these out for commercial or residential use. Martha Jane was the company's bookkeeper, responsible for collecting rent payments and ensuring that all accounts were up to date. She oversaw the correspondence of the manager, Norman Jenkins, and was essentially the head administrative honcho for one of Richmond's largest operations. Fortunately, Jenkins's office was within walking distance from home, relieving her of bus trips or counting on rides. And most importantly, the job enabled Martha Jane to do something that Cliff couldn't: save money. This would play no small role in getting the couple off the ground in just a few short years.

Between Cliff Dickman's commitment to athletics and his girlfriend, there wasn't much time left for anything else. He fared reasonably well academically, but school still took something of a backseat. Dickman took little interest in classes that seemed to have no utility—he didn't even bother buying the course textbook for psychology, and he found Philosophy 101, which he took with the great Professor Trueblood, to be a bore. Though he would later regret not paying more attention in his liberal-arts courses, his distaste for these subjects was understandable. He had trouble relating to most of his professors, for they lived diametrically opposite lives from each other—one in the ivory tower, the other on the hog farm. Dickman mostly felt embarrassed by his comparative lack of education, feeling as though he wasn't qualified to speak to his professors. Throughout his time at Earlham, he interacted only with a few down-to-earth teachers with whom he felt comfortable conversing.

He ultimately chose geology as a major. His decision was guided by the simple fact that he had grown up working outside and liked it, and geology was a rare course of study that gave him the opportunity to keep working outside. He enjoyed learning from the young, engaging geology professors, which was reflected in his stronger academic record in these classes.

Geology field trips showed Dickman even more of the world than Earlham athletics had. The first field trip was to the Palisades, cliffs along the Hudson River in New York that exhibit unique geological formations. To save money on lodging and food, the professor and students camped in tents throughout the trip.[36] The second field trip took Dickman to southern Missouri to explore lead and iron-ore mines.[37] The Earlham cohort had a frighteningly close call there. They were lowered into the mine shaft, eight levels deep, by a cable-operated cage. After they had explored the shaft, they returned to the cages for their ascent. As they waited on a cage that was hauling other miners to the surface, the cable snapped, sending the miners hurtling to their deaths. With trepidation, Dickman and his classmates rode the mine's second cage to the top, which fortunately was attached to a stronger cable.

Though academics weren't Dickman's passion, he did enjoy being a member of the student body at Earlham College. He was well known around campus for his athletic skill and also for his engagement in student life. He served on the Earlham Student Senate, which functioned like a student council and adjudicated disciplinary infractions.[38] He joined the Newman Club, a Catholic student group named after St. John Henry Newman. Dickman also was a member of the Earlham Democrat Club.[39] Though surprising in retrospect, Dickman joined because he remembered that his father, like many other farmers during the Great Depression, had always supported President Franklin Roosevelt.

Dickman garnered schoolwide attention on several occasions. For the school's May Day celebration, he performed handstands and walked on stilts in front of the entire student body. The school also hosted a fundraiser for the United Way: an election for "The Ugliest Man on Campus." It was Dickman's first big election, and he won the honor. He reported his prize to Hedwig Luerman, Martha Jane's mother, who apparently missed the joke and replied in her thick German accent, "Argh, surely there must be *someone* uglier than you."

Dickman also made interesting connections and forged wonderful friendships as an Earlham student. Two of his fellow teammates went on to particularly distinguished careers. John East, who played football with Dickman and graduated alongside him in 1953, went on to serve the state of North Carolina as a United States Senator. Tragically, East committed suicide toward the end of his first term.[40] Another notable teammate was Jim Fowler, who played baseball with Dickman. Fowler graduated Earlham with a degree in zoology, and he became a famous wildlife enthusiast, hosting the prime-time show "Wild Kingdom" and making frequent appearances on the Merv Griffin Show and the Tonight Show.[41] Dickman didn't stay in close touch with East or Fowler, but he did maintain lifelong relationships with several other teammates and their spouses.

For someone who grew up attending a farmhouse school, juggled four college sports without prior experience in two of them, and initially lacked the support of most of his family, Cliff Dickman made an astonishing success of his four years at Earlham College. He had seized the unique opportunity that his athletic gifts offered him, and he walked away from the school as a distinguished alum with the highest respect from his classmates. The 1953 Earlham College Yearbook perhaps offered the best summation of Dickman's four years of college:

> Clifford Dickman. Jim Thorpe of Webster … sixteen varsity letterman … gridiron M.V.P. 1953 … solid as the rock … never gets mad … "Glover" and campus Ugly Man … "But I don't have any skunks on my farm" … husband to be … one of the greatest guys you'll ever hope to meet.[42]

In spring 1953, Cliff became the first Dickman to graduate from college.* In attendance was Floyd, who had believed in Cliff from the start and whose tough love was indispensable in getting his brother to the graduation stage with 16 varsity letters in hand. Next to the Dickman family sat Martha Jane, beaming with pride. Five years had passed since their first date, but their wedding

---

* Cliff's younger sister Susann, who later earned a degree in education from Ball State University, was the only other member of his family to graduate from college.

bells weren't ringing yet. Opportunity had called Dickman to Earlham, but now it was duty that called: this time to service in the United States Army.

5

THE ARMY

Clifford Dickman's life thus far had been defined by diligence and toughness. But effort is only one ingredient of success—good fortune is the other. And Dickman undeniably lived a life with providential blessing on his side. Perhaps no chapter in his story makes that reality clearer than his time in the United States Army.

Dickman hadn't planned to go into military service, but he expected it nonetheless. He registered with the selective service as required by law, but because he remained in the top two-thirds of his class at Earlham College, he was exempt from the draft. Upon graduation in May 1953, Dickman and his male classmates expected to get called up to serve in the Korean War, which had been raging for three years.

The mere prospect of being drafted made a big impact on Dickman's life. During his final semester, the Dow Chemical Company had bought him a plane ticket (his first-ever flying experience) to Midland, Michigan, where he interviewed for a sales position. The company offered him a job, which paid well and offered him the hope of a bright future. But Dickman declined the offer; there was no point in moving to Michigan only to be drafted shortly thereafter.

He, along with Earlham classmates Dudley Moore and John East, expected that their lot would be better if they volunteered to serve, rather than waited to be drafted. They drove to Cincinnati to enlist in the Marine Corps, but Dickman was not accepted: he failed his medical examination for high blood pressure. It wasn't Dickman's first run-in with this ailment. Earlham had tried to stop him from playing spring sports his senior year because of his blood pressure, allowing him to carry on only after he signed a liability release. The Marine recruiter, upon seeing the results of his physical, bluntly told him he'd better call the hearse, and he gave Dickman a letter declaring him unfit for military service.

That dashed any future in the armed forces, Dickman thought, so he took a job in Indianapolis selling agricultural equipment for the Indiana Farm Bureau. But the Army, apparently undeterred by the Marines' evaluation, ordered Dickman to submit to a physical. He offered the letter from the surly Marine recruiter in Cincinnati, but the Army dismissed it and conducted their own examination. He was declared to be in satisfactory physical shape and told to immediately report for basic training at Fort Knox, Kentucky. Nothing was said about the letter from the Marines, nor did Dickman ever see it again.

Before joining the Army, Dickman took another important step in his life. On July 11, 1953, he and Martha Jane visited Jenkins Jewelry Store in downtown Richmond where Martha Jane picked out her engagement ring. The ring, which cost about $200, was paid for using money Dickman had saved from his short stint at the Indiana Farm Bureau. While the uncertainty of Army life prevented the couple from pinning down a wedding date, they were gratified to be, at long last, an engaged couple.[1]

Private First Class Clifford Dickman officially joined the United States Army on July 21, 1953.[2] He was assigned to the 3rd Armored Division, and he was supposed to be trained as a tank driver (although he never actually operated one). Dickman's basic training was brutally intense at the outset. The men learned to march, got whipped into physical shape, and ran drills—most memorably, crawling through mud under barbed wire while being shot at with blanks. The drill sergeants were merciless, screaming in the new recruits' ears that they were going to get shot if they "marched like this" or "crawled like that" on the battlefield. The fearmongering worked: Dickman was convinced that if he didn't work harder, he'd be a sitting duck in Korea. He had no history of military service in his family and simply didn't know what to expect from war.

But that fear was short-lived. Just a week into Dickman's training, the United States signed an armistice agreement with China and North Korea, bringing the chances of seeing any kind of combat from very high to very low.[3] The tone of the drill sergeants softened after that, and the day-to-day basic training became more tolerable.

Indeed, Private Dickman would quickly be relieved of virtually all of his Army obligations. When he'd arrived at Fort Knox, he'd inquired into whether the company had a football team. They did, in fact, have a six-man tackle squad, and they competed against other companies on base. Soon, Dickman's athletic reputation caught up with him, and he received new orders: he was to report to football practice every day at noon.

And so it was. Every day at noon, Dickman left basic training behind and got back to what he loved most—sports. The commanding officers were eager for their unit's teams to defeat those of their comrades-in-arms, so they cut the basic-training schedules of their best athletes so that they'd have time for practice. Even when Dickman's unit went out on "bivouac," a two-week period where the unit simulated combat and camped around the base in two-man tents, the young private was still expected to report to football at noon. Not only that, but he was permitted to sleep in the barracks at night instead of the cramped tents where his fellow trainees were. When Dickman returned to his company in the morning for his brief participation on bivouac, he didn't come empty-handed. Candles and Hershey bars were always in high demand for the soldiers away from the barracks, so Dickman bought both from the base exchange and stealthily sold them at a tidy profit to his buddies in the field—a first glimpse of his entrepreneurial spirit.

After basic training ended, Dickman was assigned to the Quartermaster Battalion, and he worked on base as a supply clerk. Yet again, his hours on duty were short. The Army's track season was coming up soon, and he needed to prepare if he was to be the base-wide winner in shot put, discus, and hammer (which, eventually, he was). The Army even sent him by plane to Fort Lee, a training base for the 5th Armored Division about 25 miles south of Richmond, Virginia, for a track meet. Upon arrival, he was picked up in a private car, driven to the mess hall, and fed a gourmet meal. Thanks to his athletic ability, the 24-year-old private was treated like a high-ranking officer. He didn't win at Fort Lee, but he was impressive all the same, throwing the 12-pound shot 49 feet and 5 inches.[4]

Thanks to his critical contributions to the football and track squads, the commanding officers quickly took a liking to Private Dickman. Captain Kenny, the leader of his company, started allowing Dickman to go home to Richmond on the weekends, even letting him bring his car back to base. Every Saturday morning, Dickman drove the three hours from Fort Knox to Richmond to visit his family and Martha Jane, and on Sunday night, he drove himself back to Kentucky. Both the every-weekend leave and on-base parking pass were unique, even unheard-of privileges. Dickman, of course, kept Captain Kenny buttered up, offering the captain his chocolate bars free of charge.

In summer 1954, new orders came in for Private Dickman: he was to report to Maison Fort in Orléans, France. Before his weekly visits to Richmond came to an end, he and Martha Jane had one last important task to attend to. Using her savings from work at Jenkins Properties, Martha Jane bought a house on Southwest 4th Street in Richmond for $15,500, which she and her fiancé picked out together. The street was lovely. Verdant trees bordered the road, and quaint abodes filled with young families lined the sidewalks. The house was on the west side of the Whitewater Gorge that divides Richmond in two. This would be a new adventure for Martha Jane, who had always lived on Richmond's east side. But she didn't cross the gorge quite yet, for the house was too much for a single resident. She continued to live in her parents' house while renting out her new property for $100 per month.

The ring and the house were purchased, and Cliff and Martha Jane were eager for their wedding day. But first, France beckoned.

★   ★   ★

The Army had remained in western Europe since the conclusion of World War II to support the continent's reconstruction. By 1950, the mission had evolved to one of deterrence against any aggression by the Soviet Union.[5] This required increased planning and coordination across the continent, and Orléans, France played an important role: the city served as a communications hub for transmissions from the United States, United Kingdom, and France into West Germany.[6] The base at Maison Fort was one of two sites on the continent that was responsible for maintaining records of every piece of Army equipment issued across Europe (both sites served as a backup in case the other was destroyed).

In August 1954, Private Dickman boarded the USS *General Harry Taylor* in New York, which carried his unit across the Atlantic to Bremerhaven, Germany. A train then carried them to France.

Orléans is an old city, situated about ninety miles south of Paris where the Loire, France's longest river, bends from its northerly direction to a westerly one. During the end of the Second World War, Orléans was a target of the Allies' bombing campaign as they liberated France from Nazi control. The bombardment destroyed the medieval glory of Orléans, but much of the city had been rebuilt by the time Dickman arrived in 1954. Fortunately, one of the city's great landmarks had survived: "Joanie on the Pony," a statue that commemorates Joan of Arc's liberation of Orléans from a British siege in the fifteenth century, when the saint was a mere teenager.[7]

The Americans lived in steel prefabricated huts at Maison Fort, simple but tolerable digs. On the Friday after arriving on base, Private Dickman inquired whether there was a football team. Indeed, he learned, there was a squad, and the next day, he met the football coach and practiced with the base's team. Before leaving practice that day, the Maison Fort football coach told Dickman that if any superior gave him trouble for attending practice, that officer should talk to the colonel.

On Monday, Dickman reported for his first day of work in the records department. When he arrived, he told the captain on duty that he needed to leave his post early for football practice. The captain, not at all amused, sternly reminded him that he was a private in the Army and that he would do a full day's work, just like everyone else. So, following the coach's orders, Dickman told the captain that if there was any problem, he ought to call the colonel. The captain, going off in a huff to investigate, was overruled by the colonel two hours later. "Private Dickman," the sheepish captain said upon his return, "you're to report to football."

Those two hours were the beginning and the end of Private Dickman's work in the Orléans records facility; his service would be athletic. Every day in Orléans, he reported to football, and eventually basketball. He was never issued a rifle, never stood an inspection, never received any orders. It was almost as if the Army command had forgotten about him. Surprisingly, his hut-mates weren't bothered by his unique treatment. They got along with him well and gave him the nickname "Jockstrap."

Like at Earlham, Army sports gave Dickman the opportunity to travel. He and his teammates journeyed across France and Germany, playing other Army and Air Force squads. He played football and basketball games, and although he trained for baseball and track in the spring, he never participated in a contest for either of those sports. One of his basketball teammates was Jim Stone, a former basketball player for Purdue and the only

69

Army servicemember with whom Dickman remained in contact in later years. Stone and Dickman must have had similar military experiences, for Stone once commented with a smile that his job in the Army was "to play basketball."[8]

Dickman had opportunities to travel independent of his athletics, as well. The Army was fairly flexible with how the enlisted men spent their weekends, so Dickman had the chance to explore nearby sites with his friends. He toured Orléans beyond the confines of his base and took a few weekend train trips up to Paris. On Christmas Eve 1954, he and a friend attended midnight Mass in Lucerne, Switzerland. At the time, the Mass was celebrated in Latin throughout the world, making the faraway churches of Switzerland and France feel just like St. Andrew's in Richmond.

Dickman marked the high point of his travels in the spring of 1955. Throughout his time in France, he had been hoping to meet Martha Jane's extended family that still lived in Borghorst and Münster, Germany. Dickman and Hedwig Luerman discussed this prospect by letter, and in turn, she alerted her relatives to the possibility of his arrival. But as the trip would require more time than a weekend, there remained the complicated matter of receiving Army permission to depart the base during the workweek.

Seeking permission for leave, Dickman approached Captain Capps's office. He first confronted the secretary working outside the captain's office. She was flabbergasted at Dickman's request. "We've had people here for two years who haven't had a single leave," she snapped, "so what makes you so deserving?" Ultimately, she said, he'd have to talk to Captain Capps himself. Entering the captain's office, Dickman politely made his leave request, anticipating rejection all the while. In a stunning reversal from his secretary, Capps replied, "Would 11 days be sufficient?"

In a simple stroke, a quick trip to visit future in-laws became Cliff Dickman's Grand Tour of Europe—an 11-day jaunt that would lead him to some of the continent's grandest cities and sites. He and a friend began the trip together in March 1955, flying on an Army mail plane to Naples, Italy. From Naples, they visited Capri by boat, and after returning to the mainland, they traveled to Rome. From there, another mail plane carried them to Marseilles in southern France. The pair split up after Marseille, with Dickman journeying north by train into Germany to visit Martha Jane's relatives in Borghorst and Münster. The extraordinary trip concluded with a quick pass through Holland, Belgium, and Sunday Mass in Paris.

Dickman's first meeting with Martha Jane's family was in Borghorst. After he arrived at the local train station, he walked a couple blocks to the town ratskeller, the Seegers' family bar that was then operated by Hedwig's sister and her husband. Of course, neither of them knew the other's language, so there was mostly a lot of handshaking and smiling. Dickman introduced himself by pointing at his chest and saying "americano," only later realizing that this is a Spanish word. Eventually, he started saying "ya" with a head nod and a smile to indicate his appreciation.

The couple drove Dickman to meet their Uncle Otto, who was overtly giddy at the prospect of meeting an American. Naturally, Otto also did not know any English, but he expressed his delight by saying "*vunderful, vunderful!*" over and over again. Dickman met Hedwig's father, Heinrich Seegers, in Borghorst as well. He was the last person in Martha Jane's American family to see him, as Heinrich died just a month later. Dickman also had the chance to pay a visit to the Luerman side of the family in Münster, home to Henry Luerman's brother, Bernhard. For Dickman, the entire trip was a special way of receiving an extended-family blessing before marrying into their clan just a few months later.

On June 9, 1955, Private Dickman departed Maison Fort for the United States. He'd spent 11 months deployed to France. Before leaving, the orderly checking him out asked for his weapon. "Jockstrap" Dickman, who had been reporting to the sports fields since the second hour of his first day of work at Maison Fort, had never been issued a weapon. The orderly, likely suspecting theft, demanded the truth, telling Dickman that he didn't care if he was a general, *everyone* in the Army received a weapon. Dickman swore that he had never gotten one, and the orderly, after being unable to find any record of a weapon being checked out to him, reluctantly let him proceed.

After disembarking in New York, Dickman had a few free days before reporting to Fort Sheridan in Illinois to be discharged. He quickly traveled by train home to Richmond. There, at Pennsylvania Station, Dickman greeted his own family and the Luermans. Under his mother's watchful eye, he opted to hug Martha Jane rather than kiss her—an act which she only forgave because of her joy at seeing him again.

After a short visit in Richmond, he drove to Fort Sheridan where he was honorably discharged. Dickman had served for almost two years, and as far as the Army was concerned, he had satisfied his obligations. For his part, Dickman was glad to be home and move on to the next phase of his life. The Army had treated him well; indeed, Cliff Dickman may have been one of the best-treated draftees in Army history. But for all the thrill of his adventures across the far reaches of Europe, Dickman knew that his future was not in the military. It lay with his family, his business, and community—right at home in Richmond.

August 20, 1955
Clifford and Martha Jane Dickman on their wedding day.

6

Putting Down Roots

By the time Clifford Dickman was back home again in Indiana, he and Martha Jane had passed the seven-year anniversary of their first date at the Maid-Rite for a tenderloin sandwich. With a college degree earned, a house purchased, and military service completed, the time to marry had finally arrived.

Family and friends gathered on Saturday, August 20, 1955 at St. Andrew's in Richmond, the church of Cliff and Martha Jane's baptisms, first communions, and confirmations. It was a beautiful summer morning for a wedding. Dickman, usually the light-hearted class clown, had a solemn, stoic air about him. Though he had eagerly anticipated this day for many years, he was bashful around older adults, and the large crowd of guests in the sanctuary made him nervous. Cliff was also keenly aware of the gravity of the occasion: the sanctity of a wedding vow was not lost on him. Each person, he believed, is always in someone else's care. For her entire life, Martha Jane had been in Henry and Hedwig's care, but soon, that responsibility would permanently shift to him. It was an undertaking unlike any he'd taken on before, and there would be no going back. As he remarked 64 years later to this

75

author before his own wedding day, "When you say 'I do' ... you really do."

But all of Dickman's anxieties melted away at 11:00 a.m. The organ sounded, the church doors swung open, and Martha Jane, escorted by her father, walked down the aisle to her groom. She wore a wedding dress with long sleeves and "white Chantilly lace and nylon tulle ... accented with iridescent sequins," complete with a cathedral-length train.[1] Unlike Cliff, the only nerves she felt were butterflies of joy; she simply bubbled over with happiness to have reached—at long last—this most special of days.

The altar was beautifully decorated with "[p]alms, vases of white gladioli, and pink carnations and tall tapers in branched candelabra."[2] Father Anthony Specuzza officiated the Mass. Cliff was joined by his brother Floyd as best man and his brother Jerome and friend Don Rohe as groomsmen. Standing next to Martha Jane was her matron of honor Hilda Dickman (who had married Jerome) and bridesmaids Corrine Dickman and Camille Gatzek. Jerome and Hilda's son Joe served as ringbearer, and Marcella Brann, daughter of Cliff's sister Bernadine, was the flower girl. Before God, their family, and their friends, the bride and groom swore their vows of lifelong fidelity to each other, and began their lives as Mr. and Mrs. Dickman.

Because the Mass was in the morning, a long day of festivities laid ahead for the newlyweds. First, a luncheon was served at the Knights of Columbus council hall, courtesy of the Luerman family. Those who attended the ceremony, about 85 in number, enjoyed a meal of chicken and ham. Soon after, the council hall opened up for a larger reception, attended by around 200 people, which featured a four-tiered wedding cake, speeches from the bridal party, dancing, and gift-opening by Cliff and Martha Jane. When all was said and done, the wedding day had gone off without a hitch.

In the early evening, Cliff and Martha Jane departed straight from the K. of C. for their honeymoon, which they spent on a small lake in northern Indiana. For $75, they rented a cottage at the lake for a full week. The next-door neighbors had young children, and when the kids discovered that the couple was newly married, they kept running over to the Dickmans' yard singing "Here Comes the Bride."

The lake was otherwise a peaceful place, good for rowboat rides and long walks. But eventually, they grew restless, so they started making some short daytrips from the lake. One such trip was to Kalamazoo, Michigan. Cliff was an avid lover of Corn Flakes for breakfast—something he had even remembered to pack for mornings at the cottage. On one sleepy day, they cruised up to Kalamazoo to take a tour of Kellogg's factory and see for themselves how Cliff's beloved Corn Flakes were made. Another day on the honeymoon, Cliff took the referee licensing exams for football and basketball. He passed the basketball exam but failed the football one, although the examiners had mercy on him and let him retake it after he told them he had made the attempt while on his honeymoon.

After the relaxing, if somewhat quirky, honeymoon, the couple returned to their new home at 27 Southwest 4th Street in Richmond. Cliff began work with Philip Thornburg, a local surveyor who hired him just after he was discharged from the Army. He had taken the job because it was outdoor work, but he quickly ascertained that surveying was not for him. Martha Jane continued her work at Jenkins Properties as executive secretary and office administrator. She had become indispensable to the Jenkins family and their business over the years, and she was quite happy to continue working for them.

In February 1956, Dickman accepted a new job with the American Agricultural Chemical Company, headquartered in Cincinnati. He worked as a fertilizer salesman, covering territory in southwest Ohio. It was a good job for a young man. The position paid an annual salary of $3,600, and thanks to a letter of gratitude that Dickman wrote to the company president in New York, he won a $1,000 bonus after just four months on the job. The role also came with a unique perk for the time: a company car, in this case, a brand-new Ford.[3]

For a new hire, Dickman was an effective salesman. Because he had grown up on a farm and his sales targets were farmers, he had no trouble understanding the needs and wants of his customers. He got along well with everyone and enjoyed the person-to-person aspect of the job.

But working for American Agricultural had one major drawback: travel. Dickman had to drive his company car around rural Ohio, often as far as Cincinnati, every day for his job. Soon, the company was encouraging him to move to Cincinnati. Cliff was hesitant about the prospect of moving, and Martha Jane was flatly against it. The couple had only just moved into their new home, and she was thriving in her position with Jenkins Properties. Not to mention, she had no desire to live far away from her parents and siblings, several of whom were still unable to drive. Once again, Dickman knew he needed to make a career change.

Cliff and Martha Jane's world changed forever in July 1956, when Cliff went to work for Whitey Kessler at his retail store, Kessler's Sports Shop. Phillip "Whitey" Kessler was an athletic legend in Richmond. He was a star basketball player for Morton High School (the previous name of Richmond High School), earning the nickname "Whitey" for the flash of his blonde hair as he streaked up and down the basketball court. [4] In 1924, at the end of his high school years, Kessler won the Gimbel Award, a high honor for the basketball player who exhibits the best sportsmanship during the Indiana state basketball tournament. [5] Interestingly, Whitey played ball alongside Weeb Ewbank, another Richmond icon who went on to lead the New York Jets to victory in Superbowl III as the team's head coach.

A decade after high school, Whitey decided to bring his athletic name and talent to the business world. On April 28, 1934, he opened Whitey Kessler's Sport Shop, advertising his grand opening in the local newspaper with illustrations of golf, tennis, baseball, fishing, and hunting gear. [6] The shop was located in downtown Richmond along North 9th Street, the northbound lane of U.S. Highway 27.

Kesslers* relied on the reputation of Whitey's high school glory days for a steady stream of business. The store, like most other sporting-goods shops, had two components: a retail business and a team business. The retail side was run by Whitey's wife, Mildred, a quick-witted, hardworking woman. Mildred operated the storefront efficiently—and mostly by herself. She ran the entire business alone during World War II, when Whitey served overseas. After the war, Whitey mostly spent his days playing cards at the country club, leaving Mildred with the tough day-in, day-out work at Kesslers. The team

---

* The apostrophe was soon dropped from "Kessler's Sports Shop."

business, where the future of Kesslers would be made, involved selling apparel, shoes, and other equipment to high school and college sports teams. Kesslers had one salesman who spent his days on the road, calling on coaches and athletic directors to make sales.

In the summer of 1956, Whitey suffered a heart attack, a surprising event for such a young and fit individual. He survived the episode, but his health had significantly deteriorated. The news spread quickly, and it made quite an impression on Cliff Dickman, still selling fertilizer for American Agricultural. With Mildred once again operating the store alone and no Kessler children in the ranks to assist, Dickman began to wonder whether he might have the opportunity to buy the shop. He knew something of the sporting-goods industry through his years of athletics, but he had never seriously considered entering for himself. Because schools generally maintained longstanding relationships with the salesmen who called on them, there simply was no room for a new entrant into the market. The only way in was to buy someone else out, and with the future of Kesslers uncertain, Dickman thought he had found an entry point. He resolved to pay a visit to Mr. and Mrs. Kessler at their new location on East Main Street.

When he arrived at the store, only Mildred Kessler was working; Whitey was still recovering in the hospital. Dickman was straightforward with her, expressing his interest in doing some work for them and eventually buying the business. Mildred was positively thrilled by this prospect. She told him that he was just what she and Whitey were looking for. Mildred asked him to come back a week later so that she and her husband could confer. When Dickman returned for that second meeting, she agreed to their plan and asked when he was willing to start. "Right away," was his answer, and he turned in his notice to

American Agricultural Chemical. It was a difficult sacrifice given how well the company had treated him. But he'd been offered the deal of a lifetime: the opportunity to keep his roots in Richmond, combine his work with his love of sports, and eventually become a business *owner*. Dickman didn't just find a job at Kesslers; he found his vocation.

Starting October 1, 1956, Dickman worked as a salesman for Kesslers, learning the bread and butter of his new line of work firsthand.[7] He traveled around Wayne County, Preble County (Ohio), and other surrounding areas, meeting with coaches and principals, sizing up athletes for their apparel and shoes, and establishing a positive name for himself. Having been a well-known athlete himself not long ago, his reputation preceded him on his sales calls. Like any successful salesman, he talked, charmed, listened, laughed, and sold. It was a good training experience for him as he prepared to take over the business. But *when* Whitey and Mildred would finally sell him the store remained an open question, as almost two years passed with little discussion on the subject.

One day in June 1958, when Mildred was sweeping the floor at Kesslers, she turned to Dickman and said she didn't think he was serious about buying the place anymore because whenever she suggested it, Cliff laughed. Dickman replied, "Whenever you're serious, I'll stop laughing." She kept sweeping, but a few minutes later, she turned and said, "Well, I'm serious." She told him the store was his as soon as he was able to get the money. Dickman couldn't believe this rapid turn of events, and he set out quickly to capitalize on her offer.

On July 1, 1958, at 28 ½ years old, Clifford Dickman became the owner of Kesslers Sports Shop, later to be known as Kesslers Team Sports. Whitey and Mildred's price tag was $65,000. The two parties never haggled over the figure, but looking back, Dickman suspects that he paid a bit much. Whitey and Mildred didn't even own the building where the store was located; they rented it from a local doctor. The price Dickman paid bought only the store name and the current inventory. Whitey and Mildred wanted the sale to be quick: there was not even an official count of the inventory before signing the deal. The retiring couple had two stipulations. First, they personally wanted to collect all receivables that were still outstanding. Second, Dickman was to be the sole owner of the business; he was not to have any partners. This strange condition proved difficult for the young man. He and Martha Jane had limited savings, and the banks refused to loan the couple any money because they didn't have enough equity in their home. The inventory in the store was the only collateral they could pledge.

As a result, Dickman surreptitiously turned to close family for help, despite Whitey and Mildred's odd prohibition on business partners. Dickman offered the opportunity for ownership in Kesslers to his siblings and Martha Jane's family, but he had only a few takers. He broke the company up into five shares, each at a price of $13,000. The first share belonged to him and Martha Jane. Another share went to Floyd, the third to his mother, the fourth to his sisters Kathleen and Dolores, and the fifth to Martha Jane's youngest brother, Bob Luerman. Bob had just one year left in college in Indianapolis, where he was studying accounting, and owning a share in the business promised him a job after graduation. With $65,000 in hand, Dickman bought Whitey and Mildred out and took over the sports shop. He was elated at his future prospects when, on his first day in charge, the store made $126.

The Kesslers had limited contact with Dickman and the store after the sale. Mildred stayed on for a short period to help with the transition. Whitey came into the store on occasion to give Cliff some unsolicited advice. He told Dickman that he needed to join Forest Hills Country Club to make the contacts he needed for success. Dickman wasn't interested in joining the club and ignored him. Another day, shortly after Cliff and Martha Jane's third child, Linda, joined the family, Whitey told Dickman that he'd never be able to afford the store with so many kids. Cliff retorted that he was the seventh child in his own family, and he sure was happy his parents had decided to have at least that many.

Whitey made his final visit to his old store in a huff. Dickman had run an ad for the store in the local newspaper, the *Palladium-Item*. Unlike Whitey's ads, Dickman included three new words at the bottom: "Cliff Dickman, Proprietor." He'd done this after speaking with disenchanted former customers of Whitey's who, upon hearing that Cliff had taken over, promised to start shopping at Kesslers again. Whitey, of course, didn't know this. He told Dickman, "Son, I want to see you succeed. But you'd better keep your name out of that paper if you want to make it in this business." Cliff felt like he owed Whitey the truth, so he shared the reactions he heard from others when they learned he was running the shop. Whitey tried to figure out who had ragged on him, but Dickman refused to say. Whitey walked out of Kesslers and never came back. His health, permanently weakened from his earlier heart attack, collapsed less than a year after he sold his sports shop. He died on April 30, 1959 at age 52, and Mildred died just two years after him.[8]

★　★　★

The new proprietor set to work at building up his business. The first matter was the name of the store. Whitey Kessler had not asked Dickman to keep the store named after him, although based on his reaction to the newspaper ad, he likely expected that Cliff would leave the name untouched. In fact, Dickman did so for strategic reasons beyond name recognition in the community. Kesslers had established strong trade credit with its suppliers, including Rawlings, Riddell, Wilson, Spalding, Louisville Slugger, and others. Those companies allowed Kesslers to pay for merchandise several weeks after receiving it. Changing the name of the store would have drawn unwanted attention to the store's new ownership, and the suppliers might have revoked the arrangement. By the time the suppliers put together that Dickman was the new owner, he had established sufficient credit of his own, and their cordial business relationships were maintained.

Dickman's next task was the matter of performance. Kesslers, like many other sporting-goods shops at the time, performed reasonably well, neither dominating the competition nor being decimated by it. In the late 1950s through the 1970s, competition in the sporting-goods market was defined by sales relationships, geographic proximity, and the brands of goods carried. In stark contrast to business competition today, price was not a basis for competition—different stores generally charged the same amount for the same product. That made it relatively easy for established businesses to succeed. Their market share was generally untouchable by intruders, who could neither offer lower prices nor woo away the loyal customers of established shops. The flip side, of course, was that established businesses faced strong barriers to growing into other markets. The outcome was a relatively stable sporting-goods market: if you owned a piece of it, you had a strong guarantee of steady business. This was especially true in Richmond, as the only competition in town (Brimm's) folded around the time Dickman took over.

Of course, this is not to say that the sporting-goods market was entirely stagnant. Some shops had comparative advantages over others, which they tried to leverage to their benefit. Larger team dealers in Terre Haute, Fort Wayne, and Dayton sometimes tried to lure away high schools and small colleges from Kesslers using their critical advantage: information. Coaches were always searching for their next opportunity—either to advance up the hierarchy of their own coaching staff or to transfer to a bigger school. The large team dealers, by virtue of associating with many schools, had inside intelligence on which schools were hiring. Kesslers simply couldn't provide the same knowledge that their larger competitors could. And of course, many of the larger shops courted their clients by offering free jackets for the coaches and principals. What they called a "perk," Dickman called a "bribe," and he refused to give away freebies. He was content to send his customers a pair of socks as a Christmas present.

But Kesslers had its own advantages which Dickman brought to the business. Time and again, customers returned to Kesslers for their lenient credit policies. Usually, schools didn't want to pay for gear until they collected ticket revenue from a few football or basketball games. Dickman willingly delivered orders to schools in advance of the season while allowing them to defer payment by several months until the ticket money came in, and he never charged them interest for the delay. This policy bought the store an untold amount of goodwill with their clients, as Kesslers's competitors typically did not allow such generous financing.

Kesslers also managed to capitalize on trade discounts with its suppliers by paying bills quickly, which usually knocked a few percentage points off their final invoice. The ability to knock out the payables immediately while delaying the receivables was unique. Fortunately, Kesslers had a strong reserve of savings in the bank, enabling them to defer cash flows for the benefit of their customers.

Kesslers's success also depended on its personnel. The store was powered by a small but mighty group. Bob Luerman, equipped with his accounting degree, joined the business a year after Dickman took over. Bob never married or had children, so he poured his heart and soul into the store. In the beginning, the retail side of Kesslers was run by Carolyn Brumfield, who assisted customers, stocked shelves, and helped with some bookkeeping duties.

Retail was the key engine of Kesslers's success in its early days, but over the years, growth increasingly came from the team business. At first, Dickman had expected to be the store's sales representative himself, traveling to schools across the area to outfit teams with Kesslers products. But he quickly learned that as owner, he needed to be present in his shop during the workday, not on the road. So he hired Dick Cox to replace him, who was quickly succeeded by Dave Martin, a basketball star from Fountain City High School.

In 1961, Martin quit, leading Dickman to make the most important hire outside the family in his career: Ray Mitrione. Born to Italian-immigrant parents, Mitrione grew up in Richmond and played football for Richmond High School and Earlham College. After two years, he transferred from Earlham and then graduated from Ball State. Mitrione served in the U.S. Army during the Korean War, and upon returning to Richmond, he worked for the YMCA and the Earlham football team as an assistant coach. When Dave Martin retired, Dickman called Ray with a job offer, and he "didn't think twice before saying yes."[9]

For 26 years, Ray Mitrione was the face of Kesslers on the road. He worked six days a week, crisscrossing Indiana and western Ohio, meeting with around 80 schools for their apparel, shoe, and equipment needs. On Saturday mornings, Mitrione generally stayed behind in Richmond and reported to the shop. The store was a home base for coaches, who like to re-live their games from the night before while enjoying Kesslers-provided coffee and doughnuts. Usually, a local radio station dropped in to interview them as they looked ahead to the next week's matchups. It was a good opportunity for Dickman and Mitrione to keep up a good rapport with their clients.

Mitrione was tremendously successful. He had a big, winning personality, and he easily made conversation with the coaches who grew to love him. Thanks to his likability and persistent efforts, he was able accomplish the difficult feat, at the time, of expanding the business into new territory, picking up schools around Indianapolis and in the southern part of the state. As a result of his success, Dickman brought him in as a shareholder, and in 1965, the company officially incorporated with Mitrione holding the sixth share. The informal ownership agreement kept secret from Whitey Kessler was at last made official.

While Ray Mitrione's star as a salesman was rising, terrible tragedy struck his family and shook the entire city. Ray's brother, Dan Mitrione, had spent much of the 1960s running covert missions for the federal government in South America. By summer 1969, Dan was living in Uruguay. The Uruguayan government faced the dire threat of a terrorist insurgency from a group called Tupamaros. Drawing on his former experience as Richmond's chief of police, Mitrione led a four-man team of American police trainers supporting Uruguayan law enforcement in their fight against Tupamaros.[10]

On July 31, 1970, Tupamaros kidnapped Dan Mitrione in Montevideo by driving into his station wagon and forcing him at gunpoint into a getaway car. The terrorist group held him for ransom: the release of all Tupamaros prisoners (about 150), or Mitrione's life. Uruguayan President Pacheco Areco flatly refused the trade.[11] The State Department immediately informed Dan's wife in Washington, D.C. and his siblings in Richmond. A ten-day saga of unimaginable stress and heartbreak followed. President Nixon, Secretary of State William Rogers, both U.S. Senators for Indiana, and countless other government officials were personally involved in the attempt to secure Mitrione's freedom.[12] Dan's wife, Henrietta, broadcasted a plea for mercy over the Uruguayan radio waves and worked with Catholic priests on a negotiation. It was all to no avail. Tupamaros eventually set a final deadline for the ransom: noon on Sunday, August 9. The Saturday night before, Ray and his brother Dominic went to St. Mary's Catholic Church in Richmond to pray for Dan. Ray, in a soft voice, told the *Palladium-Item*, "We're hoping for the best. We'll do something. I don't know what yet. But we're sitting tight.... We'll just keep on hoping."[13]

In the early hours of Monday morning, Tupamaros made good on their promise and killed Dan Mitrione. He was found dead in a car with two bullet holes in his head.[14] It was, as President Nixon put it, a "callous murder."[15] An overwhelming response of sympathy in the form of phone calls and telegrams flooded the Mitrione family. Ray said that the Uruguayan ambassador to the United States was sobbing when he called the family.[16]

The funeral, held at Holy Family Catholic Church in Richmond, was attended by both the secretary of state and the president's son-in-law.[17]

Just a few days later, Frank Sinatra, hearing the news, said he wanted to do something to help Dan's kids, so he and comedian/singer Jerry Lewis flew to Richmond to host a benefit concert in Civic Hall.[18] The venue was packed to the brim, and thanks to the ticket sales and the sizable donations chipped in by local businesses, the concert raised more than $70,000. After the event was over, Sinatra wrote a note to Ray: "It was a pleasure to be able to do, in a small way, something directly human to human."[19] It was all a beautiful witness to a community coming together in a time of heartbreak.

Throughout this extraordinarily testing time in Ray Mitrione's life, he remained committed to his work at Kesslers and his family. He was a pillar of the community, someone most local athletes interacted with at some point in their sports careers. And he was a great coworker of Cliff Dickman's and friend to the entire Dickman family.

There are three angles to the story of how Kesslers fared over the following decades. First is the retail side, where the tale is a familiar one. Throughout the 1960s and 1970s, the shop was a fixture in the community for young athletes, and in-store sales were strong and steady. But developments in the 1980s started a slow slide. The first hit to retail was Kesslers's decision to stop selling hunting rifles and ammunition: as a result of increasing firearms regulations, it wasn't profitable to continue selling these goods. The real culprit behind retail's decline, however, was price competition—something that the sporting-goods industry had rarely encountered. National retail chains, most notably Walmart, K-Mart, Sears & Roebuck, and J.C. Penney (among others), purchased merchandise in high volume from the same suppliers as Kesslers. Because they were massive buyers, they were able to secure quantity discounts that Kesslers never could have received. As a result, those stores sold the same brands at lower prices and still kept a healthy profit margin.

Another factor compounding the decline in Kesslers' retail sales was the increasing use of the credit card, especially during the 1980s. As with schools, Kesslers had maintained a competitive advantage with individual customers by allowing them to buy retail goods on credit. The shop knew many of its customers and could generally trust them to pay for their goods several weeks after receiving them. National chains, on the other hand, were either stingy in extending credit or didn't do it at all. With the introduction of the credit card, consumers could delay payment on every purchase, no matter where they shopped. The store's key competitive advantage in the face of an unwinnable price war was gone.

The retail business did not collapse overnight. From the late 1970s through the 1990s, Richmond residents slowly began to turn away from Kesslers for their shoe, equipment, and apparel needs. It was a shift that kids growing up in Richmond in the 1960s–1980s recall with nostalgia today. "Back in the day," a kid made the outing to Kesslers when it was time for a special purchase—like a new pair of shoes or a baseball bat. Kesslers often had a brand or style that no one else in the city had—indeed, they were the first in town to carry Nike shoes and Levi jeans. The clerk fitted their shoes up personally and showed them all the new lines in the top brands. It was just part of being a kid in Richmond. But as customers drifted away and margins fell, products began to disappear from the shelves. The national chains triumphed.

The team side of Kesslers, however, was a smashing success story—one which is reserved for another chapter. For now, suffice it to say that under the energetic direction of Ray Mitrione, the business steadily expanded its reach in outfitting high school and college sports teams. That provided the store with a strong launching ground for extending Kesslers to new frontiers.

The final side to the Kesslers story may seem, by modern standards, surprising for the business world: the role of family. Cliff and Martha Jane's kids were integral in powering the retail store as they grew up, and eventually, several of them would join their father full-time in leading Kesslers to new heights on the national scene. Whether at Kesslers or beyond, the Dickman children's strong sense of family identity was no accident—it was homegrown.

7

THE DICKMANS

The great British cultural critic G.K. Chesterton is believed to have said that the most extraordinary thing in the world is an ordinary man and an ordinary woman and their ordinary children.[1] Clifford and Martha Jane Dickman held many jobs and followed many passions over the course of their lifetimes—sales, office work, athletics, farming, military, construction, and politics. But their true vocation was to be a married couple and to be parents. For all that was extraordinary about their lives, family topped the list—the toughest work, the top thrill, and their lasting legacy.

The feature of the Dickman family that is most striking by today's standards would have been unremarkable at the time, and that is the family's sheer size. The first child, Debbie, was born just a year after Cliff and Martha Jane's wedding, and over the course of the next 14 years, Debbie was followed by Bob, Linda, Ted, Carolyn, Phil, Dan, and Cindy.

With two parents and eight children living under the same roof, the Dickmans had a busy, crowded, chaotic lifestyle. Had there been fewer children, Cliff and Martha Jane would have had more freedom for their own projects, more money in their pockets, more time to themselves. And had there been fewer siblings, the kids might have gotten their own bedrooms, more one-on-one time with their parents, more presents for Christmas. The large family demanded nothing less than daily sacrifice from each of its members. Perhaps this partially explains why large families are so decidedly out of vogue in America today.

But for the Dickman parents and many of their contemporaries, a large family was unmistakably a blessing, not a burden. Clifford and Martha Jane, who grew up in households of nine and six children, respectively, took for granted the idea that they would raise many kids themselves, and the prospect positively delighted them. Sacrifices were indeed made to accommodate so many people, but the mix of personalities made their home bubble over with liveliness and vitality. They wouldn't have had it any other way.

The overriding theme in the Dickman house was that the family came first. Within the family, there was a hierarchy: Martha Jane came first for Cliff, and vice versa. Notre Dame's Fr. Ted Hesburgh once said, "The most important thing a father can do for his children is to love their mother." Though it is doubtful he ever heard these words, Clifford nonetheless took the sentiment to heart. He wasn't shy about showing his affection for his wife in front of the kids. He would sneak up on her while she cleaned the dishes with big hugs, or he'd remark to the kids with a smile, "Isn't your mother beautiful?" He told the children that there was nothing they could do to come between him and their mother. He meant this not only in a metaphysical sense, but quite concretely too. At Sunday Mass, many parents strategically situated themselves apart from each other so that all the kids were within a parent's armlength. Not so in the Dickman pew. Clifford sat next to Martha Jane, and the rest of the kids filled out the row. She was first, they were second, and everyone knew it.

The couple was a united front. Cliff and Martha Jane never disagreed on anything in front of the children. An offense committed against one parent was an offense against the other too. And the kids caught on to their parents' unbreakable alliance quickly. They always knew that if one parent said "no," it was useless to kowtow to the other parent for a "yes." This unity was the firm foundation for the rest of the family.

Though devoted to each other first, the couple didn't shrink away from their parental obligations. By dinner time, Cliff usually still had unfinished work to complete, either back at the office or around the house, but he always made a point to join the others for their evening meal. Friday and Saturday nights were no exception. While many couples their age liked to hit the town on weekend nights—drinking, smoking, and dancing—Cliff and Martha Jane weren't partyers. They had many friends in their neighborhood and around the city, but they preferred to give their family priority at night. Just as there was a hierarchy within the family, so too did they prioritize family over all other relationships.

Cliff and Martha Jane viewed their mission as parents to prepare their children for adulthood, just as their own parents had prepared them. Thus, they made a home that was warm but not coddling. They didn't shower the kids with praise or smother them with hugs, kisses, and I-love-you's. Instead, the kids were regarded like adults in training from their early years, and so they were treated with fairness, dignity, and independence. Their parents' respect was how the kids knew they were very much loved.

The kids learned to earn what they had, not expect it. There were no allowances, no free gymnastics lessons or golf clubs. Not only that, but the kids were responsible for their own transportation to all their activities. Until 1972, the family had only one car which Cliff drove to Kesslers during the day, so there was simply no way for Martha Jane to transport them around town. The kids could walk, ride a bike, or catch a lift from a friend. For those events that they could get to, they often didn't have a parent in attendance. On special occasions, Cliff would come to one of the boys' baseball games, watching from his car parked just beyond the outfield fence. If they struck out, the car fired up and pulled away—partially a product of their father's busy schedule, but more so a symptom of his tenuous patience. Without a doubt, the large family meant that Cliff and Martha Jane saw less of their kids' activities than most parents get to witness.

The children managed to finance their activities by holding down jobs. The girls were babysitters; the boys mowed lawns or ran newspaper routes. Martha Jane in particular kept the pressure on them to stay busy with their jobs—perhaps because she knew it was a healthy recipe for keeping idle hands out of trouble. She solicited new babysitting or lawn-mowing clients, and she calendared the kids' appointments. When the children were younger, she kept a book with a sleeve for each one's wages. When the kids had money in their sleeves, they enjoyed the privilege of going to the bank with her and making a deposit. She had a knack for not only teaching the necessity of work but showing how it could be rewarding.

The high expectations of the house were matched only by their grade school. Like their mother, the kids attended Catholic school, and because they lived on the west side of Richmond, their home parish and school was Holy Family. At the time, the Catholic schoolteachers were overwhelmingly nuns, and they imposed demanding codes of conduct and difficult educational standards on their students. For the middle Dickman children, not even recess provided a respite from the rigors of the classroom. By the 1970s, Holy Family at last had the funds to build a separate church building (the church had previously been part of the school building). The no-nonsense priest, Fr. Robert Minton, ordered the students to haul rocks away from the construction site while on recess. While many of their peers griped about the strictness of the Catholic school, the Dickman children saw school as a natural extension of their home environment, where they were expected to behave and not complain (though admittedly, Fr. Minton and the nuns were far tougher characters than their parents).

After eighth grade, the children entered public school: Dennis Middle School for ninth grade, Richmond High School for tenth, eleventh, and twelfth. The beginning of ninth grade heralded another significant change in the Dickman kids' lives: after-school shifts at Kesslers. The store may as well have been a second home. Uncle Bob Luerman was literally family while the others, like Ray Mitrione and floor assistant Carolyn Brumfield, seemed like family. It appeared that way to the outside world too: Linda's future husband, Dave Major, initially thought that Brumfield was Linda's mother because she was always in the store.

The kids thoroughly enjoyed their after-school work. They were fortunate that Kesslers was one of the coolest stores in town, where other youth came to shop for cutting-edge athletic gear. They learned valuable hard skills—like how to letter hats and jackets, sew, build trophies, and file paperwork—and they picked up soft skills too—like how to talk to strangers and sell merchandise. Uncle Bob was their boss, and he worked them hard. They were never allowed to sit while they worked, and if they ever worked up the nerve to ask for a raise, he'd give it to them only after a tough negotiation. But it was an undeniably fun and lively environment filled with joking and teasing: an ideal job for a high schooler.

For the teenage Cliff Dickman, any money earned belonged to his family, not to him. This was a tradition that the adult Cliff Dickman was willing to drop: the money that his kids earned was theirs to keep. Nonetheless, they were expected to spend it wisely, for thriftiness was a highly valued virtue in their household. Martha Jane saved and repurposed everything she could, including aluminum foil, bread bags, and twist ties. The family rarely ate out at restaurants (though this may also have been a product of Cliff's preference for his wife's sumptuous cooking). Cliff captured his frugality philosophy by installing a sign above the paper-towel holder: "Why use two when one wipes dry?" And even still, Cliff seemed to think that his kids spent more of their money than they needed, frequently teasing them that "I could live off your scraps!"

Though the rules of the Dickman house could often be stricter than others, the kids typically didn't complain. In part, they might have stifled any criticisms out of a healthy dose of fear. Their father was not afraid to discipline the young kids with a hard spank, while the older ones were punished with a tongue lashing. He didn't resort to the crueler physical punishment of rope whipping that his father had imposed on him. The closest he ever got was in the midst of prolonged bickering between Bob and Ted. Cliff's patience ran dry, so he brought home a wooden paddle that Kesslers sold in its line of fishing equipment. The boys were instantly alarmed at the arrival of this punishment device, but it would be even worse than they feared. Their old man took the paddle to his workshop and drilled holes into it so that he could swing it faster, and all the while, the boys were ordered to stand outside and listen to the mechanical sound of their instrument of torture being fashioned. After putting it to use, Clifford hung his improvised tool above the refrigerator for all to see. That was warning enough, for he never used it again.

But putting the rare incident of punishment aside, the kids were most likely willing to follow the rules for a simpler reason: they observed their parents living by the same standards of modesty and responsibility that they were expected to exhibit. Their parents lived simply, worked tirelessly day in and day out, and didn't peep a word of complaint. For other kids who witnessed their moms and dads living by a different code, household rules seemed to be arbitrary or something from which they would eventually graduate. Cliff and Martha Jane showed their kids that the lessons they were teaching weren't just for childhood; they were the key to a lifetime of success. Not only that, but the kids were impressed by the respect that their parents had in the community. They observed the way their parents were regularly greeted around town and how they were always tied up with friends and colleagues for long chats after church. Displays like these convinced them that their parents were worth imitating.

The Dickman kids knew something else important about their family foundation: they were always treated fairly. As we will see, fairness was a pillar of Clifford's leadership style, and so too was it signature to his parenting style. Though the children came of age in varied times, had unique personalities, and posed different challenges, they were each expected to meet the same standards of behavior: to show respect for others, exercise a strong work ethic, and give high efforts to schoolwork. No one was a favorite or got special treatment. Clifford and Martha Jane understood the age-old truth that parental favoritism turns siblings against each other, and their evenhandedness was undoubtedly one of the secrets to the family bond.

But while expectations may have been the same, the kids' childhood experiences were nonetheless quite varied given their age gaps. The older kids recall their "childhood home" as being the Southwest 4th Street house, the one which Martha Jane purchased just before Cliff shipped off to France. But the family eventually outgrew the house and moved a few blocks away to 225 Northwest 7th Street, which the younger siblings remember more as their childhood home. The older kids had more responsibilities than the younger ones. Martha Jane couldn't have hoped to cook, launder clothes, supervise, and care for so many children on her own, and the kids, Debbie and Linda in particular, stepped up to assist her—which they happily did without being asked. They ended up becoming like second parents to their younger siblings.

The kids all had different personalities which melded together well: Debbie, conscientious and always willing to pitch in; Bob, an inquisitive wheeler-dealer; Linda, outgoing and a spoiler of her younger siblings; Ted, a perfectionist and goal-setter; Carolyn, determined and athletic; Phil, a teaser and nicknamer; Dan, serious and hardworking; and Cindy, a fun-natured jokester.[2] No two were the same, and while small conflicts and rivalries could spring up, those were generally short-lived. By and large, the kids complemented each other well, and they created an energetic environment which kept the Dickman house running quite happily.

There were two special treats that Martha Jane and Cliff were willing to give their children. First was the occasional camping vacation. The Dickmans started as tent campers, then they were pop-up campers, and after about a decade of experience, they became motorhome campers. Though the digs were simple in the early years, the destinations could be quite exciting. Their maiden tent-camping trip was a 17-day jaunt to Los Angeles, the family's first time ever seeing the Pacific Ocean. They journeyed to upstate New York and Maine, as well, not to mention local trips around Indiana, Ohio, Michigan, and Wisconsin.

The second treat for the Dickman kids came every Christmas Day. Cliff and Martha Jane's childhoods had a shared tradition: a generous share of Christmas presents. It had been a heavy lift for Joseph and Anna Dickman, but it was especially remarkable for Henry and Hedwig Luerman, who only had the means to repurpose hand-me-downs from neighbors so that their kids would have gifts to open. Cliff and Martha Jane likewise went the extra mile for their kids' Christmas celebrations, giving them a spoiling to last the other 364 days of the year.

But whether at home or vacation, on Christmas Day or an average day, the first and last rule in the Dickman house was love. It was present in the dinners that Martha Jane cooked for the eight growing youngsters night after night, and it was present in the way that Cliff scooped them up and whirled them around when he came home from work. Sometimes love was generous, other times it was tough—but there was no mistaking that love was their watchword each and every day.

When the kids weren't on a job or at school, they could often be found with extended family. Cliff's oldest brother, Floyd, never married and still lived on the Webster farm with his mother. Grandma Anna Dickman retained her thick skin over the years, so she and her grandkids never enjoyed a particularly warm relationship. Uncle Floyd, by contrast, was a favorite of the kids. He was funny, and he gave them access to the barns, chicken coops, and wide-open country fields. For the city-raised kids, trips to Webster were a special treat.

Visits to the Luerman side of the family were frequent, as well. Henry and Hedwig were more doting grandparents than Anna Dickman, though the kids were hardly able to decipher Hedwig's words through her thick German accent. They regularly saw Martha Jane's brother Bob at Kesslers, and they visited John, now ordained as a Catholic priest, at his parishes around the Archdiocese of Indianapolis.

The young Dickman kids shared close relationships with many of their cousins. Martha Jane's oldest sister Mary had married their childhood neighbor, Charlie Maurer, and the couple had seven children. The Dickmans even had a set of "double cousins"—the seven children of Cliff's brother Jerome and Martha Jane's sister Hilda. These cousins all lived in Richmond, so they saw each other often.

The Dickmans also enjoyed a unique bond with a couple that may as well have been family: Merle and Margaretta Bradway, better known to the kids as "Uncle Mutt" and "Aunt Greta." The couple lived two doors down from the Dickmans on Southwest 4th Street. Childless, the couple came to see the Dickmans as their own adopted family; indeed, in Greta's obituary many decades later, the Dickmans were counted among her family.[3] The Dickman kids saw the Bradway house as an extension of their own, and for their part, Mutt and Greta could usually be found at the Dickmans' house on Christmas morning as the kids opened their gifts. The special relationship that the kids had with the Bradways was something akin to Cliff's relationship as a child with the Cooley family—in both cases, a pair of neighboring families, one childless and the other with many kids, developed a lasting friendship.

Uncle Mutt took the greater interest in the Dickman kids. He taught them how to tie their shoes, and he frequently treated them to a batch of his homemade candies. Mutt was the founder of the Midwest Casket Company, which he owned and operated for 36 years.[4] When he had to make casket delivery runs, Mutt usually let one of the boys accompany him. He taught them how to play pool too, for Mutt was an outstanding billiards player.

The kids weren't the only ones who got an education from Mutt; their dad did too. Born in 1899, Mutt was old enough to be Cliff's father, and he indeed became something of a father figure to his young neighbor. Mutt was good working with his hands, especially with wood—not altogether surprising for someone in the casket industry. Cliff had some experience in building things. On the farm, he had erected concrete walls on the side of a barn, and other odd jobs had taught him how to make elementary repairs. But it was Mutt who turned Cliff into a veritable handyman. Together, the men renovated the Dickmans' basement by installing wood paneling on the walls. Mutt's instruction was indispensable to getting the job done right. For Cliff, the basement-refinishing project marked the beginning of a lifelong construction hobby. Over the years, he added countless new fixtures to his house: a patio, a deck, a backyard swing set with five

103

swings, and an outdoor fireplace. He enclosed the front porch on the Southwest 4th Street house, and he replaced the roof on the Northwest 7th Street house. Many more projects followed over the years, none of which would have been possible without the instruction of a generous neighbor.

While Mutt and Greta were quasi-family members, the Dickman family eventually gained new members by marriage. First came Marty Hanneman, then Rhonda Rogers, Dave Major, Kim Cutter, Jim Stephens, Millie Siebert, Angie Otterman, and Tony Mendenhall. Clifford and Martha Jane resolved never to relegate their kids' spouses to second-class in-law status; they treated the spouses as if they were their own sons and daughters. They attended their graduations, celebrated their birthdays, and, for those who hadn't grown up Catholic, looked on proudly and gratefully as they sacramentally joined the Church through the RCIA program. Thus were the eight spouses of the Dickman kids seamlessly integrated into the life of the family, which became only more joyful as it grew larger and larger.

As the eight Dickman kids transitioned into adulthood—graduating, moving out of the house, marrying, having kids of their own—Cliff and Martha Jane responded less with nostalgia and more with pride and satisfaction. They had set out as parents with a mission of preparing their kids to be capable adults, and their children's coming of age marked the successful completion of that mission. It was the end of an era, to be sure. But they were looking forward to the new one.

"My father," Theodore Roosevelt once said, "was the best man I ever knew." He went on:

He combined strength and courage with gentleness, tenderness, and great unselfishness. He would not tolerate in us children selfishness or cruelty, idleness, cowardice, or untruthfulness. As we grew older he made us understand that the same standard of clean living was demanded for the boys as for the girls; that what was wrong in a woman could not be right in a man. With great love and patience, and the most understanding sympathy and consideration, he combined insistence on discipline. He never physically punished me but once, but he was the only man of whom I was ever really afraid. I do not mean that it was a wrong fear, for he was entirely just, and we children adored him.[5]

The eight Dickman children could have said much the same about their father and mother alike. Firm discipline, clean living, and equal treatment were indeed the rule in their house. Yet their father and mother embraced the great virtues, refused to tolerate bad habits, and showed enduring patience and love toward their children. They were entirely just, and the kids adored them for it.

8

MAN OF THE COMMUNITY

The acclaimed social scientist Arthur Brooks has argued that there are four pillars to leading a life of fulfillment: faith, family, work, and community.[1] Over the past several decades, the balance among these commitments has grown distorted, and mindless distractions have replaced some of them altogether.[2] The causes are complex and beyond the scope of this book, but it suffices to observe an obvious, sad truth: the virtue of civic engagement has fallen sharply in recent years.[3]

But not so in the Richmond, Indiana of the 1960s and 1970s. Dedication to the community and its various civic associations was a basic tenet of good citizenship and a well-lived life. Locals were expected to take up the task of city improvement by serving in nonprofits, spearheading local-government initiatives, organizing neighborhood block parties, coaching little-league teams, and financially contributing to efforts in need of aid.

Clifford Dickman responded to the call of duty with gusto. Shortly after he took over Kesslers, with its prime location in the center of town, Dickman was invited to join the Downtown Richmond Merchants Association. The group met weekly to coordinate the operations of downtown businesses for the ease and convenience of Richmond shoppers, and he occasionally traveled to Indianapolis on the Association's behalf to speak to the General Assembly.[4] Several years later, Dickman and the Association set to work on turning Richmond's downtown into a pedestrian-only promenade, which the city maintained for about twenty years before reopening the area to cars.[5]

The decision to join the Merchants Association was an easy one for Dickman. It involved only a couple of hours per week in meetings, and it helped drum up name recognition—something the new owner of the sports shop needed. Soon, that attention led to more appointments, board positions, and fundraising roles. People were eager to have well-known Richmond residents headline their operations. The more roles that Dickman took on, the more exposure he had in the community—which led to more people seeking his support and leadership for yet another engagement.

This feedback loop repeated itself countless times. Between the time he bought Kesslers in 1958 and the mid-1970s, Dickman took on a dizzying amount of appointments in the community. Here's a sampling of them:

- Holy Family Catholic Church, Parish Council Member[6] and Head of Building Committee[7]
- Noon Kiwanis Club, President[8]
- Mayor's Advisory Committee, Member[9]
- Earlham's "E" Men's Organization, President[10]
- Richmond Athletic Booster Club, President[11]
- Richmond Area Chamber of Commerce, Board Member[12]
- Jaycees, Member and 1965 "Man of the Year"[13]
- Knights of Columbus, Member and Softball Team Player[14]

- Townsend Center, Gift Division Team Captain[15]
- Multiple Sclerosis Drive, Chairman[16]
- Heart Fund Sunday, Chairman[17]
- Morrisson-Reeves Library Citizens' Advisory Committee, Member[18]
- Head Start Advisory Group, Chairman[19]
- United Fund, Board Member[20]
- Eastern Indiana Mental Health Services, Board Member[21]
- Junior Achievement of Eastern Indiana, Board Member[22]
- Civic Theater Board, Member[23]
- Boys and Girls Club of Richmond, Board President
- Commercial Softball League, President[24]
- Junior Hi-Y Boosters Club, Director[25]
- Food Stamps for Wayne County, Committee Member[26]
- Committee to Send U.S. Athletes to 1968 Olympics in Mexico City, Local Fundraising Chairman[27]
- Quarterback Club, Board Member[28]
- Wayne County Civil Defense Advisory Council, Board Member[29]
- Public Health Nursing Board, Member[30]
- Boy Scouts, Assistant Vice President for the Eastern Section of the Crossroads Council[31]

Dickman's favorite way of serving the community was in the athletic world as a basketball and football referee. After earning his license in 1955, he first got involved by officiating an adult basketball league at the YMCA. It was a good way to make some extra money, and Dickman always welcomed the chance to be back on the court. His involvement with the Y, a Protestant organization, wasn't without controversy. When Fr. Robert Minton, the hard-headed priest at Holy Family parish, discovered that Dickman was calling games at the Y, he absurdly threatened his parishioner with excommunication. Dickman shrugged it off as a ridiculous comment, and indeed, just a few years later, Dickman saw Fr. Minton swimming laps in the Y's pool.

Refereeing basketball was tough business. Decisions had to be made on a split-second basis; there was virtually no time for Dickman to process what he saw before having to blow the whistle and make a call. Yet he improved with experience, and eventually, he worked his way up to calling high school basketball games. Those matchups came with a brutal challenge: the crowd. Basketball fans, unlike football fans, are in close proximity to the referee. On the high school courts, Dickman got used to taking heat from the crowd on the closest calls, including having one woman swing her purse at him. He generally found that if a fan was behaving outrageously, a stern warning embarrassed him enough to calm things down. It was a good learning experience for him, making his already-thick skin even thicker. Before long, the crowds hardly fazed him at all: his fellow basketball referee and business partner Ray Mitrione recalled him once sleeping during a timeout, leaning against a wall under the basket.[32] After 17 years (and now with eight kids at home), the schedule became too much to manage, as the games were often played on weeknights rather than weekends. He called his last basketball game in the early 1970s.

Football officiating was an altogether different experience, one he much preferred and continued for 36 years. Unlike basketball, he had more time to process what he was seeing before throwing the penalty flag. The angry fans were many yards away rather than a few feet, and

110

he didn't get as many earfuls from the coaches. In football, he was part of a four-man crew that traveled around Indiana together on Friday and Saturday nights to call high school games (the one exception to his and Martha Jane's usual practice of being at home on weekends). The other three members of his crew included Mitrione, who was a line judge; Troy Ingram, a back-field judge; and Wayne Van Sickle, who led the squad as head referee.[33] Dickman worked as the umpire, monitoring the gameplay from behind the linebackers. The crew became close friends and went on to work three state football championships together.[34]

For a referee, Dickman was well-recognized. Kesslers sold to many of the teams, so he and Mitrione were often acquainted with the coaches. And as he advanced into the political world, the teams were often amused to have a local celebrity put on the stripes. Dickman got a kick out of all this, but refereeing wasn't primarily about the travel and attention. Rather, it was a continuation of his own days wearing the uniform, it was time well spent with friends, and above all, it was service to the Indiana kids playing the games he had played himself not long ago.

Time at Kesslers, on the basketball courts and football fields, and in the community councils and drives had made quite a name for Cliff Dickman in Wayne County. The young man who graduated alongside only eight others at Webster High had become one of Richmond's better-known citizens. He hadn't concocted some grand scheme to make this all happen; it came organically because of his steady, honest concern for his neighbors. Now, his talents beckoned him on to a new realm that he would occupy for 20 years: government service.

Dickman's first foray into the political world began when Richmond resident Ray Zaleski approached him about running for state representative as a Republican. In Indiana, a state rep serves in the lower chamber of the General Assembly, the House of Representatives. When Zaleski approached Dickman, the seat in question covered only Wayne County.

Dickman was taken off guard by Zaleski's suggestion. He had never been active in politics, and he paid little attention to the national political happenings of the day. His only affiliation with the Republicans was that he was a registered member of the party; he'd joined after Mayor Doc Cutter, a Democrat whom Dickman supported, concluded his tenure as mayor of Richmond. Yet despite Dickman's general lack of political engagement, he had developed a reputation in the community for being both likable and engaged. That was reason enough for Zaleski to want Dickman on the ticket.

There was one issue that fired Dickman up enough to get him to agree to run for the seat in 1964: taxes. At the time, Indiana ran a sizable debt, and the governor, Matthew Welsh, proposed an aggressive tax increase to make up for the budget shortfall. Welsh called it the "2-2-2-Plan": a 2% increase in individual income taxes, a 2% increase in the corporate tax, and for the first time (and most controversially), a 2% sales tax. The sales-tax proposal was widely despised across the state, leading especially angry individuals to write "Indiana—Land of Taxes" on their license plates and earning the governor the nickname "Sales Tax Matt."[35]

Notably, and to the irritation of Cliff Dickman, the incumbent state rep for Wayne County, Ralph Waltz, had voted in favor of the sales tax despite the fact that Governor Welsh was a Democrat and Waltz was a Republican.

So Dickman agreed to take Waltz on in the primary, with the sales tax at the top of his campaign platform. He saw the new revenue measure as a slippery slope—once instituted, it would be too easy for the legislature to raise revenue for needless projects by inching up the sales tax. His campaign slogan summed his views up succinctly: "I believe in being taxed ... but not to death."[36]

Dickman's campaign efforts were modest. He didn't go door-to-door or raise significant sums of money. He tried to gain the support of party chairmen and precinct committee members, attended a few fundraising dinners for the Republican Party, spoke at some service-club meetings, and ran several ads in the *Palladium-Item*, costing his campaign $451.49.[37] Despite making little effort, he ran surprisingly well and afterwards regretted not putting in just a bit more effort. As the vote counting neared completion, Dickman led Waltz and thought he'd pulled off a victory—Waltz even called to congratulate him. But the precincts near Hagerstown, Waltz's home, were the last to report in, and when they did, Dickman learned he had been crushed in that territory. He lost to Waltz on May 5 by a difference of just 156 votes.[38]

Energized by the close call, Dickman ran again in the 1966 primary. But the game had changed, for Indiana had redistricted since the last election. Under the new rules, Wayne County and Randolph County to the north would be served by two joint representatives who would each serve both counties. The parties could each nominate two candidates to run in the general election, and the top two finishers would win the seats. Instead of one Republican winning in Wayne and another winning in Randolph, combining the two would result in a Republican coming in first place and taking one seat, while the Democrat coming in second place would take the other seat. The redistricting certainly did not work to Dickman's advantage, for his name recognition in Randolph County was far weaker than in Wayne. He came in third place for the two Republican slots.[39]

Dickman never ran for a seat in the General Assembly again, but his efforts were recognized by local political leaders. Soon, that recognition earned him a position atop the Wayne County government. On January 1, 1967, Wayne County Commissioner Carl Eggemeyer started a new term in office, but just 13 days later, he died. The other two commissioners, Herman Wambo and Byron Pike, had the authority to appoint Eggemeyer's successor. They approached Dickman about the prospect of filling the seat on the condition that when the four-year term expired, he would run for re-election. Dickman agreed and began his service on January 23. Upon being sworn in, Dickman told the *Palladium-Item*, "I am happy to have the opportunity to serve in county government.... I hope I can do the job, I will give it my best efforts, and I will be fair and square."[40]

In Indiana, each county's three commissioners perform the executive functions of county government. Their primary tasks include maintaining county-government property (*e.g.*, courthouses), supervising road and bridge construction projects, overseeing waste departments, authorizing contracts for improvement work, administering elections, and appointing other county officers.[41]

Dickman, Wambo, and Pike met in the Wayne County Courthouse on Monday mornings, opening the floor up to the public for questions and concerns. They made decisions by majority vote, although nearly all votes were unanimous. While the commissioners represented the entire county, they each hailed from one of three districts and generally were given deference with respect to matters in their own districts. That authority left room for the commissioners to play favorites, but fortunately, no such malfeasance occurred. For example, one of the key tasks of the commissioners was to pave the numerous gravel county roads with asphalt. Obviously, the commissioners faced pressure to pave their own roads or those of family and friends, but those temptations were resisted in Dickman's time as a commissioner. For his own part, Dickman even refused to pave Flatley Road where his mother and brother lived for fear of the appearance of favoritism.

Most of the decisions made by the county commissioners were uncontroversial, although there were exceptions. They had the unenviable task of deciding where to locate a new landfill—a decision that would inevitably upset those who lived near the chosen site.[42] The commissioners also had a minor tussle over whether to institute, for the first time, automatic vote-counting machines.[43] Dickman had been approached by a voting-machine salesman, and the idea interested him from the start. He invited the salesman to a Monday meeting of the commissioners, where all three showed their enthusiasm for this new innovation. But the salesman gave a word of warning: the machines were susceptible to counting errors, and if they did make such an error, it wouldn't be readily apparent. Dickman urged further deliberation once this red flag was uncovered, but the other commissioners were set on pushing forward with the new technology. He lost that vote 2–1.

The most controversial aspect of Dickman's tenure as a county commissioner was the institution of county planning. At the time, few regulations encumbered construction or land development in rural areas. But as the county grew in population and construction projects increased, the need for further regulation became evident. There were numerous examples of septic tanks leaking and causing environmental damage to others' property—incidents that could have been prevented with a simple inspection. The commissioners thus began establishing a regulatory regime for new construction projects.

The public outcry against county planning came as a shock to Dickman. Rumors and false information spread like wildfire. One citizen approached him and asked, "Is it true that if I move a head of my cattle from one stall to another, I need a permit for that?" Dickman shook his head and said, "If you really believe that, I can't help you." A newspaper ad orchestrated by the Wayne County Master Plan Opposition Organization speculated that health inspectors would start entering homes forcibly and without warrants.[44] One opponent vocalized her concern that county planning would turn Wayne County citizens into communists.[45] An even more shocking episode occurred when a woman took to the radio and claimed that if county planning became law, then the people who opposed it would be shipped off to a sanitarium in Alaska. That patently absurd comment enraged Dickman, and he publicly condemned the speaker. The ordinances passed, and county planning was easily operationalized.

As commissioner, Dickman also started to have his first run-ins with the local press. In early 1974, the county courthouse reached its capacity for staffing personnel, and the commissioners began making plans for a new building next door. The new property, then a vacant lot, was owned by the Richmond city government. While the city planned to sell it to the county, a legal obstacle required the commissioners to provide the city with a rough blueprint of the construction plans in order for the sale to close. The commissioners quickly hired an architecture firm to draw up a plan which all involved knew

116

was nothing more than a formality to facilitate the sale, not the actual blueprint. The firm proposed an eight-story building, a far cry from the two-story annex that ultimately was built on the site. But when the preliminary blueprint was released to the public, the newspaper responded by publishing the front-page headline: "County Planning 8-Story Building."[46] Dickman was outraged, believing that the paper had willfully misled its readers into thinking that the county truly was planning such an ambitious project. Dickman marched into the newspaper's offices, demanding to talk to "whatever dumbass wrote this article." The experience started him down the path of understanding the power of a headline and how the bombastic can prevail over reality in the world of journalism.[47]

Controversy, however, was the exception rather than the rule. Dickman spent nine years as a Wayne County commissioner, winning reelection by healthy margins in 1970 and 1974.[48] They were overwhelmingly good years, and it was valuable formation as he learned the nuts and bolts of local government, forged important contacts, and came to understand the true value of public service. Looking back, the commissioner years could be seen as building blocks before taking a higher step up the ladder. But to his credit, he never viewed service as commissioner as a stepping stone. He did it for its own sake, never regretting a single minute he spent serving his county.

The most tragic event to occur in Wayne County during Dickman's tenure as a commissioner—indeed, perhaps the most devastating event in the county's entire history—happened on Saturday, April 6, 1968.[49] Early in the afternoon, Cliff and Ray Mitrione were working at Kesslers. A little-league baseball team from Vandalia,

Ohio was in the store getting geared up for their upcoming season. Suddenly, there came a thunderously loud boom, and then another. Dickman and Mitrione ran out the front door and saw a column of dark smoke rising from the west end of downtown, just four or five blocks away. Dickman immediately feared, as did many other Richmond residents, that whatever explosion had just happened was no accident. Only two days before, Dr. Martin Luther King, Jr. had been assassinated. Riots were breaking out across the country, and Dickman wondered to himself whether someone had bombed the downtown in protest.[50]

After hunkering down for some time, the two walked down to Birck's hardware store, owned by Dickman's brother-in-law, Charlie Maurer. Birck's was about halfway between Kesslers and the epicenter of the explosion. Firefighters rushed past them, and the smoke grew thicker as the fire from the explosion smoldered outward. At Birck's, Dickman found Charlie and his son, Charlie Jr., sitting inside, coated in debris. The explosion had shaken the building so violently that the dust and dirt on the ceiling and walls had fallen all over them. They, like Dickman and Mitrione, were simply waiting, trying to figure out what had happened and what would come next. They had no idea that the blaze would eventually spread all the way to Birck's, destroying the building and inventory.

As things calmed down, Dickman walked closer to the explosion site, which was at the intersection of 6th and Main Streets. The carnage was devastating. Cars were flipped upside down, storefront windows were completely blasted out, and injured people were being tended to in every direction. Dickman saw one poor man with a glass shard sticking out of his neck. Many had perished in the

118

incident, and as the days went on, Dickman witnessed firefighters continue to pull bodies from the rubble.[51]

Meanwhile, there was panic at the house on Southwest 4th Street. The sound of the explosion carried across town, and Martha Jane rushed to Main Street, where she saw the smoke cloud billowing up from downtown across the gorge. The radio then ostensibly confirmed her worst fears: the host announced that "the downtown sports shop" had been blown up. It took her hours before she could finally get through on the phone to Cliff, who was able to attest to his own safety and report that *his* sports store was completely unaffected. Martha Jane was not the only one who believed that Cliff was a casualty of the explosion. Word circulated on the radio in Dayton, Ohio that the shop had been destroyed, and Kesslers customers there were relieved to hear Dickman confirm on the phone that he was completely fine.

Several days later, the cause of the explosion was determined to be a gas leak. It was an accident; there was no connection at all to the riots in other parts of the country. Gas had leaked from a pipeline under Marting Arms, a gun and ammunition shop (and probably "the downtown sports shop" the radio broadcaster had referred to). The first boom Dickman heard was caused by the gas sparking; the second was caused by the gunpowder in the basement of Marting Arms catching fire. The explosion claimed the lives of 41 people, and 120 more were injured.[52] The youngest fatality was only seven years old.[53]

The incident attracted national attention and was covered by the country's top newspapers and networks.[54] Bobby Kennedy, then seeking the Democratic nomination for president, visited the explosion site at the end of the month.*[55] The Richmond Gas Corporation, which maintained the gas lines, attracted significant criticism for its failed safety precautions. The company's fault in the matter elevated the issue of gas-line safety to the attention of the federal government, and just four months after the explosion, Congress enacted the Natural Gas Pipeline Act of 1968.[56]

In the aftermath of the April 6 horror, the community came together to heal the wounded, honor the dead, and rebuild toward the future. The cleanup fell outside of Dickman's jurisdiction as commissioner, as the explosion had occurred in the heart of Richmond city limits. But ten years later, Dickman paid special tribute to the occasion by dedicating a memorial to the victims of the explosion, which still stands at the site of the blast. He spoke proudly to the progress that the city had made since that fateful day. "I think those who died are looking down on us and are smiling," he said. "They are saying: you've done something good for the community. And we're proud of you."[57]

For almost 20 years, Cliff Dickman had called Richmond home, and throughout it all, he devoted himself to serving that home. Much like his commitments to church, family, and Kesslers, his dedication to Richmond was a pillar of his life. It therefore was only natural when a few local leaders came to Dickman, asking him to attend a small get-together where he would be the guest of honor. It was time for a bigger campaign, a higher office, and the next chapter in his life.

---

* RFK himself would be assassinated just one month after this visit.

9

"A RICHMOND MAN FOR RICHMOND'S FUTURE"

Good fortune and hard work had propelled Clifford Dickman into college sports, business ownership, and county politics. The forces of fate and effort, seemingly unstoppable when joined together, called Dickman yet again on a February night in 1975. At an informal meeting of Richmond's GOP leadership, 21 party members pressed Dickman into running for mayor of Richmond. He found it to be a seriously appealing proposition. Over the years, as he increasingly moved into the local spotlight through his various community activities, he had come to enjoy the respect and dignity that came with public service. What's more, he chalked up his performances in both county government and the private sector as successful. Why not bring that track record to city hall?

Two countervailing forces counseled against the run. First, serving as mayor would require giving up day-to-day work at Kesslers. At the time, Richmond was peaking in its population, somewhere between 41,000 to 44,000.[1] Leading a city of this size was full-time work, requiring the daily 9-to-5 and the occasional night or weekend. Second, Martha Jane was unenthusiastic about the idea.

Knowing what was coming before the meeting, she had asked her husband to turn the Republican organizers down. She rightfully foresaw the stresses of campaigning and public life. She and Cliff's status quo of steadily growing Kesslers and raising their kids was already the fulfillment of the vision she had for her family. Politics could only get in the way of that.

But for Dickman, the once-in-a-lifetime opportunity to throw himself fully into public service could not be passed up. He agreed to run on the condition that each of the 21 gathered that evening support him all the way through the primary and general elections. The Republicans, who were positively delighted at the promise they saw in unseating the incumbent Democrat mayor, pledged their commitment and ultimately kept their promises.

Dickman's first act as candidate was also the toughest: delivering the news to his wife that he'd accepted their overture and was going to run. Her disappointment was self-evident. Cliff's decision was a life-changing one, not only for him but also for her and the kids, and he'd made the decision alone. But to her great credit, even in a tough time like this, Martha Jane always remained supportive of her husband. And before long, she came to enjoy the thrill of the race and to play an important role in its eventual success.

Dickman's second act was to declare himself the first Republican candidate for mayor, which he did on February 17, 1975. "I am certain we can get the job done," he said confidently and, adding a clarion call for support, "I expect everyone to be out helping."[2]

Dickman was able to delay the true burdens of campaigning until the summer. Although he had a primary challenger, Gay Sue Hubbell, she was a relative newcomer to the political world and had no internal support within the Republican Party. On Primary Day, she lost 3,395 to 497, but she took the defeat well and pledged her support to Dickman in the general.[3]

Dickman's ambitions for November extended beyond winning the mayor's chair for himself; he also set his sights on the Republicans taking back control of the city council.[4] This was no easy task. Indiana was a Republican stronghold in the 1970s, one of just a few Republican states east of the Mississippi that broke for Gerald Ford over Jimmy Carter in 1976. But things were different at the local level. Democrats had won the mayoralty for 16 of the previous 20 years,[5] and they'd enjoyed a majority on the city council for 20 of the previous 24 years.[6]

The incumbent mayor, Charles Howell, was a newcomer to the job, having commenced his tenure only a few weeks before Dickman announced his candidacy. Byron Klute, who had served as mayor of Richmond for about 7 years, resigned to join Senator Birch Bayh's staff, and on his way out, Klute had effectively handpicked Howell as his successor. Normally, the city controller, Jerry Judge, would have succeeded to a mayoral vacancy. But in a strange turn of events, Mayor Klute swapped Howell into the position of city controller one day before he resigned, thus paving the way for Howell to become mayor.[7] It was a suspect move by the outgoing executive, one that would haunt Howell on the campaign trail.

To his credit, Charlie Howell had fairly extensive experience serving in government. He had directed the state's school lunch program, and he had also led the Indiana Department of Veterans Affairs. From there, he joined Klute's administration, serving in earnest for some time as city controller before moving into an advisory position. Howell gave himself good marks for his performance in government, reporting to the *Palladium-Item* that he'd turned a $17,000 deficit in Indiana's school lunch program into a $200,000 surplus.[8]

Whatever the merits of Howell's leadership as an appointed official may have been, his short record as mayor seemed weaker. Inefficiencies in city government frustrated many firemen, policemen, and transportation workers. Indeed, many of these city employees had expressed their dissatisfaction to Dickman before he announced his candidacy. While recent voting trends in Richmond city government worked against Dickman, he felt confident that he could reverse the tide.

Campaigning began in early August 1975. The Dickman campaign never had a single director, although Robert Reinke and Kent Klinge served as the overall strategists for the Republicans running that fall.[9] The GOP set up a small headquarters in a space next to Kesslers that Dickman himself owned. The 21 men and women who had talked Dickman into running proved indispensable, as they took the lead in volunteering their time, forging contacts with other Indiana Republicans, making fundraising phone calls, and personally committing financial assistance.

Ray Zaleski, who had first convinced Dickman to run for state representative 11 years earlier, hosted a lawn party at his house to organize volunteers and galvanize support for the candidate. Zaleski and his army had mailed about 400 invitation letters to all kinds of potential supporters—businessmen, teachers, union leaders, doctors, and more.[10] The turnout for the event—roughly 150—was considered a great success for the nascent campaign. Dickman gave his first campaign speech that evening, stressing the importance of party unity up and down the ticket. He also expressed his delight that voters from all walks of life were present at the lawn party.[11]

The Republicans began to fill Dickman's calendar with events. His 9-to-5 obligation to Kesslers was generally respected, although he attended lunch events with some frequency. Usually, he started his mornings by visiting city facilities to speak with government employees. He initially got some pushback from Howell's department chiefs for campaigning at a workplace, but when Dickman reminded them that he was on public property speaking about matters of civic concern, they usually backed off.

Dickman had not entered the race with a predetermined list of priorities. Although he was running as a Republican, local electoral contests (at least at the time) were not driven by competing ideologies or political philosophies. It came down to managerial skills and the ability to effectively work across different levels of government—county, state, and national. Thus, "good government" became the overriding theme of Dickman's mayoral campaign.

Dickman understood that the key to good government is knowing the needs of constituents, and this is what he set out to learn in his morning meetings with city employees. Dickman came not to speak, but to listen. Although his experience as county commissioner gave him some insight into where local government could be improved, he had never worked at the city level. The government employees, who freely shared their concerns and aspirations, educated him on the priorities that he needed to emphasize. As the value of these listening opportunities became apparent, he started hosting "Speak Out" nights, where citizens of the community could vent their own frustrations about local government to the receptive candidate. The first such event attracted 300 Richmond citizens.[12]

Out of these dialogues, a platform began to emerge. At the forefront of citizens' concerns was increasing crime in Richmond. Dickman claimed that crime was up over 20% since the Klute–Howell administration took over in 1968. Although he primarily chalked that up to increasing unemployment rates, he also blamed the Richmond Police Department's leadership and a lack of morale among officers. He sought to institute a merit system for the police and fire departments, whereby officers and firefighters would be hired and promoted on the basis of their competency, rather than on seniority or political connections.[13] Richmond had previously relied on a merit system, but it was abandoned in the mid-1960s by Mayor Edward "Corky" Cordell. Although Cordell was the last Republican to occupy the mayor's office, Dickman sought to put plenty of daylight between the two, publicly declaring that "I'm no Corky Cordell."[14] Summing up his case for a merit system, he argued, "Take the police and fire departments out of politics and hire and promote on the basis of merit. Eliminate the bureaucratic hierarchy and its staff and spend some of the money saved in providing services such as police and fire protection."[15]

Dickman also took a strong stand against rising city expenditures. Byron Klute had created two new positions in city hall. The first was administrative assistant to the mayor, the position Charlie Howell had held just before his midnight appointment that landed him in the mayor's chair. The "administrative assistant" was, in effect, a chief of staff—someone who kept the mayor's office organized and served as a trusted counselor. When coupled with the fact that the mayor already had a secretary to handle day-to-day administrative tasks, Dickman found the administrative assistant position to be downright wasteful. He also took aim at the other position Klute created: public safety director, who oversaw both the police and fire departments. Dickman thought this bureaucrat was a contributing factor to the demise in morale and leadership in those departments. Better to have one more police officer out on a beat than a public safety director in city hall, Dickman said.[16] He vowed to vest the police and fire chiefs with final authority over their squads.[17]

But like most other campaigns, the number one issue that Dickman harped on was jobs.[18] At the time, the United States was grappling with a recession, the nation's first financial setback since the end of World War II. The economic contraction was compounded by high inflation rates, making life hard not only for those who had lost their jobs, but also for those who hadn't seen a wage increase and couldn't keep up with rising prices. The damage had been especially severe in Richmond, with the unemployment rate lingering in the double digits throughout the 1975 campaign.[19] Dickman blamed the situation on the Klute–Howell administration, which he claimed was passive in the face of 5,000 industrial jobs being destroyed in the Richmond area.[20]

Bolder leadership and fresh ideas, Dickman believed, would poise Richmond to outpace its peer communities in the wake of the recession. He promised a "job-producing administration," particularly in the area of manufacturing, which historically was the core source of the city's employment.[21] He pledged to form a citizens' advisory committee comprised of business and labor leaders, who would be dedicated to attracting new employers to Richmond.[22] He promised to connect the city government with statewide agencies, the local chamber of commerce, and the Earlham alumni network, believing that more partnerships would inevitably stimulate local investment.[23] Dickman proposed reforms to zoning ordinances that stood as obstacles to new development, and he aspired to lower local tax rates once he had the chance to trim city expenditures.[24] He also committed himself to an open-door policy, by which he would set aside time every week for citizens to come into his office and express their views to him directly—whether that be job-growth ideas or anything else.[25]

Throughout the campaign, Dickman promised the simple but essential virtue of honesty in government. He picked on Democrats for antics like having Parks Department employees set up for their party fundraiser while on the clock, and he later charged them with having conscripted city employees to assist with their campaign efforts.[26] More broadly, Dickman thought that the city government could do more to ensure transparency and fairness. The merit system for the police and fire departments was one such example. He also promised the police and fire departments that he was willing to appoint Democrats or Republicans as their chiefs; he simply wanted "the finest man for the job."[27]

The most humorous incident of the campaign happened in September. One day, Democratic City Attorney Robert Burton found a large, colorful "Dickman for Mayor" sign set up outside his office building. A local Republican, James Backmeyer, eventually admitted to putting it there. When the *Palladium-Item* asked Burton for his thoughts on the prank, Burton replied, "I don't mind it at all. Mr. Dickman needs all the help he can get."[28]

★ ★ ★

As the campaign progressed on, Dickman hosted meet-and-greet coffees, spoke to service clubs, and continued listening to disgruntled city employees.[29] On Saturdays, Dickman and his crew of volunteers loaded up the family motorhome, newly nicknamed the "Voter Van."[30] They plastered a large "Dickman for Mayor" banner across the side, and they visited different neighborhoods for door-to-door canvassing. The campaign also hosted a few fundraising dinners and a vaudeville night, an old-timey singing event coupled with dancing and games.[31] It was during these events that Martha Jane proved most instrumental. Her poise and dedication were readily evident to all who met her, and that increased public trust in her husband.

Dickman and Howell, alongside third-party candidate Tony DeNardis, started debating each other, repeating the same arguments over jobs, city spending, and leadership in the police and fire departments. These debates were hosted by the Jaycees, the League of Women Voters, the Lions Club, and the students of Richmond High School.[32] The political world is never short of hyperbole, and Richmond's mayoral debates proved no exception. Dickman proclaimed that city hall was under "Democrat boss control," although there was no foundation for widespread corruption in city hall.[33] He attacked Howell and Klute's leadership of the police and fire departments over the past eight years as "atrocious."[34]

The Republican campaign managed to cast Howell both as an insider and outsider. Howell's numerous appointments in government, most notably his last-minute appointment by Klute, put a target on his back. The Republicans labeled him as an insider "political appointee" rather than a true representative of the people.[35] Simultaneously, Howell was portrayed as an outsider because he'd lived most of his life in Hagerstown or Indianapolis. Dickman, on the other hand, was a "Richmond man for Richmond's future."[36]

The campaigns scrambled to pick up as many endorsements as they could. Howell held a high-profile event in August featuring Phil Sharp, U.S. Representative for Indiana's 10th District (which included Richmond), and more notably, Senator Birch Bayh. Bayh was a rising star in the national Democratic Party and, to no one's surprise, was soon to announce his candidacy for the 1976 presidential election. But, Bayh told the crowd in Richmond, he preferred to "forego that subject and let time take care of that [because] the more pressing issue here is to get Charles Howell and the Democratic Action Team elected this November."[37] Sharp piled on the praise, saying that Howell was Richmond's "best lobbyist in Washington."[38]

Dickman garnered a strong cadre of high-profile supporters, as well. The governor of Indiana, Otis Bowen, held a news conference at the Richmond Municipal Airport, touting Dickman's experience as a businessman and urging voters to support him.[39] Wayne County's former congressman David Dennis endorsed Dickman in a speech to local business leaders.[40] And Elton Trueblood, the famous Earlham professor who was well-known in national Republican circles, penned a letter to the editor in the *Palladium-Item* supporting Dickman, saying, "The fact that he has been able to give himself increasingly to unselfish public service is an indication of the kind of mayor he can be."[41]

The top event of the year was a party fundraiser featuring Mary Louise Smith, the chairwoman of the Republican National Committee, as the keynote speaker. Clearly on a mission to galvanize support for Gerald Ford in the upcoming 1976 election, she spoke about the necessity of a true grassroots movement for the party. Success in local elections, she argued, was the stepping stone to victory at the state and national levels. Her directive to the party faithful was simple. "How many times yesterday did you mention Cliff Dickman's name?" she asked those gathered. "In the restaurant, the barber shop, the hardware store, across the backyard fence. How many times did you say, 'I'm for Cliff Dickman,' or 'Have you met Cliff Dickman yet? He's really impressive.' That might be all it takes to get Cliff Dickman a vote."[42]

With speeches delivered, debates argued, platforms established, and endorsements made, the campaign season at last drew to a close. Two days before the election, Dickman published a "letter to the voters" advertisement in the Sunday edition of the *Palladium-Item*. There, next to a family picture, he reiterated his qualifications and concluded, "The mayor of Richmond is a full-time position of honor and trust and I shall so regard it, if you elect me to that office."[43]

The voters of Richmond went to the polls on Tuesday, November 4. In the evening, listening over the radio at the Republican headquarters, news of the results came in: Clifford Dickman was to be the next mayor of Richmond. The party headquarters exploded with enthusiasm; the newspaper reported that the 100+ Republican volunteers stomped their feet and filled their air with cheers in support of their triumphant candidate.[44] The final vote count was 7,133 for Dickman, 6,127 for Howell, and 251 for third-party candidate DeNardis. The voter turnout rate of 57% was somewhat low for its time, though it is remarkable by today's standards for local elections.[45]

Word came in soon that Republican mayoral candidates had performed exceedingly well across Indiana. William Hudnut had won election as the mayor of Indianapolis, and the Republican candidates also triumphed in Fort Wayne, Evansville, Kokomo, Mishawaka, Elkhart, and New Albany.[46]

As the night carried on, the news just kept getting better for the Richmond GOP. The Democrats' 10–2 control on city hall was vanquished; the Republicans would enter on January 1 with a 9–3 advantage. Jo Ellen Trimble had emerged victorious in the race for city clerk, as had Darrell Beane for city judge. And in the city-council races, the Republican candidates—James Carter, Ken Paust, Roger Cornett, Rick Ahaus, Thomas Austerman, and Ken Mills—had captured six of the nine available seats. Carter, Paust, and Cornett had wrested all three of the at-large seats out of Democratic hands. It was a total sweep, one which the Richmond Republicans hadn't savored in many years.[47] And, as the public would later learn, the Republicans had pulled it off with total expenditures of $21,253, which was $1,830 less than the Democrats had spent.[48] "It was teamwork," Dickman said of the months-long effort. "We went on the offensive all the way, never on the defensive." He hadn't regretted a single moment of the campaign.[49]

Almost as soon as victory had been declared, Dickman and local Republican Party Chairman Bob Reinke hopped in the car to visit the Democrats' headquarters. Howell congratulated Dickman with a handshake and wished him well as he embarked on a new term.[50] Howell was a good sport in the aftermath, although he gave a somewhat self-congratulatory explanation for the result—that "so many Democratic party regulars said they were so confident of his victory that they didn't want to take the time to vote."[51]

The afterparty for Dickman and the Republicans carried on at the Richmond Knights of Columbus hall. Congratulations began flowing in and continued through the following days. RNC Chairwoman Smith personally called to congratulate Dickman. Indeed, just a week after the election, one particularly notable telegram arrived:

I was extremely pleased to learn of your wonderful victory. You have my warm congratulations and best wishes for a successful term.

Gerald R. Ford[52]

The transition period for the mayor-elect began right away. Just three days after being elected, Dickman announced his first appointment: local party chairman Bob Reinke would serve as city attorney. Reinke had been a close associate of Dickman's throughout the campaign, and as preparation for taking over city hall began in earnest, he was firmly set on keeping Reinke at his right hand. "I am glad and proud to serve under Cliff Dickman," Reinke announced. "My respect increased for Cliff as the campaign continued, and I am pleased he wants me to serve."[53]

The main tasks ahead of Dickman and Reinke were to fill other city-government positions and to review the various projects underway in Richmond, particularly those funded by the federal government. As Dickman would soon learn, the federal government had evolved into an indispensable source of financial support for local improvement projects. Federal funds needed to be both attracted for new projects and maintained for ongoing ones. The mayor-elect knew that he needed to be fully apprised of all these projects by Day One if he was going to hit the ground running.

The next appointment of the transition period was not announced by Dickman, but by Mayor Howell. He promoted John Newland to fire chief, a lieutenant who had spent 16 years on the fire squad.[54] Howell, of course, was still mayor and had the power to make the appointment, but Dickman was irked by the fact that he had not even been consulted given that the transition was less than two months away.

Future appointments came more slowly. Dickman took the time to consult with Reinke, the newly elected city-council members, and Tom Milligan, a Richmond resident serving as chairman of the Indiana GOP.[55] Milligan's involvement drew the ire of the *Palladium-Item*'s editorial board, which penned an article calling Milligan "an enthusiastic evangelist for the patronage gospel," where all key positions were filled by the party faithful regardless of merit.[56] In Milligan's defense, it is understandable that he wanted to fill the ranks of city government with those who would be most loyal to the new mayor. But Dickman announced that he was not averse to retaining appointees who served under Mayors Klute and Howell, and Milligan always stood in support.[57]

Dickman's most important appointment came in early December, when he named Don Meredith to the position of city controller. A graduate of Richmond High School and Earlham College, Meredith had worked in the insurance industry before becoming Wayne County treasurer in 1969. His experience as chief financial officer for the county prepared him well for the same position in service to the city.[58] The two would be extremely close collaborators in the coming years.

Another key appointment was made a few weeks later when Dickman appointed Paul "Moon" Mullin as fire chief. "Mullin," Dickman said, "is respected by his fellow firefighters and I personally feel that he will meet the challenge as a firm and fair leader of men." He believed that under Mullin's management, pride among the firefighters would be restored and Richmond's fire department would be "second to none in Indiana."[59] Dickman had only one concern about Mullin: he had a reputation for busting the jaws of guys who talked back to him. Dickman warned Mullin before taking the job that he'd have to "keep his hands in his pockets." Mullin agreed and stayed true to that commitment throughout his tenure. He would prove to be not only effective as a fire chief but also a lifelong friend to his new boss.

Dickman made good on his promised willingness to retain Howell's department heads who served well. Ralph Willis continued as city engineer, Robert Goodwin as planning director, Don McBride as park superintendent, and Louis Gibbs as police chief. Rounding out the lineup, he appointed Tim Ryder as community development director, Charles Roberts as building commissioner, and Calvin Dean as sanitary district superintendent. And in a decision that would later come to haunt Dickman, he named Jerry Haynes as transportation director.[60]

With his team assembled, the last matter was the transition at Kesslers. During the campaign, Dickman had made clear that if elected, he would not sell his interest in Kesslers. But he had unequivocally promised to be a full-time mayor, so the daily work of running the shop would be left to Bob Luerman. Fortunately, Dickman and Luerman had worked together for 16 years, and the latter was well-prepared to take the reins. Kesslers had propelled Dickman into serving as an active community member in Richmond, and he walked away confident that the store was in the most capable of hands.

New Year's Eve celebrations on December 31, 1975 were particularly special across the United States. The upcoming year marked the nation's bicentennial—200 years since the Declaration of Independence had been signed. And they took special prominence for Cliff Dickman and his family, for the next day would be his inauguration.

The evening's festivities were grand in Richmond. Though it was a Wednesday, churches opened for worship. Hundreds turned out on the downtown Promenade late at night, where they were entertained by the sights and sounds of bell ringers, fifers, firecrackers, horns, and drummers. As midnight approached, local McDonald's owner Dana Weigel presented a replica of the Liberty Bell to Mayor Howell and Mayor-Elect Dickman. Midnight struck, the bell rang, and the crowd cheered and broke out into "Auld Lang Syne."[61]

At noon the next day, in the city-council chambers in the Richmond Municipal Building, Judge James Puckett swore in Clifford Dickman as the 26th Mayor of Richmond.[62] He entered into a long succession of outstanding Richmond citizens to have served as the city's chief. Richmond's second mayor John Finley wrote the poem "The Hoosier's Nest," the first writing to dignify Indiana's inhabitants as "Hoosiers." Mayor James Hibberd was a forty-niner who rushed for California gold, James Ostrander was a West Point graduate and major in the Army during the Civil War, and Thomas Bennett even served the Idaho Territory both as its governor and its representative to Congress in between two terms as mayor of Richmond. Other occupants of the office had entered with experience in medicine, law, the military, insurance, education, and law enforcement.[63]

Dickman brought business experience to the office, something relatively unique compared to his predecessors. That experience had taught him pragmatism, which would become a defining hallmark of his administration. But the virtues he carried into office went further than that. He possessed an indefatigable work ethic that was drilled into him on the farm, a toughness and grit that was beaten into him on the football fields and basketball courts, and a steadfast dedication to the common good that he had practiced ever since calling Richmond home. Forty-six years of all-American formation had prepared Dickman well to lead his community.

Following his oath, Dickman took the podium to deliver his inaugural remarks to the overflow crowd. First, he apologized to those standing in the back, joking that his large family had taken up so many of the seats.[64] After a hearty laugh from the crowd, Mayor Dickman delivered a short, eloquent address. His words are worth quoting in full, for they are, in many ways, even more pertinent today than when they were first delivered. He spoke:

> On November 4, 1975, the voters of Richmond chose the Republican party to lead our city for the next four years. Today, January 1, 1976, we accept this challenge and we are now charged with this responsibility.
>
> We accept this assignment with humbleness and sincerity and that we be reminded, should we forget, how we got here. Government is for all of us, not just a select few. If there would be but one wish for our administration, it would be that we stay close to the citizens and remember that we are their employees.
>
> We in the United States have the finest government on earth, regardless of all its faults. We are gathered here today, each and every one, with a little different philosophy and each and every one has the right to exercise his opinions and beliefs within the rights of all. We call these rights 'Freedom.'

Our freedom today is going through one of its strongest tests as we are about to celebrate our 200th birthday. It is being lashed at and criticized by her own people more than anyone else in the world. Let us hope and pray that this Bicentennial year will turn us around and make us proud that we were born in the United States of America.

Today, let us be ever mindful of the job that lies ahead. Let those of all political faiths join together, as much as possible, for better government, for a better Richmond. Let us allow the issues to flow, the debates to occur, and the truths to seep through. In the end, let us remain friends, for we need each other here on Earth. Above all, let us keep God in our hearts and in our minds and that we move forward for a better Richmond, a better community, a better nation, and a better world.

I am humbled by the responsibilities vested in me as mayor of your city. I ask for your help and your prayers in guiding the City of Richmond over the next four years, and I and my family pledge our best to set a good example.

With this said, let us begin the task that lies ahead. Thank you very much for coming here today and may each and every one of you have a very happy New Year.[65]

10

THE FIRST TERM

"A mayor does all sorts of things," Clifford Dickman reported after 100 days in office.[1] His lengthy experience in business and county government had made him as ready as anyone to take over Richmond city hall. But no amount of preparation can completely prepare a person for all the surprises and challenges of taking the helm of his home community.

No day is the same for a mayor, but Dickman was able to ease into a stable routine. The day started with his 8:30 a.m. arrival at city hall. His trusty secretary, Lois Brown, was on hand to provide him with a brief preview of his schedule.[2] Brown was instrumental in managing the mayor's workload—Dickman called her his "right arm." She booked his travel, typed up minutes and correspondence, set up meetings, and coordinated his appearances around town.[3] She remained in her role for seven of Dickman's mayoral years.

Another critically important member of Dickman's government was the city clerk, Jo Ellen Trimble. Dickman hadn't appointed Trimble to her job; the office was independently elected. Fortunately, the two turned out to be a great duo. She came to her position with excellent bookkeeping and organizational experience, having served as a secretary in Richmond Community Schools and in the Indiana Secretary of State's office.[4] As city clerk, Trimble was responsible for managing municipal records, such as ordinances and contracts. She was often the first person to identify appointments that the mayor needed to make, and she kept him abreast of other bureaucratic issues that required his involvement. Lois Brown and Jo Ellen Trimble laid the groundwork for Mayor Dickman's success.

Each day was full of meetings with contractors, city-council members, department heads, or constituents. The high-energy, person-to-person aspect of the job suited Dickman well. He'd never been one for quiet office work—he'd chosen to steer clear of that life when he took on a geology major at Earlham. And indeed, one of the things he loved most about the sporting-goods industry was that it kept him on his feet talking to customers. Serving as mayor required him to be even more social. When the inevitable bout of paperwork would strike, he'd usually work through it in the waiting room rather than his private office, hoping that a constituent would walk in and give him an excuse to chat rather than read.[5]

Constituent communication was important work, and Dickman tried to interact with Richmond citizens every day. One fruitful way of doing so, he found, was to go out for lunch, usually with City Controller Don Meredith. Dickman was well-recognized around town, and people frequently approached him with ideas, compliments, or complaints. Unsurprisingly, the last category was the most frequent he heard. Sometimes, he learned valuable information about a problem that demanded action from the city. Other times, he knew a situation was out of his hands, but he felt it was his duty to let the citizen have his say nonetheless.

Another important alliance Dickman maintained was with the local press. Today, the Internet allows newsworthy events to be transmitted without an intermediary, but in the 1970s, all news was filtered through media establishments like radio stations and newspapers. The sole newspaper in town, the *Palladium-Item*, was Dickman's primary means of mass communication with the people of Richmond, so to remain popular with his voters, he needed to be popular with the *Palladium*. Fortunately, that was virtually never a problem. One of the *Palladium* staff writers, usually longtime reporter Fred Lord, visited Dickman at city hall almost every day. The regular, face-to-face interactions forged an amicable relationship. Dickman also benefited from his sister Dolores's position as secretary to the newspaper's proprietor, R.G. Leeds. Dolores was a lifelong supporter of everything about her brother—from sports to college to politics. Her good standing in Leeds's office certainly didn't hurt Dickman's relationship with the newspaper. Dickman often spoke during his mayoralty about the three great powers in America—government, labor unions, and the press.[6] At least in Richmond, Mayor Dickman viewed the press as wielding its pen for good.

When not meeting with a news writer or a constituent, Dickman could often be found meeting with a department head. The leaders of the city departments were like his cabinet; they were not only in charge of their respective domains, but they also advised Dickman (and each other) on the biggest issues facing the government. Dickman gathered his department heads for a meeting every week and gave each the opportunity to provide updates and receive feedback. At the close of every meeting, Dickman warned his staff that they would be offered gifts and favors in exchange for influence, and that these overtures should always be rejected. He once phrased it to the newspaper this way: "I tell my staff they can make honest mistakes, but be sure they're honest ones. They know if it is a crooked mistake, I will help take any step needed to see justice done."[7]

An early scandal in Dickman's tenure proved that he would stand by his team when he believed they had been honest. In May 1976, the Indiana State Police, with the cooperation of several Richmond police officers, raided a bar that had been suspected of hosting illegal gambling. The State Police hadn't informed Richmond Police Chief Louis Gibbs about the raid, even though it happened on his turf with the help of his own squad.[8] As later became apparent, Wayne County Prosecutor Gerald Surface and the State Police had jointly decided not to inform Gibbs because he was a regular patron of the bar and friends with one of the owners.[9] Speculation swirled that Gibbs himself had participated in the illicit gambling. Gibbs didn't help his cause when he told the *Palladium-Item*, "When it comes to a choice between this job and friends, I'll take friendship."[10]

Dickman stood by Gibbs's side throughout the controversy. He understood why Surface and the State Police hadn't informed Gibbs of the raid, but the attacks on Gibbs's character crossed the line. Asked about Gibbs's friends-come-first quote, Dickman contended that Gibbs must have been misquoted or taken out of context, because "only a fool would say that."[11] And when asked whether he would accept Gibbs's resignation, Dickman expressed doubt, saying, "I think I'd be doing a great injustice to the man to even think about it."[12]

Six weeks after the raid, Gibbs felt that he'd lost too much credibility to lead the police department effectively. He submitted his resignation, which Dickman accepted with regret.[13] On Gibbs's recommendation, Dickman appointed Charles Chris as his successor.[14] The entire episode was unfortunate for Gibbs, especially considering that no evidence of wrongdoing was ever uncovered. But he was very grateful that the Richmond mayor had stood beside him. Gibbs had been a Democrat from the Howell administration that Dickman had decided to keep on staff. From then on, Gibbs remained one of Dickman's strongest supporters.

Dickman confronted another dilemma early in his tenure, one which prefigured larger battles to come. In its waning days, the Howell administration negotiated a three-year contract with the fire department, shortening their work week from 56 hours to 50.4 hours without any salary adjustments. This was allegedly the shortest week for any fire department in Indiana at the time. For Dickman, the contract created a public-safety problem. Because the department had the same number of firefighters working fewer hours, there were fewer men ready to respond to an emergency.[15] Indeed, some stations had only two firemen on duty at a time, which certainly wouldn't have cut the mustard in the event of a large blaze. Dickman and Fire Chief Mullin spent 14 months hammering out an agreement that finally resolved the dispute. In exchange for a $1,000 raise, the firefighters agreed to resume their 56-hour weeks.[16]

This wasn't Dickman's last run-in with the fire department over labor issues.[17] Just a few months after the issue of hours was resolved, the administration faced a heady battle on wages for the upcoming year. Lurking in the background of these negotiations were the terrible events transpiring in nearby Dayton, Ohio. There, the firefighters had gone on strike, and as the homes of 13 families burned down, the Dayton firefighters idly stood by and watched.[18] It was a horrendous act, and Richmond officials feared that if an agreement with their own department was not reached, the city could witness similar tragedies.[19]

Mayor Dickman, though a tough negotiator, always kept an open mind to the labor requests from city employees. But when unions threatened to strike, he had not one iota of tolerance. In August 1977, the firefighters' union rejected the city's offer of a 4% salary increase and preliminarily voted to strike.[20] Dickman condemned the strikes, threatening to dismiss any firefighter who walked out and declaring that there would be "no amnesty" for anyone fired.[21] The public outcry against the Dayton strike and Dickman's strong tone likely convinced the firefighters to back down on their threat of strike and to accept the city's agreement. Afterward, Dickman immediately restored an air of cordiality, saying that "Richmond has one heck of a fine fire department and police department ... I am just real pleased with them, and whatever we can see to give them in salary increases in the future, we are going to do everything we can."[22]

The key factor driving both the salary demands of city employees and the city's inability to pay was the rampant inflation of the late 1970s and early 1980s. A consumer good that cost $1 when Dickman entered office cost $1.83 when he exited it.[23] This pressured laborers to demand salary increases that may seem high but were understandable given the times (for example, the police tried to bargain for an 11% raise one year).

Further compounding the budgetary problem was the city's constrained revenue stream. In 1973, Governor Otis Bowen, on a crusade of tax relief for Hoosiers, steered a property-tax bill through the General Assembly. The law gave counties a choice. Option 1 allowed counties to adopt a small *income* tax, but as a result, the state government would freeze the total amount of *property*-tax dollars the county could collect. Under Option 2, the county collected no income tax and didn't face a cap on the collection of property-tax *dollars*, though it did impose a ceiling on a county's property-tax *rate*.[24] Wayne County, like many others, opted for Option 1 and imposed a 1% income tax, which capped its property-tax dollars. The problem for Option 1 counties was that the state government never adjusted the cap on property-tax dollars for inflation. Over time, municipalities were left with no choice but to make deep cuts to increasingly expensive services.[25]

Clifford Dickman was no cheerleader for tax increases, but he recognized that the 1973 law left local governments hamstrung. In a State of the City speech, he memorably quipped that the city was "almost as poor as a fence mouse," for Richmond was powerless even to maintain its existing level of basic services.[26] On one occasion, he and Evansville Mayor Russell Lloyd, Sr. approached Governor Bowen about the problem, but Bowen shrugged them off. Dickman surmised that he was quite proud of his tax-cutting legacy and remained oblivious to the problems on the ground. Nonetheless, the pressure from local government eventually came to the attention of the General Assembly, which responded by lifting the property-tax cap by 5% for 1978 and 8% for 1979.[27]

Another funding problem for cities was their reliance on federal revenue sharing: block grants that local governments received from Congress in exchange for complying with federal conditions. Richmond had increasingly turned to federal funds since Indiana's 1973 reforms. Dickman frequently vocalized his opposition to the principle of revenue sharing.[28] It forced cities to become reliant on the power brokers in Washington rather than take responsibility for their own collections. When cuts to federal revenue sharing were enacted, the city was hung out to dry. Dickman also thought revenue sharing was "a bad investment," claiming in one op-ed to the *Palladium-Item* that for every \$1.43 in taxes that an Indiana citizen sent to Washington, only \$1 was returned.[29] But the reality was that, without fundamental changes in state taxes, cities needed the federal funds. Though Dickman opposed the principle, he bowed to common sense and fought for the city to win federal dollars whenever he could.

Ultimately, spending cuts were the only tool in Dickman's budgetary toolbox. Keeping salary increases manageable for city employees was obviously one important component of his strategy. Police cars couldn't be replaced, special training for firemen had to be cut, recreational activities in the city parks were reduced, and personnel was shared among city departments. "These are all very tough decisions to make," Dickman said, "but they have to be made."[30] He tried to be creative. For example, Dickman noticed that the city collected trash on federal holidays, and on those days, the sanitation workers collected time-and-a-half pay. Seeing the additional wage expense as wasteful, Dickman skipped one day of trash collection each week a federal holiday occurred.[31] Though plenty of citizens responded negatively to this policy, it demonstrated his ability to think unconventionally in order to steady the city's balance sheet.

Spending cuts rarely make for popularity in government, and Mayor Dickman took plenty of heat for his budget trimming. But popularity was never his lodestar—good government was. And when he wasn't simply trying to keep the ship of government afloat, Dickman was able to work toward the big-picture progress in good government that he'd campaigned on.

One of his first initiatives was the institution of a merit system for the Richmond Police Department. The movement toward merit systems had been gaining momentum across Indiana in the 1970s. The goal was to remove promotion decisions solely from the hands of a police chief (or, in some cities, the mayor himself) so that merit, rather than favoritism, prevailed. It was broadly supported by the officers and had been an important promise of Candidate Dickman.

It was a good issue for the new mayor to take on early in his tenure—straightforward and noncontroversial.[32] Dickman and the city council formed a study commission, which eventually recommended the formation of a seven-person, nonpartisan body to make promotion and disciplinary decisions for the police department.[33] Together, they would decide based on written examinations, oral interviews, and administrative reviews of performance records.[34] Dickman approved of the proposed plan, and the council unanimously enacted the merit system into law in May 1977.[35]

Dickman had also campaigned on the idea of building a civic center in downtown Richmond, a place where the city could host conventions, concerts, plays, and other public gatherings. Dickman himself had only tempered enthusiasm for the idea, but local-tourism proponents were eager to see such a facility in Richmond. Dickman gave his blessing to a study committee headed by Ken Paust, a local businessman and Chamber of Commerce committee member.[36] The idea garnered a great deal of interest at first—a crowd overflowed the city-council chamber in September 1976 for a debate on the purchase of several parcels of land for the center. The price tag was $300,000, but the Chamber promised $270,000 in annual revenues from the center, not to mention the hundreds of thousands of dollars in positive externalities for the city economy.[37]

A week later, the council passed a resolution to purchase the land, but the State Board of Tax Commissioners invalidated the ordinance because it hadn't been passed by a 2/3 majority.[38] That decision killed all momentum for the project. The convention-center idea, commented the *Palladium-Item*, had "burst upon the local scene with a bang, maintained the clash of opposing voices for more than a month and then faded with a whimper almost as suddenly."[39] The mayor, still unconvinced of the wisdom of a convention center, was content to let the issue recede from public debate.

Dickman's most important goal was bringing jobs to Richmond. The city had been dealt devasting employment blows in the Klute administration, leading Dickman to declare that the lack of jobs was the biggest problem facing the community.[40] He quickly learned, however, that it was counterproductive for a mayor to lead the charge in selling the city to would-be employers. Large companies were leery of their plans being leaked, and political actors like mayors couldn't be trusted to keep a secret. Instead, prospective employers turned to local businessmen who could surreptitiously sell the merits of the community. At the time, Richmond was fortunate to have an outstanding ambassador to the business community in Arthur Vivian, the operator of a local Buick dealership who was deeply passionate about his Richmond home. As a founding member of Wayne County's chamber of commerce, Vivian took the lead in attracting industry to the area.[41]

In fall 1978, Richmond hit the jackpot. Thanks to Vivian's outreach, Chrysler announced the construction of a 600,000-square-foot transaxle plant in Richmond that promised to employ 1,400 people.[42] It was a massive score for a city of 40,000. Some Richmond residents found it too good to be true and doubted whether Chrysler would follow through with its plan.[43] But Cliff Dickman wasted no time in preparing for Richmond's newest corporate citizen, and he started work on extending Industries Road to reach Chrysler's 80-acre plot of land on the northwest side of town.[44] Chrysler broke ground on its plant in November in a ceremony attended by Dickman and Indiana Lieutenant Governor (and future Governor) Robert Orr. Dickman proclaimed that the coming of Chrysler was "one of the greatest days in our city in a long time."[45]

But just after the new year, the skeptics' fears were realized. Chrysler installed a new president, Lee Iacocca, who embarked on a massive cost-cutting mission to salvage Chrysler's deteriorating financial condition. The company reneged on its plans for Richmond, instead deciding to expand its extant operation in Kokomo, Indiana for building the transaxles.[46]

Local leaders were stunned, including Dickman, but he immediately tried to strike a positive tone, claiming that Chrysler had been pleased with its reception in Richmond. Dickman promised Chrysler that should their economic prospects improve, Richmond "will be waiting with open arms for their return." He told the newspaper, "We almost had another good one, but like a fish on the hook, it got away. We will just keep on fishing and some day...."[47] The *Palladium-Item*'s editorial board credited this optimism, noting that it might provide the spark needed for another employer to take advantage of the economic opportunities in Richmond. And with Chrysler's financial situation on the rocks, the newspaper even questioned whether Richmond dodged a bullet in having Chrysler terminate its plans sooner rather than later.[48]

Dickman kept at it. After Chrysler announced its change in plans, he called Lieutenant Governor Orr to ask the state's economic-development board to remember this episode when steering future industrial opportunities around the state.[49] By the end of 1979, a West German diesel-engine manufacturer promised to bring several hundred jobs to the city.[50] Yet even that prospect eventually fizzled out. During Dickman's tenure as mayor, Richmond failed to notch any new, large-scale employers.

But the success of a town isn't merely measured by how many manufacturing titans it can woo. Undoubtedly, Richmond would have been better off had Chrysler made good on its commitment, but it's folly to not recognize that the sword can be double-edged. With all the tax breaks and taxpayer-funded development projects that small cities offer to industrial behemoths, it's costly for cities to compete for new jobs. And if the corporate giants pack up and leave a community en masse, the vacuums left behind—vacant property, joblessness, lost tax revenue—can shred the economic and social fabric of a community.

Dickman understood the key truth that economic success ought to be counted by the number of well-paying jobs in a community, not the number of corporations. So in the wake of the Chrysler announcement, he continued to proclaim that Richmond was open for business, large or small. He believed that compared to other Indiana cities of its size, Richmond was one of the best situated because it had preserved its core downtown area.[51] Nonetheless, he continued to press for development on the city's fringes. One of his best job-growth initiatives was to expand Industrial Parkway on the eastern side of Richmond, an effort to entice manufacturers wanting easy access to Interstate 70. Over the years to come, many such enterprises set up shop along the new road, and they have remained committed to Richmond for several decades.

Dickman marked several other important achievements in his first term. He oversaw the completion of two skywalks downtown, the widening of Williamsburg Pike, and extensive sidewalk-repair projects. [52] He spearheaded legislation and negotiations to close down a local "massage parlor" (called "Caesar's Palace"—"massage" was a euphemism).[53] Dickman instituted a program to give citizens more responsibility and authority in reporting crimes, and he added buses to the city fleet that were capable of loading riders in wheelchairs.[54] All of these— to say nothing of addressing the day-in, day-out challenges that come with leading a city—Dickman marked as proud achievements.

Two predicaments that Dickman faced during his first term merit particular attention. As any Hoosier will be unsurprised to learn, both involved two key forces: cooperation and cold.

The first came in February 1977, just over a year into Dickman's tenure. America was facing a critical natural-gas shortage. The problem had been attributed to a variety of causes. First, temperatures had been frigid for several months nationwide, and the extra energy required to heat homes and businesses drained the country's natural-gas supply. Some also blamed a decrease in gas production on federal price controls, which lowered revenues for gas companies and consequently deterred production. Others still blamed the energy companies for using natural gas to generate electricity when other fuels could have been used instead.[55]

Whatever the cause, Richmond had a problem on its hands. The natural-gas crisis had caused a massive substitution to fuel oil, and now it too was in short supply. On February 1, the local fuel-oil distributors informed the mayor that their supply allocations would not be enough to serve the city for the month if temperatures continued to linger at frosty lows. And without fuel oil, many Richmond citizens wouldn't be able to heat their homes. The county's largest dealer, Sun Oil Co., reported that it had sold 1,000,000 gallons of fuel oil in January but had only 460,000 gallons for February. The kerosene and coal stockpiles, the dealers said, were almost depleted already.[56]

The mayor immediately set to work on a citywide conservation effort, telling the newspaper that "[w]e're all in this together."[57] He summoned a meeting of the Wayne County civil defense board, county sheriff's office, city police department, Red Cross, Salvation Army, and local utilities.[58] Together, they started working on a contingency plan in the event that the fuel-oil supply threatened to hit zero. If that risk became imminent, then the remainder would be distributed where it was needed most—the hospital and homes. Factories, stores, and schools would have to sacrifice their allocations.

But Dickman was determined to prevent that worst-case scenario from materializing. On the morning of February 2nd, he made a public appeal for all thermostats to be lowered to 60 degrees in an effort to save energy. He also started meeting with businesses across the city, requesting that 60-hour-a-week shops reduce their hours to 42 and that 60-plus-hour businesses cut to 54.[59]

The mayor's plea seemed to work. Although he had no way of tracking whether the conservation efforts were succeeding overall, almost all stores heeded his appeal for good citizenship and cut their business hours as requested.[60] The only businesses that pushed back on his plea were the grocery stores, which cited the wide-ranging shopping habits of their customers as evidence that they needed to stay open longer.[61] But eventually, even they got on board with at least some hourly reductions. Four days into the conservation effort, Dickman expressed his gratitude that citizens and businesses alike were all chipping in and doing their part.[62]

Good news eventually came in the form of good weather: forecasts for the weekend of February 12–13 predicted a burst of warmth, which would alleviate pressure on the fuel-oil supply.[63] With positive predictions from the distributors, Dickman declared that the crisis had passed, though he asked citizens to continue conserving the still-reduced supply. He added that low thermostat settings help homeowners save on utility bills and remarked, in true Dickman form, "Ours is not going back up at our house." The entire conservation effort had been completely voluntary, and its success, along with good weather, had staved off a true calamity. As City Controller Don Meredith put it, the "cooperation from not only the businesses, but all the citizens, is very admirable and speaks highly of the citizens of Richmond."[64]

Bad weather precipitated a far greater crisis one year later—indeed, it was one of the worst weather disasters in Richmond's history. The story begins with another of Dickman's creative cost-cutting decisions. Going into the winter of 1978, the mayor scaled back the city's usual purchases of salt for de-icing the roads. He had two qualms with salt: its high price and its corrosive effect on cars. Instead, he thought, the city could mostly get by with a cheaper mixture of sand and calcium chloride.

Unfortunately for Dickman, the winter of 1978 was brutally cold and relentlessly snowy in the Midwest. Starting in mid-December, Richmond perpetually had snow on its streets and sidewalks, and a month later, Dickman's salt-cutting decision was in full public scrutiny. The sand, it turned out, had been a mistake: it had no de-icing effect whatsoever. Sand could help provide traction when it had direct contact with a tire, but the continually falling snow covered the sand and made it useless. Plowing was the only effective method the city had for improving the roads, which worked well for snow removal but couldn't melt the ice. As a result, the roads remained quite hazardous for driving all the way into late January. The *Palladium-Item* Sunday edition captured the public's frustration by publishing a large front-page photo of a protestor—standing in front of a snow-blanketed city hall and garnering support from honking cars—holding the sign: "Clean City Streets or Clean City Hall!"[65]

Two days later, Tuesday, January 24, Dickman and Transportation Director Jerry Haynes admitted that the city had no road salt. Morton Salt Company offered to sell salt to Richmond, but the city had to send a truck to Toledo, Ohio to pick it up. Haynes expressed skepticism, claiming that a Toledo shipment could deliver only 15 tons of salt when the city needed 150–200 tons.[66]

By Wednesday, the situation had not improved—rain, snow, and sleet mixtures had only made the roads slicker. The newspaper featured a front-cover photo of a teenager ice skating on a downtown street. And the forecast didn't promise any relief—another two to four inches were expected overnight.[67]

But no forecaster, mayor, or protester could have predicted the reality that struck Richmond in the early hours of Thursday, January 26. In what would later be known as the Great Blizzard of 1978, wind gusts up to 50 MPH, near-zero visibility, freezing temperatures, and significant precipitation joined together to create the perfect storm. The new snow—six inches' worth—wasn't the main problem; the wind was. It drove the 20 inches of snow already on the ground, plus the six new inches, to create massive drifts—some of which reached two stories high.[68] It was unlike anything Richmond had seen in living memory. Doors and windows were closed in, vehicles were trapped, and roads were completely buried.[69]

Dickman had been up most of the night. The city council had gathered at his house for a late-night impromptu meeting, and he'd been on the phone trying to coordinate snow-plowing efforts. But as Dickman quickly learned, plowing that night was a lost cause. The powerful winds simply pushed the mountains of snow back onto any freshly plowed roads. Until the blizzard abated, human efforts were fruitless.

In the early morning, Mayor Dickman declared a state of emergency. The city was effectively shut down. Schools, businesses, and roads were closed. Electrical outages were widespread, and repair crews couldn't reach the power lines to make the fixes. Deliveries of basic necessities—bread, milk, prescriptions—were halted. And just outside the city, livestock perished in the frigid air.[70] The situation was calamitous.

The city's small fleet of plowing trucks was no match for the blanketed roads, so Dickman went to work enlisting private contractors to help with road-clearing efforts. Other city vehicles were pressed into service, especially with delivering food and other necessities to people who couldn't get out of their homes. Here, private citizens once again stepped up to the plate: local auto dealers donated their cars to the city for transporting supplies around town.[71] Other volunteers who owned snowmobiles and four-wheel-drive vehicles went out on their own to rescue fellow citizens who were stranded in their cars.[72]

Help soon arrived from outside sources. The Indiana National Guard delivered food and supplies to homes and freed vehicles that had been trapped by snow drifts.[73] President Carter declared a state of emergency in Indiana the next day, and the federal government eventually promised to reimburse municipalities for 75% of snow-removal costs.[74]

Over the next few days, the overwhelming priority of the city government was getting snow off the roads. With temperatures not appreciably rising, the snow wasn't going to simply disappear; it had to be moved somewhere. And that meant that it had to be pushed into parking lots, front lawns, and even driveways—which led to no shortage of grumbling to the mayor. There was, of course, nowhere else for it to go.

But progress and warmer weather eventually came. Major thoroughfares were cleared first, and inch by inch, residential streets again became passable. On February 1, with the city officially out of crisis mode, Dickman delivered his thanks to the efforts of government employees and altruistic private citizens alike:

> To those who volunteered with four-wheel drives, snowmobiles, and various other vehicles go the greatest thanks as they helped countless persons who were in dire need.

> For those who checked on their neighbors and friends goes another great deal of gratitude, and for the one who picked up his shovel and dug in, I say, 'thank you.'

To the local news media, particularly the radio stations, we are all indebted for their patience in communicating with all of us.

I also wish to thank the city departments who did everything possible to help our citizens be as comfortable as conditions permitted. Our medical agencies carried on with limited staffing as did all essential service groups.

Let us hope that what has occurred is now history and may the records pile up in ice and snow [and] never be broken.[75]

As life returned to normal, local politicos and news writers inevitably started playing the blame game. While anyone can nitpick the run-up to the blizzard, it was ridiculous to blame anyone for the complete shutdown brought on by the blizzard itself. It truly was a once-in-a-generation event in Richmond—there has been nothing like it since 1978. But to his great credit, the mayor wasted no time in trying to learn how the city could grow from this episode. He formed a special advisory committee of citizens and city-council members to study how the city could better manage large snowfalls.[76]

The three Democrats on the city council, perhaps eager to deny Dickman a comeback after the blizzard, announced that they wouldn't serve on the advisory committee. It was a bad move. The not-so-pleased mayor retorted, "I didn't realize it was a Republican snow. I thought it belonged to all of us."[77] The *Palladium-Item* wasn't happy either. Its editorial board charged: "The [Democrats'] boycott is either because the councilmen think serving on the snow committee is too much work, or it is a childish act of partisanship at its worst."[78] But the snow committee forged ahead, and with its recommendations approved by the city council, Richmond entered the 1979 winter with three new spreaders, two new four-wheel-drive trucks, a newly repaired front-end loader ... and plenty of salt.[79]

Fifteen months out from Richmond's next local election, the big question began to arise: will the mayor seek a second term? Though Dickman publicly remained noncommittal, he'd always known he wanted to run again.[80] He made it official in January 1979 during a speech to the Board of Public Works and Safety. He opened with a word of thanks to the city employees who had furthered his initiatives, but he reminded them that the task of improvement was never complete. He asked for the voters to keep their faith, as "we all want to continue serving them."[81]

Dickman faced no opposition from his fellow Republicans in the primary. The Democrats fought for their party's nomination in a four-way race, with Charles Hart emerging as the nominee.[82] But a few weeks later, Hart withdrew for unknown reasons.[83] The Democrats called on Reverend Otis Barber, pastor of Second Missionary Baptist Church and a graduate of Earlham's School of Religion, to accept the nomination.[84] Things looked extremely auspicious for the Republicans. On a national level, public opinion for President Carter and the Democrats was sliding. And locally, the Democrats had been able to field only their second-place candidate.

But despite the odds against them, Barber and the Democrats hit Dickman hard. Barber attacked Dickman's policy of permitting leaf burning in the autumn, which had generated considerable local ire. He railed against excessive costs in running city departments, the poor quality of the streets, the suspension of trash collection around federal holidays, and mismanagement in applications for federal funding.[85]

Dickman and the Republicans ran on every incumbent's favorite word: experience.[86] The campaign claimed that crime had been reduced by 14% over the past four years, 50 miles of streets had been paved, 4,000 new private-sector jobs had been created, and 87 public-sector jobs had been trimmed from the city's payroll.[87] Out of these encouraging accomplishments, a punchy campaign slogan emerged: "Dickman: The Man, The Record."

In September 1979, with the election about six weeks away, the Indiana Association of Cities and Towns named Richmond as winner of the Community Achievement Award, an honor marking "exceptional local government and achievement." Mayor Dickman accepted the award on the city's behalf in South Bend.[88] Though the *Palladium-Item* cheekily thanked the mayor "for taking the bows for the city," Dickman heaped praise on the staff workers in the city departments. "They're all the ones who have done the work, and I think they feel a sense of pride that it is all worth the effort."[89]

As the campaign entered the final stretch, endorsements poured in—Congressman Phil Sharp and former Mayors Klute and Howell for Barber;[90] Senator Richard Lugar,[91] former Congressman David Dennis,[92] Lieutenant Governor Orr,[93] and Earlham's Professor Trueblood[94] for Dickman. The *Palladium-Item*'s editorial board also came down for Dickman, though their endorsement was less than enthusiastic: "The preponderance of evidence is that, despite some problems, the Dickman administration has the skills and the experience that makes it more likely to provide the kind of leadership the city needs as it enters the 1980s." The paper criticized both campaigns for lacking "any great vision or inspiration on new directions," and while crediting Dickman's experience, it criticized his mistakes as "expensive on-the-job training." It lukewarmly concluded, "[A] Second Dickman term seems in the best interests of the city."[95] After the election, Dickman said this op-ed stung him more than anything during the campaign. "How anyone can be so hypocritical and tear me up three different ways and then in the end say they endorse me?" he complained.[96]

Dickman also absorbed a harsh attack from Barber's campaign manager, Karen Bertsch. In the days before the election, she penned a letter to the editor explaining that she had entered politics in reaction to a speech that Dickman had given to the Optimist Club one year into his mayoralty.[97] In the speech, Dickman lamented Richmond's high unemployment level and blamed the situation in part on "all the women that have gone to work." The result, he explained, was that "those who really need a job can't get it," and that "some guys with families [are] being pushed out by women."[98] These comments rattled Bertsch, and she charged Dickman with being insensitive to the contributions of women employed outside the home. Her letter quoted with approval the words of an anonymous Republican lawyer: "Any woman who would vote for Cliff Dickman would be a fool."[99]

Dickman's 1977 speech rankles modern sensibilities, and the quotations cherrypicked by the editorial can give a negative impression. But for several reasons, it's clear that the outsized rhetoric of the columnist and the anonymous lawyer is no more than political hyperbole. The mayor was a strong supporter of Richmond women—whether they worked inside or outside the home.

For starters, consider the full context of his speech. Dickman's concern was that if a single family occupied two jobs, then another family might have no job at all. This is what he meant when he said, "The man holding down two jobs *or* with a wife working is going to have to be willing to pay the bill for the man who is being forced out of a job."[100] In other words, if a family's sole breadwinner couldn't land a job, the rest of society would pick up the tab via welfare checks. The main point of Dickman's speech was to acknowledge his perception of this tradeoff, not to condemn working women.

Next, take a comprehensive look at Dickman's political activity over the years. As Bertsch's editorial itself pointed out, more than 50% of American women worked outside the home at the time. The mayor had no desire to alienate such a substantial proportion of his voters. To the contrary, he unsurprisingly sought out the vote of the female electorate and supported policies that improved their livelihoods. He spoke to numerous women's groups about his candidacy both in 1975 and 1979.[101] Richmond women gladly contributed their efforts to his political organization, and Dickman lent his support to Republican women running for other positions in city government. In policy, Dickman vocalized his support for the forward-thinking idea of subsidizing homemakers, saying that "the government could pay a household X amount of dollars if one of the parents stays home." And he added, "Maybe it would be the man who stays home if the wife has the better job."[102]

Finally, consider Dickman's own experiences with working women. Though his mother did not work outside the home, Dickman always described her as one of the hardest-working individuals he'd ever known. Several of his sisters were employed throughout their adult lives. His wife's wages had enabled the couple to buy their first home. He consistently praised City Clerk Jo Ellen Trimble and his administrative assistant Lois Brown, recognizing that he couldn't succeed as mayor without either of them. And although he couldn't have known it at the time, his four daughters and numerous granddaughters (not to mention in-laws) went on to have flourishing careers—something in which he took great pride. The idea that Cliff Dickman opposed women working outside the home is belied by the story of his life, and the voters of Richmond soundly rejected it in 1979.

As the campaign entered its final stretch, the candidates themselves swung harder at each other. At a debate, Barber accused Dickman of over-delegating to his department heads. "I hope you never get chewed out by me," Dickman snapped back. "I may seem like just a nice guy, but just try me. A few of my department heads have, and they found out what can happen."[103] Barber railed against the city's failure to lock in road-salt contracts at low prices and the poor quality of the streets.[104] Dickman defended his performance during the blizzard and highlighted the new labor contracts he'd negotiated with city employees. He pointed to the city's new neighborhood-watch program, the merit system for police, and the budget savings that the city had achieved.[105] In sum, he confidently declared, the last four years were the best Richmond had ever seen.[106]

That was a bold claim, but the voters seemed to agree. On November 6, 1979, Richmond re-elected Clifford Dickman as mayor by more than a 2–1 margin—6,211 to 2,923.[107] The Republicans swept the election: Trimble won re-election as city clerk, and the Republicans took seven of the nine seats on the city council.[108]

Barber and Dickman were gracious to each other after the election. A *Palladium-Item* photo captured their handshake as Barber conceded, both men with earnest grins on their faces.[109] Dickman admitted to the *Palladium* that he'd expected the landslide, saying that the Democrats didn't have any issues to campaign on. And of course, he was flattered that the people of Richmond had hired him back for four more years. "I don't think people want a change, and evidently that showed up in the voting," he said. Turnout had been low—only 48% of registered voters cast a ballot, Richmond's lowest in 28 years. But it didn't bother the victorious mayor, who remarked, "I think apathy kind of comes from when someone does a good job and they (the voters) don't think there's any reason to get out there and vote."[110] The *Palladium*'s editorial board congratulated Dickman and said, more warmly than in the campaign, that "the Dickman team clearly has earned four more years" and that "the voters have chosen well for continuation of good city government through 1983."[111]

Though victory had been virtually assured from the start of the 1979 campaign, Dickman was gratified to win the confidence of his fellow citizens. But the next four years would test Dickman far more than his first term had. They would require more than just the political experience the voters had valued. They would demand energy, grit, and faith.

11

A New Decade

"Honesty, sound judgment, and implementation of sound plans"—these were the hallmarks of government that Mayor Dickman promised to the people of Richmond in his second inaugural address. "I do not ask the staff just to strive for these attributes, I expect it of them, as I expect it of myself."[1] He would not let himself down on this score, though disappointingly, the same could not be said of one of his staff.

The mayor's second inauguration not only marked the beginning of a new term but also the beginning of the 1980s. Dickman took to the pen and explained his goals for the decade to *Palladium-Item* subscribers. He began with a lofty political goal: his ardent wish for the federal and state governments to devolve more authority to municipalities, especially tax-collecting power. He then turned to the mundane, day-to-day work ahead for the city. Most pressing was a $40 million sewage-separation project that would soon rip up roads across Richmond.[2] "[A]ll of us will be perturbed and disturbed until it is complete. I warn you now to get braced, grit your teeth, and bear with us." His letter also reignited an old war that had silently simmered over the past several years: annexation.[3]

Annexation is the process of adding territory to a city. Sometimes, citizens living on land outside city limits consent to being annexed, but usually they resist it.[4] The people living on Richmond's fringes were in the latter category. Many had strategically located themselves to be near the jobs, restaurants, and activity offered by the city while avoiding the higher tax rates that in-town residents paid. If they were annexed, then they too would pay Richmond taxes without any new benefits in return. The very principle of annexation bothered them too, as the city council could annex adjoining land without any say from the people living there.[5]

From the perspective of city officials, however, annexation was a necessity. In the 1970s and 1980s, suburban flight was unfolding across America, even in midsize cities like Richmond. Developers bought cheap, open land outside city limits and built up new neighborhoods. City dwellers flocked to these developments, which offered lower taxes, larger plots of land, and freshly built homes. The problem, from the government's perspective, was that the city's official population shrank, which reduced the allocations it received from the federal and state governments. All the while, the suburbanites continued to work Richmond jobs, enjoy Richmond city services, and drive on Richmond streets—all without paying the taxes of a Richmond citizen.[6]

Richmond hadn't annexed any territory since Mayor Doc Cutter's administration in the 1960s. Knowing the opposition that lay ahead, Dickman nonetheless began work on annexation within a few months of becoming mayor. "Any city that is alive and healthy cannot be standing still," he said. "Like any business or individual, a city cannot be stagnant."[7] But his first-term annexation efforts failed. The city council passed an ordinance to annex 776 acres on the east side of town, but the state tax board overturned the enactment.[8] For the rest of Dickman's first term, annexation talk had lain dormant, including on the campaign trail. But the night Dickman was reelected, he declared his intention to pursue annexation yet again.[9]

Just days into his second term (and on his 50th birthday), Dickman announced his specific plans at a speech to the Lions Club. The city hoped to annex 332 acres on Richmond's west side—a square tract with Round Barn Road on the western border, Salisbury Road to the east, U.S. 40 to the south, and College Corner Road to the north.[10] The acreage under consideration was far more modest than the last time around. But nonetheless, the plot was home to about 750 people living in 250 residences, so it promised a significant population addition (and therefore a significant revenue increase) to the city.

Opposition flared up immediately. During the first-term annexation battle, a group called "Citizens Against Annexation" (CAA) had formed, and they banded back together for the 1980 fight. They weren't shy about their hostility to the proposal. One resident, responding to the argument that Richmond's suburbanites take advantage of city services without paying their fair share, said, "If they don't want us to use their streets, just let us know and we'll go somewhere else." Many of them took aim directly at Dickman. CAA's vice president said, "The mayor's wasting the federal money he gets right now. He can't take care of the streets he's got already."[11]

The old football player had no fear of taking hits from the CAA, so he attended one of their meetings. It was not a productive session; they mostly berated him. But while there, he learned something disheartening. While the residents opposed the tax increases (about $100 annually for each annexed citizen) and railed against the undemocratic principle of annexation, they had another concern that wasn't reported in the newspaper. They believed that, if annexed, their children would have to switch from Centerville schools to Richmond schools, an outcome they didn't like because Richmond schools had more black students. This was factually inaccurate; annexation would not have affected school districting. But even so, Dickman was disappointed by the undercurrents of racism that animated some (though not all) of the opposition.

If anything, he was only more motivated to press on. In August 1980, the City Plan Commission split 5–5 on a procedural vote to advance the measure to city council, but after further study, they agreed to annexation unanimously.[12] The final vote was set for December. CAA kept up its barrage of criticisms and organized protests in front of city hall (one of their signs read "Mayor Dickman: Annexation of Center Twp. Is Un-American!" with a sketch of the Stars and Stripes ripped in two).[13] But Dickman was confident that annexation would pass. The Republicans, who generally favored annexation, had a 7–2 majority on the council. With victory seemingly certain, Dickman left town for a conference in Atlanta.[14]

The council shocked the town when it voted 5–4 against annexation. Three Republicans had silently been wavering on the issue, and they joined the two Democrats in rejecting the proposal. One councilman was swayed by the strong opposition the residents had displayed, while another thought adding more territory to city control would increase expenses more than city revenues.[15] Dickman was "heatedly disappointed," condemning the council members for neglecting their duty to their constituents—the Richmond residents who were unfairly subsidizing those living in the proposed territory.[16] But the defeat was conclusive, so Dickman made no more attempts at annexation during his tenure.

Dickman largely pressed on with the same initiatives and faced the same challenges as he had in his first term. Budgetary pressures abounded, and at the beginning of Dickman's second term, the belt-tightening was at its peak. President Carter pledged to slash around 25% from the federal revenue sharing program as part of his broader push to cut the national government's spending. Dickman went to D.C. to hear the details of the planned cuts, and though he understood the grim implications for Richmond's budget, he agreed with Carter's objective.[17] The results of the 1980 census didn't help Richmond's budget either: the city's official population shrank from 43,999 to 41,261, a 6.2% drop.[18] That loss reduced allocations from the state and national governments, which were made on a per-capita basis.[19] Meanwhile, inflation reached its peak in 1979 and 1980, making spending cuts harder than ever to stomach. The primary casualty of the tightened budget was the roads, as the city was unable to repair potholes on newly paved streets. The police and fire departments also suffered, as they were unable to hire new members or upgrade aging equipment.

The people of Richmond suffered in the early 1980s too. The new Federal Reserve Chairman, Paul Volcker, relentlessly attacked inflation by hiking interest rates.[20] It was healthy medicine for a monetary system spinning out of control, but there was a price to be paid—a reduction in consumption and, by extension, devastating job losses. The United States found itself in the grips of a recession, and the auto industry was particularly affected.[21]

That spelled doom for eastern Indiana, which was particularly reliant on auto-industry jobs.[22] Richmond's unemployment rate hit 14% in the summer of 1980, and it lingered at high levels until reduced inflation allowed Volcker to end his tough program.[23]

Though these economic matters were largely out of the city's hands, the Dickman administration nonetheless continued its day-to-day work of making Richmond a better place to live. Federal grants were thinning, yet Dickman zealously pursued them to develop poorer areas of town.[24] The mayor successfully fought an initiative from the state government to convert the local State Hospital, a mental-health institution, into a prison.[25] Alongside the Chamber of Commerce, he oversaw the opening of a trail in the Whitewater Valley Gorge cutting through the heart of town.[26] He overcame stiff territorial opposition to extend roads around the edges of town, thoroughfares that are taken for granted today.[27] And he organized concerted cleanup efforts across the community, emphasizing the need for citizens to look after their own neighborhoods.

Dickman also continued to confront labor strikes. Though confined to the private sector this time, the 1982 strike against PRC Recording Co. was serious enough that the mayor had to step in. What started as peaceful picketing for higher wages by the International Brotherhood of Electrical Workers quickly turned dangerous. Strikers burned a PRC security vehicle, threw rocks, and blocked non-striking employees from reporting to work, leading to the arrest of 26 people.[28] Dickman deployed Richmond police to the site and informed the governor that intervention from the Indiana State Police might also become necessary. He saw arguments of merit—and points of failure—from both sides. Dickman viewed labor unions skeptically, and he thought PRC management had made a fair offer after negotiations. But he also warned the company that "if their goal was to reduce wages substantially, we aren't out there to protect management and enable them to cut wages.... If the company's intent was to cut wages $2 an hour, I think that's wrong."

At the end of the day, Dickman was committed to being impartial toward both sides. "We have to stay in the middle. Our goal in the city is to keep people from getting injured and property damaged."[29] But despite Dickman's ostensible respect for both parties, the strikers despised him all the same. Several months into the strike, the union representative said that Dickman was merely a puppet for the PRC plant manager, who actually ran the city. The strikers made effigies of Dickman and the plant manager and hanged them on "gallows" (pickets) outside the plant gate. [30] With inflammatory words and acts like these, the police department feared for the mayor's safety. At a parade that summer, four officers accompanied Dickman's car—the first and only time he received special protection in politics. Fortunately, no danger ever materialized, and the PRC dispute was eventually resolved peacefully.[31]

Serving as mayor often took Dickman outside the city. He traveled to Washington, D.C. with some regularity, meeting with members of Congress and federal agencies in the never-ending battle to direct funds to Richmond. But the most important of Dickman's out-of-town commitments was his participation in the Indiana Association of Cities and Towns (IACT). The IACT is a non-partisan organization made up of mayors across the state. Its main task is to voice the concerns shared by municipalities to the General Assembly. The member-mayors gather for meetings to establish their priorities, and they frequently appear before legislative committees and subcommittees to explain those goals to state representatives and senators. In Dickman's time, the Association spurred some critical policy achievements in the statehouse, including the Indiana Home Rule Act of 1980, which delegated more governing authority from the state to cities, and raising the burdensome property-tax ceiling.[32]

Dickman joined the IACT in his first term and rose through the ranks—serving as second vice president, then first vice president, and finally president for a one-year term beginning in September 1982.[33] He forged valuable contacts in Indiana politics along the way. One of the country's best-known Republican mayors at the time was Indianapolis's William Hudnut, who became Dickman's friend and golf buddy. Dickman even advised Mayor Hudnut as the latter weighed the decision to run for governor (he did not).

Dickman succeeded Hudnut as the chairman of the Indiana GOP Mayors' Caucus in 1980 after Lieutenant Governor Robert Orr won the governorship.[34] Orr had also been a pal of Dickman's, both in his lieutenant days and after. Dickman supported his candidacy by serving as cochairman of the Mayors for Orr Committee. The new governor did not disappoint: Dickman found Orr to be more agreeable to work with than his predecessor, Otis Bowen.[35]

Through the Association of Cities and Towns, Dickman also got to know Richard Lugar, a former Indianapolis mayor and longtime U.S. senator. Along the way, he met a bright young staffer for Lugar named Mitch Daniels, the future Hoosier governor and president of Purdue University. Dickman also welcomed then-Representative (and future Vice President) Dan Quayle to Richmond in

his bid to unseat Senator Birch Bayh, which was ultimately successful. [36] And, of course, Dickman became
well-acquainted with mayors across the state, taking special pride in representing them as IACT president at conventions hosted by the National League of Cities and at
presidential briefings in the White House.[37] His service
to the Republicans and to good governance in Indiana was
widely admired and appreciated, and some politicos
would not forget that service when it came time to select
candidates for higher offices.

One IACT event remains unforgettable to Dickman.
He was running late for a meeting with his fellow mayors
at the Atkinson Hotel in Indianapolis. Dickman dashed
up to the eighth floor, but first, he needed to make a trip
to "the john" (a favorite of his euphemisms). He rushed
into the bathroom stall, but looking down, he noticed
something unusual on the other side of the divider—two
small, pointy-toed shoes pointing in the opposition direction. He burst out as quickly as he could, and because the
meeting proceeded uneventfully, Dickman thought he'd
been spared of the embarrassment. But at an IACT meeting six months later, the story of his inadvertent trip to
the ladies' room at last came out, and everyone had a good
laugh about it. The Association was more than just an ad-
vocacy group or networking opportunity for Dickman.
With Republicans and Democrats alike, he found true
friendship.

Dickman delighted in the unique life experiences that
being mayor afforded him. As the public face of Richmond, he appeared at countless events around town and
beyond. He presided over ribbon-cutting ceremonies and
welcomed new employers to Richmond—even donning

Mickey Mouse ears when Disney Music set up a distribution center in town.[38] He "enjoyed" the special privilege of having a spot in the county's underground bunker in the event of nuclear war.[39] Dickman was also a regular on the local speaking circuit, with gigs ranging from the Rotary and Kiwanis Clubs to the YMCA to the U.S. Army Reserves. [40] He dedicated weeks to recognize various causes—Boy Scouts Week, Constitution Week, Free Enterprise Week, Kiss Your Baby Week, Be Kind to Animals Week, and even Weights and Measures Week, to name a few.[41] Dickman awarded keys to the city to distinguished residents and guests, threw first pitches on Opening Day, saluted Richmond High School sports teams as they went off to important contests, and represented Richmond around America—from San Francisco to Indianapolis to Washington, D.C.[42]

Some vignettes of Dickman's time in office are worth recounting. In the fall of 1980, the mayor had the privilege of welcoming incoming freshmen to his alma mater of Earlham College. Before introducing Dickman, Earlham President Franklin Wallin joked to the liberal student body, "A more partisan Republican you will not find." At this, the students chuckled, although a small few gave him a smattering of claps. Dickman took the podium and told the tiny minority of applauders, "The two of you are invited to stop by my office any time." All the students roared at this joke, and Dickman pressed ahead by urging the new arrivals to join the football team. "Richmond would really enjoy a winning season. It might hurt the grades but what the heck." The Republican had captured the goodwill of his new Democratic constituents, and he walked off the stage "amid boisterous applause."[43]

As mayor, Dickman took the lead in celebrating the accomplishments of Richmond citizens. And during Dickman's tenure, no son or daughter of Richmond achieved more on the national stage than Vagas Ferguson.*[44] A 1976 graduate of Richmond High School, Ferguson had been a sensational running back for the Red Devils.[45] He went on to run the football for Notre Dame with outstanding success; to this day, he has the third-most career rushing yards in Fighting Irish history. [46] Ferguson played a few years in the NFL, but before his transition from college to the pros, Richmond held a grand banquet to celebrate the hometown hero.

With more than 500 in attendance, the event was headlined by Irish head coach Dan Devine, who had tremendous affection for his star player. "I would have pushed a peanut all the way here with my nose. Nothing could have kept me from coming here," Devine said to the Richmond crowd. "I know he's a great football player, but he's also a great person, a great human being, and I love him."[47] Local Notre Dame grad Ray Zaleski, a New England Patriots receivers coach, a Dayton sports broadcaster, and Mayor Cliff Dickman took the podium to shower more praise on Ferguson. Dickman noted that Ferguson's humility stood out to him more than any other quality. "Not only is he a credit to this community, but to Notre Dame—and that's the best football school in the country," Dickman said. "When you're a credit there, that's the best."[48]

---

* A close runner-up was Richmond's Weeb Ewbank, who coached the New York Jets to victory in Superbowl III and took his place in the Pro Football Hall of Fame during Dickman's tenure as mayor. Dickman was part of the entourage accompanying Ewbank to Canton for the induction.

While some Richmond natives brought honor to their hometown, others brought shame. In the late 1970s, Americans began voicing concern about the activities of a cult society known as "Jonestown," named after its leader, Jim Jones. A Congressman from California, Leo Ryan, traveled to the cult's home base in the jungles of Guyana to investigate. The cult ambushed him and four others at the airstrip, killing them all. Knowing the national uproar and retribution that would follow, Jones orchestrated a mass suicide of all cult members by cyanide poisoning. It was wretched—more than 900 people died at Jones's command.[49]

The entire nation was horrified, but the tragedy hit especially hard in Richmond. Jones had grown up across the county line in Lynn, Indiana (he and Dickman spent their boyhoods only about 10 miles away from each other). Jones graduated from Richmond High School, as did his wife, Marceline Baldwin, and the couple had married in Richmond too. Though their cult took root elsewhere, Richmond residents remembered the couple—indeed, Baldwin's parents and sisters lived in Richmond at the time of the tragedy. "Aghast" was how veteran *Palladium-Item* reporter Fred Lord described the local reaction, noting that the town talked of little else for a week. Mayor Dickman described the events as "an unbelievable tragedy. As I've gone from place to place in the city this week, I believe the residents are as baffled as I am."[50]

Jonestown was a dark chapter, but the community had much to be proud of during Dickman's years in office. For one, "the City of Roses" had reached peak recognition for its floral heritage. With more flowers growing under glass than any other city in the world, Richmond planted an annual tradition in 1972—the Rose Festival. It started as a small carnival, but within a few years, it quickly blossomed into a fixture of summertime. The celebration usually lasted three to five days, bringing out thousands of locals and thousands more from out of town. It featured amusement rides, food vendors, concerts, pageants, museum and factory tours, exhibitions, and parades.[51] And it was all made possible by an army of volunteers and dedicated community leadership.

The mayor was not responsible for coordinating the Rose Festival, but he did play a prominent role in it.[52] He formally commenced the celebrations with a proclamation, hosted a mayor's breakfast, and rode with Martha Jane near the front of the parade line, which featured about 100 cars and floats.[53] Though the mayor was front and center for the festival's signature events, Martha Jane took a greater role in planning the event as a member of the welcoming and hospitality committee.[54]

Celebrities sometimes graced the Rose Festival, and in 1982, Dickman played an unexpected role in trying to recruit one. Some locals had heard the pop singer Barry Manilow give a radio interview in which he'd mentioned an unfavorable visit to Richmond early in his musical career. The Rose Festival chairman talked the mayor into writing a letter to Manilow, seeking to make amends by inviting him to sing at the festival:

Dear Mr. Manilow:

Say it isn't so! But if it is so, and you apparently said it was, won't you give us a second chance? If this doesn't make sense, please read on....

After explaining the radio interview and the details of the festival, the mayor's letter concluded:

You'll find the key to the city awaits you, opening the doors which were locked on your first visit. You'll find a figurative, perhaps a literal, bed of roses awaits you. And most of all, you'll find awaiting you an acceptance far different than the one you described on the radio show. Will you come? Will you give us a second chance? We hope so.[55]

Manilow responded with a letter to Dickman. Though he declined the invitation, Manilow was quite cordial:

Your letter was greatly appreciated.... I do remember Richmond. It gives me chills when I think of it. But it's not Richmond's fault. I played at the Holiday Inn [at the Blue Note lounge] accompanying a girl singer named Jeanne Lucas. We called ourselves 'Jeanne and Barry' and we were awful.

Thank you very much for your lovely letter and gracious invitation.... My best regards to you and the City of Roses.[56]

The Dickman–Manilow exchange was as amusing as it was unexpected.

Though some efforts to recruit well-known characters to town failed, others succeeded. An especially notable figure who came to Richmond during Dickman's mayoralty was Martin Luther King, Sr., who spoke at Earlham College on the 10th anniversary of his son's assassination. George Sawyer, a local attorney, had convinced King to visit Richmond. Speaking with a reporter at Sawyer's house before going to Earlham, King spoke of his son's dream. "We've got to get rid of this color thing once and for all," King declared. "Just as my son said, and I agree with him, each individual has to be judged by the content of his mind, not his color."[57] Meanwhile at Richmond

High School, with rain falling upon them, Dickman, Martha Jane, and City Councilman Marion Williams led a civil-rights march of 250 people to Earlham College for the speech.[58]

King delivered an impassioned Christian sermon of forgiveness to the 2,000-person crowd gathered at Earlham, with Senator Birch Bayh and Congressman Phil Sharp in attendance. "You're looking in the face of a man who carries no ill will in heart for his enemy. I refused to stoop low enough to hate anyone." He went on, "I do not hate the man who took the life of my namesake…. I don't hate the young man who came in my church and shot my wife to death after 48 years of happy marriage. It left me awfully lonesome, but I don't hate him." The audience poured out tears and applause, and Dickman presented King a key to the city.[59]

Whether the city was being dealt a blessing or a blow, Dickman was out in front. But he wasn't the only one affected by his position: his family had to live in the spotlight, with all its attendant benefits and burdens. The kids' experiences varied by their ages. The oldest, Debbie, was married and living in Wisconsin during her father's years in office, so she was more removed from the vicissitudes of public life. The youngest, Dan and Cindy, were in grade school during these years, so they reveled in their mini-celebrity status—though their parents' hobnobbing after Sunday Mass tested their patience. For the kids in the middle, public life had its ups and downs. Because of the watchful scrutiny of their classmates and the other parents, the Dickman teenagers sometimes felt like they were living in a fishbowl. And their father knew they faced this pressure, warning them that others were waiting for them to fail so they could tell the newspaper. If

THE MAN, THE RECORD

that happened, he warned, they wouldn't get bailed out by him or Martha Jane. Perhaps because they didn't get any special treatment from their parents (and their friends knew it too), the eight children by and large lived like ordinary Richmond kids.

Supporting a family of ten on a single local-government salary wasn't easy. Dickman's salary ($29,000 in 1982) was higher than many other Indiana mayors of comparably sized cities. [60] But inflation consistently topped his annual salary increases, so the real value of his wages steadily declined. "Our steaks now are rare," he reported, adding the punch line, "That's because they are few and far between." Ever the handyman, Dickman cut the family utility bill by creating plastic frames to insulate the edges of their windows and doors. The Dickmans virtually never went out to restaurants, clothing purchases were axed, and the motorhome stayed parked at home. But, Dickman reflected, "It's causing us no real hardships, nor is frugality keeping us from enjoying life." [61]

From the mayor's perspective, his public position earned something far more valuable than money: the community's respect for the family. Martha Jane especially, he found, was widely admired around Richmond. With her husband frequently on the road or stuck in the office, she had primary responsibility for keeping the large family nourished and in line. The kids' achievement in school and their work ethic on display in lawnmowing and babysitting jobs reflected the success of Martha Jane's daily parenting work. All this, coupled with her unfailing kindness toward friend and stranger alike, won her the esteem of many in Richmond. Her husband was proud and fortunate to have her standing by his side.

180

Looking back on his mayoralty many years later, Dickman credited the respect that she and the rest of their family received as his favorite aspect of the job.

Through the years, Dickman demonstrated a signature governing style and core political philosophy. First, as might be expected from a four-sport athlete, Dickman was not afraid of conflict. "I make my stand known on any matter or issue," he said, "and you don't make everyone your friend this way."[62] Both parts of that sentence were plainly true. Consider how he went into the lion's den by attending an opposition group's meeting during the annexation fight. Or how about this anecdote: one summer morning, fast-food establishment Frisch's Big Boy posted an odd message on its letterboard—"Did you wave at the mayor when you passed him?"[63] The backstory became clear later. A few days previously, Dickman had passed two police officers in their car. He waved to them, but they didn't wave back, even though they had clearly seen and recognized him. Dickman hauled both men into his office for an explanation, though they didn't disclose why they were upset with him. (Frisch's was a favorite of the police department, which is probably why it took a jab at Dickman.) All the same, Dickman was happy that the conversation with the officers happened. "I think if you discuss problems, most of the time you can resolve them."[64]

The waving incident may seem silly, but it reveals how Dickman didn't sweep disagreement under the carpet; he aired it out. Healthy conflict was an inevitable by-product of his commitment to honesty and his responsibility as mayor to listen to the concerns of the people. For Dickman, if there was no conflict, that could only mean that people were hiding their real views or refusing to engage with dissenters—both of which he found to be detrimental to a free society. "The only way I know is to tell it like it is," he said. "If you try to be somebody else, you turn out to be phony."[65]

Another theme of Dickman's mayoralty was his constant emphasis on bringing government closer to home.[66] Over the years, power had become increasingly concentrated in Indianapolis and Washington, D.C.—a trend which Dickman detested. This system stripped cities and counties of the power to raise their own funds. Instead, they had to beg for it from the higher powers and comply with their onerous demands. Cities became reliant on these funds for operating even the most basic services like street lighting.[67] Indiana towns, he told a gathering in Terre Haute, "are having to hold their services together by Scotch tape, baling wire, and prayer."[68] He considered that an unacceptable state of affairs.

Notably, however, Dickman was not a libertarian who wanted to slash the role of all government to a bare minimum. This was a common label slapped on most Republicans of the age, especially Ronald Reagan.[69] But the president, as purveyor of "New Federalism," believed in reducing *federal* power so that state and city governments could respond to their own problems with fine-tuned solutions. That was a vision which Dickman supported "100 percent plus."[70] As other mayors, including William Hudnut in Indianapolis, railed against cuts to federal revenue sharing, Dickman stood behind the president, promising that Richmond would find more sustainable sources of income.[71] The *Palladium-Item* called Dickman's response his "basic conservatism" and approved wholeheartedly.[72]

As federal funds for cities decreased into the 1980s, Richmond felt the pinch. There was a price to be paid for cities relying less on Uncle Sam: the money had to be collected elsewhere. Dickman appeared before the Indiana General Assembly to plead for a state-tax *increase*—an abomination by libertarian standards. But after stripping his city's spending down to the bone, there was no solution left but to add money to the government's coffers. "All I say is, God help us if something doesn't happen," he told the representatives.[73]

As part and parcel of Dickman's close-to-home vision of politics and civil society, he also believed that citizens needed to step up to the plate and take personal responsibility for their city. He thought that he could pinch Richmond's pennies if citizens took over basic responsibilities which, in his view, the city never should have taken on in the first place. With citizens taking charge of the common land around their own property, Richmond could cut services like street sweeping, litter collection, cutting back dead trees, and sidewalk repairs—all of which would further reduce the city's reliance on federal funding. And, Dickman believed, it would teach younger citizens the importance of caring for their home community.[74]

The final theme of Dickman's mayoralty was his commitment to fairness, the virtue which he aspired to exercise above all else. He viewed his own role, fittingly, as a referee between competing interests. During his first campaign, he vowed to hire the best department heads he could, whether Republicans or Democrats. He tried to be fair to his first police chief, Louis Gibbs, when Gibbs was under fire from the county prosecutor. Dickman struck a balance between homeowners and business owners during the fuel-oil crisis, between unions and management during labor strife, and between firemen and taxpayers during salary negotiations. "Fair and square" was his mantra from his first day in office as county commissioner until his last as mayor.

A letter from a constituent captures the community's perception of Dickman's integrity and commitment to getting the job done right:

I guess votes are like nickels.

My father told the story of a well dressed gentleman and a young lady who spotted a nickel on the sidewalk at the same time. It was apparent that she was going to pass it by so he picked it up.

"A well-to-do man like you stops to pick up a measly nickel?"

"Young lady, I have to make over 10 cents to keep 5. It took me one second. That's $6.00 per minute, $360 per hour, over $14,000 per week, or almost ¾ million per year. I don't make that much."

Your conduct in office collects nickels every day....[75]

Much like the writer of this letter, the people of Richmond came to know Mayor Dickman as a leader who addressed conflict head-on, tried to shift government closer to home, and exercised fairness without fail. Of all these traits, Dickman's commitment to fairness would be tested more than ever as he entered the final and most trying of his years in office. But his last quarter in politics began not with distress or difficulty, but rather on a note of hope and excitement: when Clifford Dickman ran for Congress.

12

CONGRESS AND CHEMSCAM

The story of Clifford Dickman's run for a seat in the United States House of Representatives begins in the most unlikely of places—a third-grade classroom. It was early 1980, and Dickman had been invited for a Q&A with Baxter Elementary School students. After assuring the inquisitive youngsters that he had no ambitions to run for president, one of the more acute questioners asked, "Do you want to be in Congress?" "I don't know," the mayor replied. "I think it would be great to be in Congress and would be interesting, but to run for it, that's the problem."[1]

The question wasn't just on the minds of elementary-school students. Several local politicos—most notably Dickman's former campaign managers, Bob Reinke and Kent Klinge, plus former state and Wayne County GOP chair Tom Milligan—were eager to oust the incumbent congressman, Philip Sharp. The common-sense Richmond mayor, they thought, could be just the candidate to do so. The three men promised Dickman that they would line up all his events, forge contacts, and manage the campaign for him. For his part, Dickman reported by summer 1981 that "I have not said no" to their overtures.[2]

Congressman Sharp had four terms in the House under his belt. Born in Baltimore, Maryland, Sharp spent his childhood in the small town of Elwood, Indiana. After earning a Ph.D. from Georgetown and teaching political science at Ball State, Sharp went to work as an aide for U.S. Senator Vance Hartke, a Democrat representing Indiana.[3] Sharp ran against 10th District Congressman David Dennis three times, finally succeeding on the anti-Nixon wave of the 1974 midterms.[4] Dennis was an easy target for the Democrats that year. As a Republican member of the House Judiciary Committee, Dennis had staunchly defended the president throughout the Watergate investigation and voted against forwarding articles of impeachment to the full House (though in Nixon's last days in office, Dennis pivoted to favor one article of impeachment).[5] Dennis's miscalculation made way for Sharp to finally win the seat, and he had retained it ever since.

In December 1981, Clifford Dickman made his candidacy for the Republican nomination official. "My wife, Martha, and my family join with me in the belief that Phil Sharp needs to be replaced," he announced to a crowd of supporters at city hall. Citing his 25 years of experience in government, business, agriculture, and community service, Dickman declared himself ready for the task. His overriding theme was agreement with President Reagan's program of "new federalism." As the president set out to restore power to states and municipalities, Dickman wanted to provide a voice and a vote in support. He likened his own excitement for the race to the way his Earlham coaches pumped him up before games. He was ready to go out and win.[6]

After the announcement, Dickman immediately set off to canvass his new electorate in the family motorhome, which had long banners bearing his name taped to the sides. [7] In tow was former Congressman Dennis, who sported a Dickman campaign button and introduced him at all his events that first day. [8] Reinke, Klinge, Milligan, a political consultant named J.C. Beck, and an entourage of other supporters accompanied the candidate too. [9] They had a lot of ground to cover. After the 1980 census, Indiana had drawn new congressional district lines, so the bulk of the former 10th District had become part of the new 2nd District. The territory included Muncie, Franklin, Columbus, Winchester, New Castle, Rushville, Shelbyville, and Greensburg—all of which Dickman visited the day of his announcement. It was Republican-friendly territory, though less so than the old 10th District. [10]

The campaign mostly involved returning to the same cities and towns Dickman hit during his first day on the trail. Usually, he'd attend Lincoln Day dinners or similar GOP functions, speak to a group of the party faithful, answer their policy questions, and, with any luck, collect a few contributions from newfound supporters. [11] Dickman was joined at these events by his primary opponents. A month before Dickman declared, Ken MacKenzie of Muncie entered the race. The youngest of the candidates, MacKenzie nonetheless had a compelling background. He'd graduated from Purdue, served in the Army, worked as a legislative aide in Washington, and then was director of public affairs for the Ball Corporation in Muncie, which produced the famous Ball mason jars. [12] Ralph VanNatta joined the race in late January. He had served as Shelbyville's mayor and commissioner for the Indiana BMV, and he'd been on the verge of winning the nomination for lieutenant governor. [13] His statewide experience, VanNatta believed, gave him an edge in the race. Claiming that he and Dickman had the same conservative views, VanNatta nonetheless believed he was better known in the district. Dickman silently agreed with this.[14] Nonetheless, the Republican county chairmen in the district declared that the race would be a close one.[15]

In stark contrast to the primaries of today, the candidates ran less against each other and focused more of their criticisms on Sharp.[16] The party—and each of the primary contestants—stood united behind the Reagan program, and they further agreed that with unemployment and interest rates still running high, the economy ought to be the key issue of the campaign.[17] With so much policy agreement among the candidates, the real question facing the Republican voters was which of the three men had the best shot at winning the general election in November.

While the economy is a typically reliable topic to campaign on, the candidates faced a difficulty in their messaging: there was a Republican in the White House, so it was hard to pin the economic woes of the day on the Democrat congressman—rather, it was the Democrats who held that political ammo against the Republicans. What's more, the 2nd District candidates faced the reality that even in the Republican-leaning territory, Sharp was well-liked by the voters. He'd developed a reputation for successfully helping constituents navigate the federal bureaucracy, and he had an affable, authentic personality.[18] There was no doubt about it: Dickman and his fellow Republican hopefuls were swimming against the current.

Dickman, eager to stand out in the field, directed his attacks on Sharp for misusing government funds. He accused Sharp of abusing the "franking privilege," which allows members of Congress to send official-business mailings to constituents without paying postage. Sharp was then representing the 10th District, but Dickman charged that he had franked mail to territory in the new 2nd District. The only explanation for this, in Dickman's view, was that Sharp was using his mailings for campaigning purposes—and doing so on the taxpayer's dime.[19] Dickman also suggested that Sharp used public funds to travel to areas joining the new 2nd District. These attacks drew strong rebuke from Sharp's press secretary, who called Dickman's accusations "ridiculous."[20]

When he wasn't taking shots at Sharp, there was one key theme from Dickman's mayoralty that he sought to drive home in his speeches around the district: he wasn't a partisan hack, but rather an independent-thinking, common-sense advocate for good government. Sure, he had a conservative perspective and was a supporter of the president, but at the end of the day, he approached each decision on its merits—not with preordained conclusions. Thus, when constituents asked him policy questions he didn't know the answer to, he considered his conceded lack of an answer to be a strength. Candidate Dickman promised that if the voters sent him to Washington, he would learn about problems and evaluate responsive legislation on a case-by-case basis, not bind himself to a strict platform or the demands of party whips.

During the congressional campaign, life dealt the Dickman family a series of tragic blows that they never could have anticipated in such rapid succession. It started in mid-January 1982, when Henry Luerman, Martha Jane's father, suffered a heart attack. After a few days in the hospital, he died on January 18 at age 81.[21] Only three weeks later, Hedwig Luerman was found dead in a chair in her home, still holding the Sunday morning newspaper in her hands.[22] As if the loss of two parents in less than a month wasn't enough to grieve, Martha Jane's brother Bob Luerman passed away on February 23, only two weeks after Hedwig.[23] Like his father, Bob had heart trouble all his life. Though he didn't admit it until his final weeks, he couldn't even walk the two blocks between Kesslers and the bank without resting. Because Bob had never married, he'd lived his whole life with Henry and Hedwig. All three residents in the Luerman house had died unexpectedly in the course of five weeks.

But the tragedies were not confined to the Luerman side of the family. In March 1982, Cliff's brother Jerome, who was married to Martha Jane's sister Hilda, was diagnosed with lymphoma and given a dire prognosis. Fitting with his character, Jerome stayed tough, telling the whole family, "I'm gonna whip this thing." But the cancer was relentless, and he died at age 54 in December 1982.[24] It was a terrible loss for Cliff and Martha Jane's family, but far more so for Hilda, who had lost a father, mother, brother, and husband in the course of one year.

With one heartbreaking development after another, the Dickman family couldn't quite shake the feeling that some further tragedy was on the cusp of befalling them. But the family soldiered on in every way. Jobs were worked, homework was completed, food was prepared, sports were played, Masses were attended, and yes, even campaigns were still run. Yet in the midst of the family tragedy, the last item on that list became a great chore. Dickman wanted to spend his free moments with the family who needed him, but he was instead whisked around the state to deliver political speeches to strangers.

As the primary drew nearer, Dickman found himself facing the worst of all campaign debacles: a money problem. His fundraising had been strong at the beginning.

With about a month to go before primary voting, he expected to spend $75,000, a good chunk more than MacKenzie and far more than VanNatta.[25] But the campaign contributions dried up, making it impossible to reach that benchmark.[26] Dickman couldn't finish the race with a strong advertising operation.

The wheels were coming off the wagon in other ways. Dickman was disappointed when his friend, Indianapolis Mayor William Hudnut, declined to endorse him or any candidate in the 2nd District primary. Hudnut had privately encouraged Dickman to run but publicly opted to stay neutral. The same was true with J. Roberts Dailey, the Indiana Speaker of the House, who had also nudged Dickman to run against Sharp but was pressured into endorsing MacKenzie by his fellow Muncie Republicans.[27] Dickman was most let down by a pro-life group's decision to endorse VanNatta; he thought he'd been the most vocal opponent of abortion on the campaign trail. A reporter harshly summed up Dickman's situation in the final stretch of the campaign: "In the game of political endorsements, Richmond Mayor Cliff Dickman is becoming the girl nobody minds being engaged to but who can't seem to get to the altar."[28] By the end of the campaign, the *Indianapolis Star* had concluded that Dickman was "a long-shot bet" but "still a factor in the race."[29]

In the early hours of voting on Primary Day, it became clear that the battle was lost. Turnout was light in Wayne County, where Dickman needed a colossal showing to build a margin.[30] The votes were totaled: Dickman suffered a landslide loss to Ralph VanNatta, with Ken MacKenzie coming in second.[31] The final count was 22,429 for VanNatta, 19,343 for MacKenzie, and 10,784 for Dickman.[32] Dickman fared well in his home county, but not well enough. He garnered 4,919 votes compared to the 2,846 combined total of VanNatta and MacKenzie.[33] By

191

contrast, in MacKenzie's home county (Delaware County), the hometown candidate won 5,259 votes, compared to Dickman's 614.[34]

Dickman took the defeat well. "We gave it a good try," he said. "We thought we could win. I never enjoy losing a political race, but there are other much more important things in life." He wished his opponents well, saying that he had no hard feelings and that it had been a clean campaign.[35] But he was harsher on his own organization, blaming his candidacy's demise on the lack of money. "You need funds to run for Congress," he stated straightforwardly. The campaign's final bill was about $68,000, but a good chunk of that money had never been raised. Dickman pledged to take on the debts himself, and he did—setting him back almost $30,000 personally.[36]

Though he didn't regret the experience, he was not keen to repeat it. There was a wide gulf between an 11-county electorate and a citywide one, and he much preferred the latter. For one, he struggled to remember names of people he met out of town, which caused some offense. He felt that he was constantly having to butter up the egos of committee chairmen around the district, which the tell-it-like-it-is mayor despised. And in the midst of all the family tragedy of February and March 1982, he saw more clearly than ever where he was needed—right at home in Richmond. In hindsight, he didn't know how he could have balanced a family of ten in Richmond with weekly commutes to Washington, D.C. It was a truth that Martha Jane had realized all along. While she had given all the support she could to her husband's congressional bid, she was more relieved than disappointed to put this campaign behind them.

While a Dickman–Sharp contest may have been spirited and even fun for the Richmond mayor, it was unlikely to have been fruitful for him. Capitalizing on the "Reagan recession," the Democrats had a favorable swing nation-wide in the 1982 midterms. Phil Sharp held his seat against Ralph VanNatta, taking more than 55% of the vote.[37] Ken MacKenzie had his shot against Sharp two years later, and he too was defeated by a sizable margin.[38] The congressman even went on to defeat an ambitious 29-year-old Hoosier named Mike Pence in 1988.*[39] Sharp held the seat until 1995 when he retired from public office.[40]

With the race for Congress behind him, one might think that Clifford Dickman finally had the chance to ease into a slower, more normal pace of life. But alas, the summer of 1982 was far from calm for Richmond and its mayor. The brutal strike at PRC Recording was ongoing, Jerome Dickman was dying of cancer, Cliff's son Bob was hastily learning the ropes of running Kesslers following Bob Luerman's untimely passing, and the other mayoral duties of the day pressed on. Then, in August 1982, a story broke in the *Indianapolis Star* that would haunt the rest of Dickman's days in office.

"Chemscam." It would become the largest corruption scandal in Indiana in 30 years, and it was being investi-gated across all levels of government—the FBI, Indiana State Police, State Board of Accounts, and county prose-cutors. The probe had started after an audit of the city of Greensburg revealed something highly unusual. For no discernible reason, the city's chemical purchases had soared from $6,000 in 1976 to more than $114,000 in

---

* Pence later held the seat (which became the 6th District) between 2001 and 2013, vacating it to serve as governor of Indiana. In between Sharp and Pence, the seat was held by David McIntosh, yet another distinguished Hoosier who had co-founded the Federalist Society as a law student.

1979. Investigators soon discovered a bribery scheme: the Greensburg mayor and street commissioner agreed to purchase chemicals for their city from a certain vendor, and in exchange, they personally received a cash kickback. Similar arrangements were uncovered around the state, and indictments were soon issued against local-government officials in Seymour, Noblesville, and Frankfort, not to mention the salespeople perpetrating the schemes. By August, it was clear that an entire web of government officials and chemical companies were involved. More than a dozen communities were investigated, including Indianapolis, Anderson, New Castle, Terre Haute, Logansport, Martinsville—and Richmond.[41]

The day after the *Star*'s damning statewide report, Wayne County Prosecutor Gerald Surface publicly announced his ongoing probe into Richmond's city government, which had secretly been proceeding in collaboration with the state. Surface's office had been scrutinizing some chemical-purchase oddities on the city's budget reports. For example, in the sanitary district, chemical costs increased from $55,000 in 1979 to $99,000 in 1981. In the Parks Department, chemical outlays totaled $5,000 in 1979 and rose to $14,000 by 1981. The department heads offered explanations for the cost increases and provided their accounting records for inspection.[42]

Dickman responded quickly with an order to audit each department's chemical purchases. He promised transparency, but he also expressed faith in his department heads. The *Star*'s report, he contended, had made Richmond "appear guilty by association" because the city had been grouped in with other communities where mayors and departments heads were already indicted. He also criticized the investigators' accounting procedures, claiming that the cost increases were distorted because supplies other than chemicals were included in the figures.[43] He nonetheless was willing to cooperate with the probe and get to the truth of the matter.

The offices of the prosecutor and city controller pursued their investigations over the coming months. Eventually, Gerald Surface requested a grand jury, which Judge J. Brandon Griffis impaneled on December 7, 1982.[44] The grand jury issued its first subpoena a few days before Christmas: a demand for the city and county's financial records.[45] The mayor quickly complied, though he knew of "no local wrongdoing or problems."[46] He was fairly convinced of his team's innocence. For example, when the sanitary district hired legal counsel from Indianapolis to advise them on the grand jury's probe, Dickman immediately terminated the representation. He not only had faith in his team, but his political instincts told him that the hiring of a lawyer looked like an admission of guilt.[47] And from Dickman's perspective, "[t]he sooner this (the investigation) is over, the better."[48]

The six-person grand jury's investigatory sweep was hard to predict, especially because its proceedings were secret. In January, it subpoenaed all financial records related to the sanitary district's scrap-metal sales.[49] But a few days later, the grand jury honed in on the real problem by demanding records on the city's purchases of asphalt materials.[50] And that led to the identification of a new target: Transportation Director Jerry Haynes.[51]

Haynes had been a fixture of Dickman's administration from the beginning. Though Dickman hadn't known Haynes before becoming mayor, he had nonetheless been very pleased with Haynes's performance over the years. At the regular meeting of department heads, Haynes always expressed willingness to assist his fellow department heads with their work, and he'd been a steadfast partner of Dickman's during the 1978 blizzard crisis.[52] But after Haynes became the new target of the investigation, Dickman grew wary of his transportation director, saying that if Haynes had done anything wrong, he would have to stand on his own.[53]

Dickman's distrust stemmed from the newfound connection between the asphalt purchases and Haynes, which struck a chord in Dickman's own mind. Long before the Chemscam scandal broke, Dickman had been visited in his office by the president of Magaw Construction, a local asphalt company. Magaw was a regular supplier of the city's, but the company president asked the mayor why the city purchased an asphalt crack-sealing chemical from an outfit in Kansas City rather than locally from Magaw. Dickman promised to inquire. Haynes told Dickman that Magaw's crack-sealing agent wasn't thick enough for the city's purposes, so the transportation department purchased it elsewhere. That explanation seemed persuasive enough, so Dickman dropped the matter.[54] Little did Dickman know at the time that this was a lie, and Haynes, eager to avoid further scrutiny, surreptitiously switched the department's purchases of the agent to Magaw. The asphalt company's president was happy, so he never raised the issue with the mayor again.

Of course, had Magaw's president told Dickman that Haynes had started buying from his local company, Dickman would have known that Haynes had lied. And if Haynes had never switched suppliers, then the asphalt president would have continued haranguing Dickman and likely would have debunked Haynes's explanation for ordering from an out-of-town supplier. The communication breakdown prevented Dickman from seeing the truth of the matter himself. And the truth, as Dickman would finally learn, was that Haynes had been profiting personally by his dealings with the Kansas City company.

Haynes spent 75 minutes with the grand jury on January 28 and then returned for another round of testimony on the 31st.[55] The grand jury reached its decision on February 4. Haynes was indicted on 168 counts of bribery and 4 counts of conspiracy to commit theft. The grand jury also charged two salesmen and two Kansas City-based chemical companies on various counts.[56]

Up to this point, the mayor had not yet confronted Haynes one-on-one about the matter, as he didn't want to interfere in the grand jury's investigation.[57] Haynes had been publicly refuting any wrongdoing, and that had been good enough for Dickman, who wanted to believe that his subordinates wouldn't lie. After the indictments came down, Dickman ordered Haynes into his office, demanding to know once and for all whether Haynes had accepted bribes. Haynes merely replied, "If they want to get me over a cup of coffee, I guess they can." The odd metaphor was Haynes's way of denying that he had done anything wrong. But Dickman had reviewed the evidence himself, and he saw the shifting look on Haynes's face. He knew that Haynes had lied to the public and was lying to his face that very day. Dickman suspended Haynes without pay on the spot. The two never saw or spoke to each other again.

The allegations against Haynes were damning. He was accused of bilking the city out of $160,000 for chemical products that were never even shipped. In exchange, Haynes allegedly collected a "commission" of almost $80,000.[58] Haynes had been accepting bribes for years—as early as January 1977, Dickman's second year in office. It started small with a $48 kickback, but slowly the bribes increased into the low hundreds, then the high hundreds, then eventually to $1,000 per incident.[59] Haynes's dishonesty hit the city government like a thunderbolt. Ken Mills, president of the city council, considered the loss to the public trust most devastating. "Public officials really are different than the average person because the people have put a special trust in you." Fellow councilman Jack Elstro phrased it another way: "No one is above the law, and people in politics, most of all, should show a greater responsibility in not only his or her duties for the public, but for all of us."[60]

Yet as the mayor himself said, "Nobody is more upset than I am that there are people who have been dishonest."[61] No doubt that was a true statement. At every department meeting from the very beginning, Dickman had concluded by warning his fellow public servants that gifts, favors, and even cash would be offered to them in exchange for favorable deals with the city. They were to resist these overtures at all costs, Dickman sternly warned, for if they didn't, "I'll help them put the rope around your neck."[62] Haynes had heard these admonitions for seven years, and yet week after week, month after month, he continued to cheat his own city. For the mayor who prioritized honesty and fairness above all, Haynes was the ultimate disgrace.

But the grand jury's work wasn't finished yet. Recall that in January, it had also subpoenaed records on the sanitary district's sales of scrap metal. Among other things, the sanitary district was responsible for collecting trash and operating the landfills. Its employees had a longstanding practice of selling junk in the landfill to scrap yards. The proceeds would sometimes go to a discretionary fund, which was used to pay for the department's Christmas parties or for employee travel. On other occasions, the employees were permitted to pocket the money earned from scrap sales.[63] Dickman didn't have a huge problem with it. If the landfill could be kept cleaner by incentivizing employees to haul out scrap to recycling centers, Dickman didn't mind if the sanitary district had a fund for its Christmas parties or even if the employees got to keep the money themselves.[64] But the practice had "disaster" written all over it. The district hadn't established any accounting procedures for proceeds earned from scrap sales. The cash from the sales was simply kept in a desk drawer and paid out for expenses as they came up. Indeed, even after a burglar stole $1,375 in cash from the drawer in 1981, the scrap-metal cash earnings continued to be stored there.[65]

The grand jury handed down three indictments against sanitary district superintendent Ed Goodknight on April 18, 1983. The first charge was by far the most serious: misappropriating about $3,000 from the desk-drawer fund. The second charged Goodknight with having a sanitary district employee transport his family to Richmond from the Indianapolis airport, and the third accused him of selling a lawnmower to the district without disclosing that he owned it.[66]

Goodknight maintained his innocence fiercely. He wrote a memorandum to Dickman detailing his withdrawals from the desk drawer. Some of his alleged withdrawals, if true, were worrisome. For instance, he was charged with using the funds to pay travel expenses for the spouses of city officials on a business trip to Atlanta.[67] Some of his withdrawals had plausible explanations but still raised an eyebrow. For instance, Goodknight used scrap-metal cash to buy a bottle of scotch for a meeting at his house with an engineering-firm executive, where Goodknight dissuaded the executive from charging the city 7% interest on overdue bills. Perhaps the purchase was legal as it was used for a business purpose, but undeniably, it was a terrible look for a government official to buy booze using city cash stuffed in a drawer.[68] Other withdrawals were wrong but obviously not worthy of criminal prosecution. For instance, Goodknight borrowed (and repaid) $15 to buy a new baseball mitt for his son. Clearly, he should never have done this, but no reasonable prosecutor seeks jailtime for a person who borrows $15. The *Palladium-Item*'s executive editor summed up the Goodknight situation well: "All may be ethically insensitive and unwise for the boss of a place. But are they criminal acts, and was there intent to defraud the taxpayers?"[69]

For Dickman, the answer was "no." He concluded that the indictments against Goodknight were too minor to warrant suspension from his position, and in any event, he thought Goodknight was innocent of the charges. Goodknight, he said, may have been guilty of "poor judgment. I don't know if it's dishonest." And for years, Dickman had pledged to stand by his team if they made *honest* mistakes. "I'm only trying to be as fair as I can. I have [to] do what I think is fair and just," the mayor said. But Dickman knew that his decision not to suspend Goodknight would take a toll on him, for another storm was brewing: his third mayoral campaign.

From the very beginning of Chemscam, which broke 15 months before Election Day 1983, Dickman was acutely aware that the corruption scandal portended a hard path to reelection. At the height of the grand jury's investigation into Jerry Haynes and Ed Goodknight, Dickman publicly confessed, "It may be the end of the line for me. I feel like a victim of circumstances."[70]

He was indeed in trouble. Chemscam had crashed all of Dickman's political momentum, and the Democrats found new enthusiasm to oust the mayor and his fellow Republicans from city hall. They ran six primary candidates for mayor, four for city clerk, and a whopping four-teen for the at-large city-council seats (the Republicans ran four).

Dickman, however, had a more immediate problem than anything posed by the Democrats. For the first time as an incumbent, he faced a primary challenge, and it was a strong one. City councilman Jim Carter had announced his candidacy for the Republican nomination only days after the grand jury was formed. He attacked the city's performance on the ongoing sewage-separation project, and he criticized Dickman's view that cities ought to increase their tax rates. [71] Chemscam, Carter believed, would give him just the boost he needed to seize the GOP nomination.

Dickman contemplated whether to run again very carefully. He wanted "the best person around for the Republican Party in the general election," and for a while, he wondered whether that might be someone else.[72] But at the end of February 1983, he decided to go for it. Being mayor "is the toughest job," a statement that was never truer than when Dickman said it. But he'd received enough encouragement from the party and the wider community to want to try again.[73] He also thought that declining to run would either be an admission of guilt or make him look like a quitter when the going got rough. He was neither of those things and adamantly refused to have people think of him as such.

The fact that the people of Richmond still supported Clifford Dickman's candidacy in such a time of upheaval is a reflection of something important. At no point was Dickman ever investigated for or accused of public corruption. He was never even approached with a bribe, unlike the mayors of other Indiana towns. Perhaps that was because Richmond was too large of a city for a contractor to directly deal with its mayor. But a more likely explanation is this: any would-be briber probably knew that an attempt to curry favor from Dickman would be utterly futile, given his incessant refrains that honesty and fairness were his guiding lights in government. The people respected the mayor not only because he had the fortitude to reject a tempting bribe, but more so because he wouldn't let the temptation come within a country mile.

But widespread agreement on the mayor's innocence was not a ticket to reelection. Some faulted the mayor's governing style for not catching Haynes earlier. The *Palladium-Item* accused his "laissez-faire" approach of two weaknesses: "insufficient oversight of department heads, and an excessive loyalty to appointees even when they may be wrong."[74] His motto, the paper asserted, was "[s]tand by your man."[75] Local Democrat Andrew Cecere said that Dickman's administration had "fail[ed] to grasp the tenor of the times," throwing Richmond into a state of "stagnation."[76] Primary opponent Jim Carter piled on. He argued that Richmond "cannot afford to simply coast into the future led by a mayor whose administration has lost the confidence of large numbers of local citizens."[77]

Dickman had indeed proved too trusting of Haynes when he initially denied wrongdoing, but in the mayor's defense, it's not clear how much he could have done to avert Haynes's theft. The city had a meticulous requisition process which ran through the city controller's office, and the mayor wasn't expected to oversee individual funding requests.[78] Amidst an investigation by the State Board of Accounts, the accountant made clear that Haynes's fraudulent purchases were too small and spread out for anyone, including the mayor or even the city controller, to detect. And although the accountant recommended that the city hire an internal auditor and central purchasing agent, she insinuated that even those precautions likely wouldn't have stopped Haynes (and, as Dickman pointed out, those precautions weren't free—they might have cost more than Haynes's theft).*[79] At the end of the day, the city's department heads were vested with authority and trust, and Haynes abused his.

Objective evaluation and reasoned analysis, however, does not make for good political theater. On the primary campaign trail, Councilman Carter accused Dickman of running a "loose operation," and Carter promised that he would appoint only "well-qualified people, who won't abscond with the funds or make fictitious invoices."[80] Dickman, undoubtedly frustrated by the mounting pressure, hit back hard at Carter. "God help us if things change in this community on the Republican side," he warned, adding, "Ask the people who know this man (Carter) in [his] past ventures."[81] At a primary debate hosted by the Townsend Center, the *Palladium-Item* reported that Dickman was "exploding at the podium and exclaiming that ... 'when you're the mayor you have to make the call and that's the one that counts.'"[82] In one of the final debates, Carter wrapped up one of his attacks on Dickman with the caveat, "Don't get me wrong, the mayor and I are good friends"—to which Dickman replied, "we *were*," only half-smiling.[83]

Dickman survived the primary challenge, but only barely. The day after the election, his margin of victory was 21 votes.[84] But after a recount requested by Carter, the final margin narrowed to 11.[85] After the victory was

---

* This is not to say that there was no way the city could have stopped Haynes. For example, perhaps if the city had required a second individual to certify that a requisitioned shipment actually arrived, Haynes could never have perpetrated his fraud. The point is that there were no obvious gaps in the city's purchasing practices. That is why the State Board of Accounts absolved Dickman and City Controller Don Meredith of any blame.

official, Dickman felt lucky: "If you win by one, you're still the winner. I get to celebrate twice."[86] The relief was felt by Republicans across the state. Even Governor Orr had taken notice, scribbling at the bottom of a congratulatory letter: "Whew!!"[87]

But even before his wafer-thin margin was sliced in half, Dickman knew what the primary voting foreshadowed. His incumbency advantage against the Democrats was nil—he carried an incumbency liability. Yet he was a fighter and would give the general campaign every drop of energy he had. In terms natural to him, he said, "I hope I'm shooting the free throw at the last minute and make it—again."[88]

The Democrats nominated Frank Waltermann for mayor. Waltermann, a local funeral director, had Richmond politics in his blood—his father Joseph Waltermann had served a term as mayor in the late 1930s.[89] His campaign theme was that after numerous labor strikes and corruption among government leaders, the city was divided and in need of "a new breed of leadership." "I make this promise: Richmond will heal well and prosper again under my leadership," Waltermann proclaimed.[90] He too had faced a tough primary, beating former Democrat councilman Phil Marino by 69 votes.[91]

After the primaries, the mayoral campaign was put on hold for a few months—an act of mercy for Dickman, for the Chemscam investigation reared its head once again. The grand jury had now been impaneled for five months, and Wayne County Prosecutor Gerald Surface was still hellbent on adding more charges against sanitary district superintendent Ed Goodknight. In late May, after Dickman and City Controller Don Meredith had been subpoenaed to testify, the grand jury delivered yet another indictment against Goodknight, only this time it had nothing to do with scrap metal or even chemical purchases.[92] The latest count accused Goodknight of purchasing modular furniture in order to prevent competition from other furniture suppliers, who couldn't match the specifications of the modular pieces already purchased.[93] Yet again, Goodknight might have displayed poor judgment in his furniture purchasing, but the idea that Goodknight had intentionally obstructed competitive bidding on office furniture was an enormous stretch.

Dickman continued to believe in Goodknight's innocence, but he'd lost much of his confidence in Surface's investigation. For one, the mayor pointed out that Goodknight was merely one member on a board of commissioners; only the entire body could act. If the furniture acquisition was really a crime, Dickman wondered aloud, why not indict all the commissioners? Likewise, if Goodknight's spending from the city's scrap-metal sales was a crime, then why not charge the many sanitary district employees who sold landfill junk to recycling centers for personal profit? It didn't add up. So Dickman turned his ire on the prosecutor's office, which he suspected to be motivated by vindicating the extensive time and effort it had already poured into the investigation.[94]

But with a campaign on the move, Haynes awaiting trial, and Goodknight facing his second round of indictments, the pressure to suspend his sanitary superintendent was strong. Dickman had already declined to suspend Goodknight after the first indictments, but now the decision confronted him again, and he found it to be "the most difficult I've ever had to make in my eight years [as mayor]." Here, his innate instinct toward fairness collided with his need to present a clean, functioning administration to the voters of Richmond. "I'm just not happy about what we may be forced to do. I don't think it's fair, and I don't feel very good about it."[95]

Eventually, the pressure was too much—not for Dickman, but for Goodknight. The latter felt that he couldn't effectively do his job while facing the indictments, and with the sanitary district working on the $40 million sewage project, the city needed a superintendent who could give 100% to the job. Begrudgingly, Dickman agreed with Goodknight's assessment and suspended him without pay. "It's not the happiest day in my life," Dickman said, "but you have days like that, I guess." But even still, he fiercely maintained Goodknight's innocence on the day of the suspension.[96] Although the *Palladium-Item* also harbored doubts about the criminality of Goodknight's actions, the paper credited Dickman for making the right call on a tough decision.[97]

Not long after the difficult decision on Goodknight, the Election of 1983 resumed in earnest. Frank Waltermann's campaign was marked less by a new vision for the city and more by the promise of new personnel. Waltermann didn't belabor the Chemscam scandal explicitly, but implicitly, his campaign was completely centered around it. Voters "don't trust any politicians," he claimed. "They think they're all crooks.... That's sad. The apathy and distrust."[98] The Democrat's promise was simple: integrity in government.

Perhaps part of the reason why Waltermann didn't suggest a grand new direction for Richmond was because he tended to agree with Dickman's approach on many issues. Both agreed on the desperate need for an influx of jobs, controlled city spending, and an enterprise zone that favored business expansion in poor parts of town.[99] Dickman was somewhat more pessimistic than Waltermann about the city government's ability to influence private-sector development—for instance, Dickman argued that a new department dedicated to economic growth would be impractical given budget constraints.[100] By the end of the campaign, he accused the Democrats of making "pie-in-the-sky promises."[101]

Waltermann unsurprisingly picked up the endorsement of labor unions.[102] Dickman had been tough with unions, though he'd tried to treat management and labor equally in the midst of the PRC Recording strike of 1982. With two months to go before the election, an AFL-CIO council hosted a rally in front of city hall, and the union's president invited Dickman to read a proclamation designating "Salute the American Worker Day" in Richmond. But before he could even finish reading the brief statement, the union drowned him out in "boos," and Dickman stalked away from the podium.[103]

The Dickman–Waltermann contest attracted the attention of the state political parties, which poured extra resources into the local campaigns.[104] Dickman benefited from both Indiana senators endorsing him. Senator Richard Lugar said, "At this critical phase of the [economic] recovery, the need is clear for solid and experienced leadership. No one fits this definition better than Cliff Dickman."[105] Senator Dan Quayle made a special visit to Richmond, touring the new sewage-treatment plant that had been part of the $40 million sewage overhaul in Richmond. Quayle was impressed. "People will look back in 30 years and say that Mayor Dickman sure had a lot of foresight because we sure needed this [treatment plant]," the senator declared. He called Dickman "a truly outstanding mayor." While in the sanitary district's administration building, Quayle took note of the modular furniture that had resulted in a criminal indictment for Ed Goodknight. Ironically, Quayle admired it and said, "We're supposed to get this in the Hart [Senate Office] building." "Be careful," Dickman cautioned.[106]

Dickman's most heartfelt endorsement came from the mayor of Shelbyville, then the youngest mayor in Indiana. In a letter to the editor, he wrote that "Cliff Dickman is known statewide among other mayors as a proven leader and a man who has been dedicated to his city government. I have felt very fortunate in knowing Mr. Dickman, and the city of Richmond is fortunate to have such a great man leading their city."[107]

Somewhat surprisingly, Dickman also picked up the endorsement of the *Palladium-Item*. The newspaper recognized Dickman's depth of experience: nine years in county government, eight years as mayor, and statewide recognition as a past president of the Indiana Association of Cities and Towns. Waltermann, the paper thought, hadn't demonstrated that his experience or knowledge would improve the administration of city government. The editorial board was willing to evaluate Dickman on his own merits and trust that his administration could turn the page on Chemscam.[108]

But Dickman knew that his prospects at winning a third term were slim. At one of his first debates with Waltermann, held at Richmond High School, Dickman sensed the students' overwhelming enthusiasm for his competitor, and Dickman knew this to be a proxy for what their voting parents at home were feeling. Just a few days before the election, Dickman told a reporter, "I don't know what it'll feel like to be out of office.... It kind of scares me." He had no regrets: "I've done things the way I thought they should be done. If people don't like that, then they don't want me for their mayor, and I don't want the job. If there's one thing I've learned in politics, it's that the best man doesn't always win."[109]

The people of Richmond rendered their verdict against Dickman on November 8, 1983. It was a brutal beating—9,431 for Waltermann, 4,023 for Dickman. The Democrats swept most of city hall and turned a 9–3 Republican advantage into a 10–2 Democratic one. Jo Ellen Trimble lost the city-clerk race after eight years on the job, and Ken Paust and Ken Mills, who had sixteen and twelve years of city-council experience, respectively, lost their seats too. [110] Indeed, Democrats had triumphed across the cities of Indiana that year, winning 71 out of 115 mayoralties. [111]

Dickman conceded to Waltermann only two hours after the polls closed. Outwardly, he accepted the defeat with grace and wished his successor well. But it was hard for the natural-born competitor to lose, and it stung even more to have been beaten so badly after eight years of devoted service to the people of Richmond.

Though he'd foreseen the outcome, Dickman was intensely disappointed by how the Chemscam scandal had plagued his candidacy. From the day the investigation was announced in August 1982 until Election Day 1983, the newspaper had constantly and brutally hammered the city government. But besides the perfidy of Jerry Haynes, Dickman had been pleased with the city government's operation on virtually every front. The police, fire, streets, and parks departments were firing on all cylinders. And even though Goodknight and the sanitary district were under heavy scrutiny, Dickman was nonetheless quite proud of the district's success in its challenging sewage projects. All this, however, was clouded by the scandal, and Dickman found it deeply unfair. He never doubted that he was the right candidate for Richmond in 1983, but he also knew he'd never really stood a chance. "It's about like a fighter in the ring that's on the ropes, and one blow comes after another and to have overcome that—it would've been one heck of a victory."[112] But he had kept his personal integrity throughout the scandal, and he was gratified by that. "I'm a survivor," he said of Chemscam. "I came through that and I survived."[113]

The Chemscam saga requires a short epilogue. Jerry Haynes eventually pleaded guilty to accepting bribes, and he was sentenced to two years in prison.[114] "I feel sorry for him," former Mayor Dickman said, "but I have no sympathy for him."[115]

In December 1983, the charges against Ed Goodknight were dismissed.[116] Dickman reinstated Goodknight with backpay immediately, but Waltermann, who took office only weeks later, dismissed him immediately.[117] Goodknight was an easy target, for even though he was no longer under scrutiny, he was the symbol of the old regime the voters had convincingly sent packing. Goodknight was never indicted again.

Nonetheless, Wayne County Prosecutor Gerald Surface's investigations into city corruption carried on into 1984, yet again shifting focus far from the initial inquiry into chemical purchases. Surface empaneled another grand jury, which spent two and a half months looking into alleged fraud in the sewage-separation project. No one was ever charged, though the sanitary commissioners and project engineers were upset at having their names dragged through the mud. Dickman, by then a private citizen, was infuriated and called this latest probe "a Gestapo operation." He'd supported the initial investigation into illegal chemical purchases, but as its focus shifted to sales of scrap metal, sewage spending, and even furniture purchases, he'd increasingly lost his patience. The investigations, he said, did "an awful lot of damage to the whole community."[118]

Dickman's distrust of Surface would eventually be vindicated, for Surface ironically ended up being the greatest disgrace of all the Chemscam cast of characters. In 1990, Surface was convicted of dropping drunk-driving charges in exchange for bribes from a local attorney.[119] It was a horrific breach of public trust, and it earned him an eight-year sentence at a federal prison camp in west Texas.[120]

Frank Waltermann was inaugurated as mayor of Richmond on January 1, 1984. The new mayor inherited a parting gift from the outgoing administration: a state-designated "enterprise zone" on the northeast side of town. Businesses located in the zone received massive income- and property-tax advantages, all with the hope of spurring 400 new jobs there.[121] Dickman, though sorry to not oversee the success of the new initiative, was proud of this final addition to his legacy. Waltermann was excited about this new step in Richmond's growth too. [122] He respected the achievements of the Dickman administration.

All the same, a few days into the job, Waltermann terminated many of Dickman's department heads, including City Controller Don Meredith, Fire Chief "Moon" Mullin, Police Chief Charles Chris, Ed Goodknight, and two other sanitary district employees.[123] It was no surprise; there was a new boss, so it was time for a new team. Many of Dickman's department heads had become his friends over his two terms in office, and these relationships would deepen further in the years to come, especially with Moon Mullin.

Waltermann served two terms as mayor, and after declining to run for a third term, he was succeeded by Republican Roger Cornett in 1992. Waltermann and Dickman always got along well, just as they had during the

1983 campaign. Six months into Waltermann's tenure, the two raced each other in go-karts in the "Rose City Grande Prix," and a couple years later, Waltermann even invited Dickman to participate in a "roast" against him.[124] Dickman delightfully and good-naturedly obliged his successor.

Clifford Dickman had been "proud to [be] mayor and foolish enough to want to do it again."[125] Though a third term was not to be, he still had much to look back on, much to take pride in, much to be thankful for. "What a pleasure it has been to work with you over the last eight years," Dickman told the city council in his final meeting as mayor.[126] It was true. Over his many years since leaving office, Dickman has never hesitated to say that for all the job's challenges, serving as mayor of Richmond was the greatest experience of his professional life. And just as he'd learned to do on the Webster ball diamond and the Earlham gridiron, he'd left it all out on the field.

13

A FAMILY ENTERPRISE

As Clifford Dickman prepared to walk out the door of
city hall on New Year's Day 1984, he knew he'd lost more
than a political position. He'd lost his job, his very liveli-
hood. It was a level of career uncertainty that he hadn't
known since the summer of 1949, when he quit his night-
shift job at Johns Manville with vague hopes of finding a
better opportunity elsewhere. Thanks to a visit paid by
the football and basketball coaches at Earlham College,
Dickman hadn't been let down then: their scholarship offer was one of the watershed moments in his life. Thirty-
five years later, Dickman was invited to embark on yet
another trailblazing course—only this time, the opportunity was offered by his own son.

Upon starting his first term as mayor, Dickman had
turned the reins of Kesslers over to Martha Jane's
brother, Bob Luerman, who had worked there ever since
he'd earned his accounting degree. Luerman was more
than capable of taking the helm. He had a dogged work

213

ethic, solid business savvy, and plenty of bookkeeping experience. Plus, having no family of his own, Luerman was 100% committed to the store: Kesslers was his life's work. Yet with Dickman gone, not even a workhorse like Bob Luerman could fill the gap while staying on top of his own tasks. He needed help, and fortunately he had to look no further than Bob Dickman, Cliff and Martha Jane's second child and eldest son.

When his dad was sworn into office in January 1976, young Bob Dickman was beginning his final semester at Richmond High School. Like his siblings, Bob had been working for Kesslers after school for many years, but unlike the others, Bob dreamed of joining Kesslers full-time one day. He loved the products they sold, he enjoyed interacting with coaches and players, and he was attracted to the family-business culture of the store. So when Bob Luerman called his nephew to make a job offer, Bob Dickman didn't think twice before saying yes. He took a light load of courses in the spring semester so that he could report to work by noon, and after graduating that summer, he went full-time right away.

Kesslers was still a small team in the mid-1970s. The two Bobs ran the store's operations from its downtown location. Ray Mitrione was the only road salesman for the company's team division, selling sporting goods directly to high schools and colleges. As such, Mitrione spent most of his days away from Richmond, calling on athletic directors and coaches around eastern Indiana and western Ohio. On the retail side, Kesslers employed a couple assistants who stocked shelves, assisted customers, and sewed patches onto letterman jackets.

Bob Dickman and Bob Luerman worked well together. With such a small staff, they each had to be a jack of all trades. One day, you could find them placing inventory orders, unloading shipments off freight trucks, stocking shelves, attending buying-group meetings, and filling customer orders. The next day, they'd be tracking receivables, taking deposits to the bank, cutting payroll checks, waiting on customers, stringing tennis rackets, and building trophies. It was an endless stream of hard work, but that was nothing new for the uncle and nephew.

The sporting-goods industry hadn't changed much over the 1960s and 1970s. Kesslers continued to enjoy exclusive-dealing agreements with the top sporting-goods vendors like Nike, Converse, and Levi's, which made it the only store in Richmond selling these hotly demanded products. Over the years, Kesslers kept up its membership in a buying group—a collection of sporting-goods dealers who placed orders together to capture discounts from vendors. As such, Kesslers enjoyed strong relationships with other dealers in the industry, who implicitly agreed to not encroach on each other's customers or territory. "Just do your million" was the mantra. And indeed, Kesslers, like its peers, was doing about $1 million in annual sales in the mid-1970s.[1]

Things were steady, but they wouldn't stay that way forever. The retail industry, which at the time was contributing the lion's share to Kesslers's bottom line, started changing in the 1980s. The exclusive-dealing agreements that Kesslers enjoyed with Nike and other vendors were disappearing. Now, a shopper could find these coveted brands at JC Penney's or K-Mart—often at a much cheaper price. And small retailers couldn't compete with price cuts of their own, as high inflation had significantly driven up business costs. The margins were squeezed. Every year, sporting goods was becoming a tougher industry for making a living.

Kesslers was rocked in 1982 when Bob Luerman, following his father Henry and mother Hedwig, unexpectedly passed away. Suddenly, at age 24, Bob Dickman was the boss, and he felt like he had the weight of the world on his shoulders. For months, Bob was working around the clock, trying to carry the immense workload of his uncle by himself. Only after he hired an assistant to help with administrative tasks did the load begin to lighten.

Then, just two years later, Kesslers's lead shareholder and former president was voted out of the mayor's office, and he needed a job. For Bob, there was no question that his dad would come back to work for Kesslers when his term ended. But Cliff was not so sure. He knew of the store's tight margins and the difficult business environment for sporting-goods dealers in Indiana. There wasn't room for him anymore, he told Bob, not enough money coming in the door to feed two families. Bob refused to accept this for an answer. Well, Bob replied, what if we grow the business so that it can feed more families? That was an idea the elder Dickman could agree to. Despite his protests, he really did want to return to Kesslers, and the chance to do something bold with the business was intriguing.

The two shook hands on Bob's proposition, and with that, a new era in Kesslers history began. Gone were the days of maintaining steady local business, of serving the same customers in the same territory. The mission was now growth, the leadership was now multigenerational, and the stage would soon be national. It would be unlike anything that Cliff could have imagined when he'd first set out as the proprietor of Kesslers in 1958—but then again, nothing in his life went as expected.

★　　★　　★

Growth in the fragmented, territorial industry was exceedingly difficult. Unsurprisingly, the father–son pair had a rocky start. Their first attempt at expansion was to open a retail shop in the Richmond Square Mall in the summer of 1984. Retail shopping had increasingly moved from the city's downtown toward strip malls located near the interstate, and the Dickmans hoped that establishing a secondary presence there would bolster their sales.[2] The results were mixed. The new storefront wasn't a failure, but it didn't deliver the boost they needed to "feed more families." They needed to try something bigger.

Their next expansion attempt fared much better: the purchase of Hartzlers Sporting Goods based in Fort Wayne in 1985. Having a second location in Fort Wayne gave Kesslers the unique opportunity to "throw a ring around the eastern Indiana area," Cliff said.[3] While Kesslers got a sales boost from Hartzlers's three retail stores, the greater long-term opportunity hinged on its Fort Wayne-based team division. Hartzlers, like Kesslers, had only one team salesman, but the doubling of the sales force and customer base introduced the beginning of a fundamental shift in the Kesslers business model—away from retail and toward sales to high school and college teams. It also marked an important addition to the company's management: the hiring of Bob's younger brother Phil, who agreed to run the Fort Wayne operation after graduating from Indiana University in 1986.

Soon after, Kesslers made its second and third acquisitions: Team Sports of Indiana, located on the west side of Indianapolis, and Kokomo's Sanburn's Sporting Goods.[4] On the Kokomo deal, Cliff's negotiating skills came in handy. Sanburn's was a strong force in central Indiana, but in order for the deal with Kesslers to go through, the company needed to trim the liabilities it owed to its vendors. So Cliff picked up the phone and called Sanburn's creditors directly. He put it to them plainly: Kesslers wouldn't be able to purchase Sanburn's if that meant having to cover the payable in full. But if the creditor would agree to knock 50% off, then Kesslers would buy Sanburn's and guarantee that the lower debt would be repaid. Not only did Cliff's logic persuade the creditors to agree to the plan, but they also trusted his promise to pay the renegotiated amount, for they knew by reputation that he was a fair, honest businessman. Thanks to the negotiations, Kesslers closed the deal with Sanburn's, and it went on to apply this tactic in subsequent acquisitions. After Terre Haute's McMillan Sports (1991) and Portland's KC Sports (1993) came aboard, the Dickmans stepped back and recognized something extraordinary: in just a handful of years, little Kesslers Sports Shop of Richmond had become the largest sporting-goods dealer in Indiana.[5]

Acquisitions took a pause at this point, for the expanded nature of the business created several snags for Kesslers. The most ominous problem was financial. Kesslers had traditionally operated with low debt and strong cash reserves. This offered them unique advantages, such as inventory discounts for making payment early and the ability to sell on credit to their customers. But after the acquisitions, Kesslers's checking account began to bleed fast. For example, the company paid $240,000 for Hartzlers, which evaporated their cash savings and forced them to borrow from the bank. That made it harder to keep up their pay-early, collect-late policy. An even bigger cashflow problem was to "cover the float." When Kesslers absorbed an office, it immediately had to start covering the new outpost's expenses (most notably payroll), but it took

218

some time before they could finally capitalize on new revenues, like collecting outstanding invoices. Once things stabilized and the office finally turned a positive cash flow, Kesslers scooped up another company, so all the new cash, not to mention more borrowed funds, had to be funneled into the acquisition. From the outside, Kesslers seemed to be on fire with growth. But from the inside, the company's resources were strained to their limits.

After the Terre Haute and Portland acquisitions, the cash-flow problem climaxed, and Kesslers was in legitimate danger of folding up. The store had been maxing out its line of credit for years, and the bank was getting antsy about their ability to ever pay down the debt. Kesslers's profitability wasn't the issue; rather, it was that all their money was tied up in inventory, an asset that couldn't pay the bills or the bank. The loan officer gave them a stern warning: get the cash-flow problem under control or have the debt accelerated, which would mean the end of Kesslers.

The bank's shot across the bow caused Cliff to question the future of his store. Kesslers, he thought, ought to consider selling the inventory, paying off the bank, and closing up shop, which would at least guarantee the shareholders some return on their investment. In many respects, these doubts were quite uncharacteristic of the man who had taken on sizable financial and political risks throughout his life. Fortunately, however, Bob and Phil wouldn't hear of it. They believed in their growth strategy, their new employees across the state, and in each other. They asked their dad to hang in there, and seeing his sons' passion, Cliff readily agreed.

That episode reflected something more fundamental about the father–son nature of the business. When the senior Dickman returned to Kesslers after being mayor, he never declared himself the boss. Instead, he took a more supportive role, putting in the same hard work as his boys but trusting in their vision for the future. He was the company president, but he saw a transition under-way: Kesslers was becoming their business. And in all the boys' initiatives, whether wise or foolish, he supported them all the way—both morally, in building them up with his words, and physically, by giving all his energy to get-ting the job done right.

The bank's warning lit a fire under the Dickmans, so they went to work on reshaping their strategy. First, they came to grips with a hard truth: their retail shops in the satellite locations were failing. It was a tough realization. Retail was part of Kesslers's DNA: it had been the entire foundation of the business in its earliest days. But after taking an honest look at the books, the trend was written on the wall. Kesslers's future was in the team business, not retail. They closed the retail fronts in Kokomo, Terre Haute, and two of the three Fort Wayne locations.

Second, Kesslers started cutting back on the size of its inventory. This was easier said than done. In the pre-Internet age, it was very challenging to keep up-to-date inventory counts in all the stores, so each location carried an excess to be sure it could fill all orders. If Kesslers was going to run a leaner operation, it needed the ability to get accurate, on-demand inventory counts in all offices.

That led to another breakthrough in the business: the use of new computer technology. In started when Bob met with a computer salesman who sold a software package designed for jewelry stores. The package ostensibly had no use to Kesslers, but the salesman was confident that the developers could fine-tune the software for the sport-ing-goods industry. After some back and forth with Bob on what such an interface would have to be capable of,

Kesslers bought the system. The price tag was $75,000, which Cliff initially thought to be an enormous waste of money for such a speculative piece of technology. But yet again, he trusted the judgment of his business partners, and he was right to do so.

The software was a game-changer, as they were finally able to keep real-time tallies of their inventory. Knowing what they had on hand, they were able to order only the inventory they truly needed, and in turn, they rebuilt their cash reserves and paid down their debt. Eventually, the software enabled them to go even further. Kesslers salesmen could input their orders into the program from any of the store's computers, and the orders were printed, filled, and shipped from Richmond. This consolidation of inventory brought enormous cost savings. The old jewelry-store software package, which had been customized in large part thanks to Bob's conversation with the salesman, became known as SportsPak, and before long, it was the standard software in the industry.

With the business growing rapidly and the stock of inventory converging in Richmond, Kesslers's headquarters needed to expand. The company had been operating out of its same storefront on East Main Street ever since Cliff started working there in 1956 (though he had expanded it in the 1960s by purchasing the building next door and knocking out the dividing wall). Now a six-city operation, the store had outgrown its shell. So in the summer of 1990, Kesslers moved down the block from the 916 address to 930—better known as the "old Evans and Romey building" which was then a furniture store.[6] The new headquarters offered six floors connected by freight elevator for inventory, screen-printing, retail, office space, and eventually embroidery. The move also coincided with Phil's transfer from Fort Wayne back home to Richmond, for he, Cliff, and Bob had decided that it was time for management to all work from the same place.

And so, over the mid-1990s, Kesslers shored up its foundations: building its reputation in new locations, incorporating SportsPak into its business model, training its 65 employees, and drawing down on its debts with the bank.[7] All this was setting the stage for Kesslers to take the next leap: growth outside Indiana.

No milestone marked Kesslers's transformation into a national company more clearly than the phone call Clifford Dickman received in the summer of 1995. Congratulations! the caller told him: you've been selected to join the National Sporting Goods Association's ("NSGA") Hall of Fame.

Dickman couldn't believe it. The NSGA, which represented 22,000 retailers, was the largest sporting-goods trade association in the country, and its Hall of Fame was the highest honor the sporting-goods world had to offer.[8] Dickman's predecessor inductees included household names in sporting goods—A.G. Spalding (basketballs), John Riddell (football helmets), W.C. Coleman (camping gear), Doug Easton (baseball bats), and Adi Dassler (founder of Adidas)—and later inductees included Nike's founder Phil Knight, Under Armour's Kevin Plank, and the Cabela family of outdoor-recreation fame.[9]

For Dickman, the honor itself was astounding, but it was most heartfelt because Bob and Phil had secretly nominated him. "I think these guys fooled a lot of important people," the patriarch said with a smile. The truth was that they hadn't fooled anyone.[10] A business friend from Dayton, Ohio served on the Hall of Fame's selection committee, and he could think of no one more worthy than the purveyor of Kesslers. Still, Cliff heaped the praise on his young business partners, saying, "If it wasn't for them, I probably wouldn't be in business."[11]

The entire family journeyed to Chicago for the induction ceremony on July 18, 1995. It was a swanky occasion—the "biggest thrill of his life," as Dickman described it at the time.[12] The events began the night before the induction with a special reception at the Chicago Yacht Club. The next morning, he had a place of honor at an industry-wide breakfast meeting, and that evening, he and two others were the prized honorees during a banquet downtown at the McCormick Place Convention Center. Keynoting the event was General Colin Powell, still riding a tidal wave of popularity from his leadership in the Gulf War. With more than 500 people in attendance, Clifford took his place in the National Sporting Goods Hall of Fame and offered a few words of gratitude to the general and the audience. The honor was well-deserved. As Bob put it, "I think his success has been good, clean living and honest, hard work."[13]

It wouldn't be the Dickmans' last brush with the NSGA Hall of Fame. In 2019, 24 years later, Bob Dickman was inducted for his own role in steering Kesslers's growth in the 1990s and 2000s and for chairing the NSGA Board of Directors in 2009 and 2010.[14] They became one of only two father–son pairs in the Hall of Fame's 65-year history.[15] For Cliff, whose greatest pride in his business career was passing the store on to the next generation, there was no higher honor or award than seeing Bob take his own place in the Hall of Fame.

★   ★   ★

In 1997, Jack Davidson, the owner of Columbus, Ohio-based Agler-Davidson Sporting Goods, reached out to Bob. Davidson had sold his retail division but couldn't find a buyer for his team business. Not wanting to hang his salesmen out to dry, he turned to Kesslers, the only sporting-goods shop in the region to have expanded their team division. Would they be interested in taking his team business free of charge and hiring his salesmen?

Cliff, Bob, and Phil quickly agreed that it was an opportunity of unique proportions. Their store was already noteworthy for acquiring team divisions outside its home city, but the chance to do so outside of its home *state* would put Kesslers in a league of its own. They accepted Davidson's offer, hired his salesmen, and began expanding the Kesslers name into central Ohio. Though Davidson had pitched his business free of charge, that didn't mean he had gifted Kesslers a gold mine. Yet again, the store had to cover the float, paying salaries to the new Ohio employees and taking over Agler-Davidson's outstanding payables well before they realized any additional revenue from the acquisition. But having been chastened by their talk with the bank several years earlier, they now absorbed the upfront financial drag of the acquisition smoothly.

Not long after, Koenig Sporting Goods in Cleveland sold their retail division and closed up shop. The team division, not having a thoughtful boss like Jack Davidson, had been left standing out in the cold. Having heard the good fortune of their fellow sporting-goods salesmen in Columbus, the Koenig team reached out to Kesslers, which eagerly brought them onboard. That gave Kesslers's team division full coverage of Ohio—the east covered by Cleveland, the center covered by Columbus, and the west covered by Richmond, just across the state line. The same year, Kesslers acquired Gerry & Al's Sporting Goods in Rantoul, Illinois, which combined with the Terre Haute office and the soon-to-be acquired Crown Point location to give Kesslers a strong presence in the Land of Lincoln.[16] In just one year, Kesslers had doubled in size.

The team divisions that Kesslers bought all had a common feature: they came free or very cheap because they were operating under distress. Why were these other companies struggling? One explanation might be the "just do your million" mentality that was so pervasive in the industry. Companies were too comfortable with the business they had. They weren't thinking about how to serve their customers better, and they weren't coming to terms with the big changes, like computer technology, that were already transforming the industry. Kesslers, on the other hand, had long since lost faith in the status quo. Their motto became "grow or die." And indeed, as their competitors failed to grow, they began to die off.

As Kesslers swelled, it attained economies of scale that their competitors lacked. In buying larger quantities from suppliers, Kesslers was able to purchase at lower rates than their fellow sporting-goods dealers. And by controlling more territory, they were able to insulate themselves from competition and charge higher prices. Without the advantage of size, the other stores couldn't make the margins they needed to survive.

Kesslers's competitors weren't happy to see them succeed. The unspoken agreement had been to stay in your own territory, and Kesslers was brazenly breaking out of theirs. Some complained to their vendors, who had promised that they, not Kesslers, would have primacy in selling that vendor's products in their territory. In turn, some of the vendors half-heartedly told Kesslers to back down—though frankly, they weren't upset by the prospect of more of their product being sold, no matter who was selling it. Another competitor spread something of a conspiracy theory: that a supplier, Russell Athletic, was financing Kesslers's acquisitions so that it could eventually take Kesslers over and sell directly to customers. Still others turned their ire on Kesslers by kicking them out of buying groups, which stung after being affiliated with these associations for so many years.

Kesslers was indeed the industry disrupter, and there was much to miss about the "just do your million" days. But the truth was that the business world was permanently changing: the power of computers, direct sales from suppliers to customers, pinched margins, and the introduction of sporting goods in general retail stores meant that there was no going back to the halcyon days. What made Kesslers different was that it recognized and adapted to these changes. If it hadn't jumped out in front, another company would have. What's more, the store wasn't joining forces with the biggest kids on the block; it picked up struggling shops and hired their employees, who otherwise would've been out of work. From the perspective of these industry veterans, like the Koenig salesmen in Cleveland, Kesslers didn't ruin the good old days; it cast them a lifeline.

In the midst of the growth in Ohio and Illinois, Kesslers made another key hire: Cliff's youngest son Dan. After graduating from Indiana University, Dan had gone to work as a CPA in Atlanta for Crowe Chizek, which turned out to be invaluable training for his second job as chief controller for Kesslers. Cross-office recordkeeping in the 1990s was exceedingly challenging, and Dan's new procedures streamlined the process. He also had more technological prowess than his father and older brothers. Up to that point, Kesslers's SportsPak software relied on dedicated data lines to transmit orders and inventory counts across offices. These lines were enormously expensive to maintain; a single data line from a satellite office to Richmond often cost thousands of dollars every month. But Dan foresaw the explosive potential of the Internet, so he transitioned all the locations to dial-up connections, putting a huge dent in monthly expenses and positioning the business well ahead of its competition.

Perhaps the biggest miracle in the entire Kesslers story was that a father and three sons could work together so well. It was especially remarkable given their close quarters: the three boys' offices were adjoined to one another, with Dan and Phil on the ends and Bob occupying the middle. Naturally, the Dickmans traded different points of view on all kinds of topics, but never once did they fight. When a decision was made, they all rallied behind it. Dan credited it to everyone knowing their place: "We all get along well with each other and we know our roles. I think that's a successful formula to have with any business."[17]

Two other Dickmans were pivotal players for Kesslers during this period too. Martha Jane started supervising the accounts-payable department shortly after Cliff returned to the business. Stretching back to her days collecting rent payments at Jenkins Properties, she appreciated the importance of getting bills paid in full and on time. Though Kesslers leaned heavily on credit with vendors during its tight years, Martha Jane's meticulousness and plain decency meant that every bill was paid well before coming due. This earned Kesslers goodwill and additional credit with its suppliers, and both proved to be vital resources when cash flows were stretched thin.

The next key family hire was Carolyn Stephens, Cliff and Martha Jane's third daughter. Carolyn had been working as a nurse in Richmond when her father and brothers asked if she'd consider running Kesslers's new embroidery department. Machine-embroidery technology had recently taken the critical step of connecting to external computers. This allowed numbers, names, and logos to be embroidered onto jerseys more quickly and accurately than ever. Carolyn learned the technology, and over the next 20 years, she headed up a tight-knit department of embroiderers. Kesslers's new service flummoxed their competitors, many of whom didn't offer in-house embroidery. It also stymied their suppliers' efforts to sell directly to customers; only a dealer like Kesslers could offer this level of customization. And as with any family business, the department was in hands that everyone could completely trust.

The acquisitions also introduced Kesslers to those outside the family who would evolve into key agents in the company's development. After the Agler-Davidson pickup in Columbus, the Dickmans welcomed Steve Carloni aboard. Steve became like another brother to the three boys over the years, and he was soon a leader in identifying potential office locations and closing acquisition deals. Mark Helmond, who'd joined Kesslers after the Indianapolis merger, was instrumental in forging strong relationships between Kesslers and its vendors. And in Richmond, Kesslers scooped up Denver Baker, who brought a sharp eye for identifying the hottest footwear of the year and ensuring that it was stocked on Kesslers's shelves and advertised in its catalogs. These three business partners, and many others, remained with the company for decades.

At the turn of the millennium, with a strong economy and the full leadership team assembled, Kesslers was firing on all cylinders. Hickok's Team Sports in Atlanta, Georgia and Sportsman's Corner in Gulfport, Mississippi joined the team, thereby extending Kesslers beyond the Midwest. The store also embarked on a new component to its growth strategy: opening locations of its own by hiring salesmen away from competition. This led to new offices in Evansville; Cincinnati; Springfield, Illinois; Knoxville, Tennessee; Tulsa, Oklahoma; and Little Rock, Arkansas. [18] With improved technology, streamlined accounting procedures, and risk diversified across offices, each new location seemed easier to open than the last. Some of these offices included small retail stores, but at this stage, establishing strong team divisions was the dominant goal.

In large part, Kesslers was successful in wooing team salesmen from new territories because of its name-recognition. No other sporting-goods dealer came close to having the national reputation that Kesslers now enjoyed. And sometimes, Kesslers leveraged that name-recognition and made a splash. In closing the deal with the Koenig salesmen, Bob, having just earned his private pilot's license, flew the Kesslers team to Cleveland in a six-seat Piper Lance. The salesmen, who'd never seen a display like that in the sporting-goods world, were stunned: *this* was the leader of the industry.

But even more so, it was the plain likeability and trustworthiness of the Dickmans and Carloni that won over many of Kesslers's new employees. In Springfield, as the team pitched the Illinois salesmen about joining Kesslers, Bob highlighted the youthful energy of Kesslers leadership and what a fun, exciting environment that fostered. About 5 minutes later, Bob conspicuously pulled out his pill box and took some medication while the group looked on, prompting Phil to comment, "So much for young, healthy leadership!" The salesmen thought the episode was hilarious—not to mention a very authentic look at their potential business partners. These weren't tycoons; they were a down-to-earth Indiana family, a group of people they could trust. This genuineness was the Dickmans' secret sauce to hiring new salesmen, and of course, the boys had learned it from their mom and dad.

During later rounds of Kesslers acquisitions and office openings, Clifford began to take a backseat in management. To be sure, he was at work every day, and he was the closest advisor that Bob, Phil, and Dan had as they went about the country expanding the business. But those three were now out front, and he eased into a supporting role.

He and Martha Jane kept the home fires burning when the boys were gone, ensuring that the bills were paid, inventory was arriving on schedule, and Richmond's retail customers were satisfied. Cliff took on ambitious handyman projects too, most notably in the Richmond facility's basement. When Kesslers bought the building, the basement was really two basements that were separated by a 32-inch-thick wall of concrete. Because the freight elevator could reach only one of the basements, the second was entirely wasted space. For 30 grueling days, the 67-year-old Dickman connected the two rooms by boring 500 ¾-inch holes on both sides of the wall in the outline of an archway, taking a sledgehammer to it, and hauling away more than 12,000 pounds of concrete.

From his earliest memories, Clifford Dickman had been trained to work; he didn't know any other way to live. "Retirement" simply wasn't in his vocabulary. Well into his 70s, Cliff still regularly traveled across the state on business. He installed basketball goals for Kesslers customers, drove a trailer (called the "Sports Express") to schools for coaches and athletes to sample new shoes, and completed minor renovations to satellite Kesslers facilities. But eventually, his years began catching up with him, and so did Martha Jane's—she wrapped up her 15-year tenure at Kesslers around the year 2000. By about 2005, Cliff stopped traveling out of town on business and mostly worked as the Richmond office's maintenance man—no small task considering the building's age and six floors. Finally, in the early 2010s, the time came to officially retire. Clifford Dickman cashed his final paycheck over 55 years after cashing his first one.

By the time Dickman's schedule started winding down, Kesslers was completely unrecognizable from the tiny storefront Dickman had gone to work for in 1956. When he began, annual sales were $100,000; by 2004, they were $30 million. It had mostly been a retail store at the beginning; now, more than 90% of sales came from on-the-road sales to high school and college teams. Dickman had employed just one salesman and a few storehands at the beginning; now, there were 65 salesmen and 180 employees overall, 40 of whom were in Richmond. What had begun as Whitey Kessler's local shop in 1934 had become the largest dealer of team sporting goods in America, spread across 19 offices in eight states.[19]

The biggest change, however, was that the store wasn't actually Kesslers anymore. In 2004, it merged with Dallas-based Collegiate Pacific, now known as BSN Sports. The decision was a difficult one, but the far-flung company was becoming more challenging to manage than ever. Technological change was accelerating, and to stay apace with other dealers, significant, expensive updates were needed in short order. Competitors were incessantly trying to poach Kesslers's salesmen—a result of Kesslers not requiring its sales staff to sign non-competes. In short, while Kesslers was enjoying a period of success, it would be eclipsed if it didn't keep expanding—"grow or die" was not only a motto; it was a reality. After 20 exhausting years of constant change, the next stage of growth in personnel, office space, and technology was one which the Dickman brothers didn't want to take alone.

The boys asked for their parents' blessing before giving up the family business after so many years, and it was granted. There was plenty of nostalgia to go around in closing the book on the "Kesslers" name—the name of Whitey, who'd become a Richmond sports legend almost 100 years ago; the name of the shop where young Richmond athletes equipped themselves for decades; the name of the place where Cliff had earned his living and his growing family had centered its life. Yet this was not the end of the Kesslers story; it was just a new chapter. Today, though the Richmond retail shop is closed, BSN Sports continues to operate an office out of the old Kesslers headquarters downtown. There, you'll find the three Dickman brothers—still working out of the same adjoining offices they occupied 25 years ago; still in touch with their industry colleagues from days long past; still selling the same basketballs, batting gloves, and ball caps that, as young boys, they stocked on shelves under the watchful, loving gaze of their father.

"The story of Kesslers Team Sports is that of a hardworking family that owned a local business that has grown to become one of the most successful in its field," the *Palladium-Item* said as the store prepared to change hands.[20] "I didn't envision this," Clifford Dickman told the newspaper. "But I've enjoyed every minute I've been in the business. The main thing you don't forget is the loyal customers you've had over the years."[21]

It was a classic Dickman statement: it wasn't the trappings, it was the people. It wasn't the faraway travel that made him love Earlham athletics; it was the teammates. It wasn't the office that made him love being mayor; it was the constituents he served and who appreciated him in return. And it wasn't money or sporty products that made him love Kesslers; it was the customers, the employees, and the business partners, especially those with whom he shared a name.

14

"DRIVE ON"

With the benefit of hindsight, many people can identify events from their early years that illuminate their lifelong character. An extrovert, for example, might look back on how, as a kid, she always made new friends on vacation, or a teacher might remember how he always had a book in his hands. This is certainly true of Clifford Dickman. One of the distinguishing features of his character is dogged determination: his refusal to quit no matter how challenging the circumstances. That was on display from his earliest days as a ball player, when he outhustled everyone on the court until the final buzzer, even if the scoreboard showed an insurmountable deficit.

Tough basketball games may have refined his persistence; so too did later episodes in life, like the Chemscam saga and Kesslers's wake-up call from the bank. But of all the obstacles Dickman has faced, the simple act of growing old has tested his grit and resilience more than any other. It has demanded nothing less than "defying Father Time," as the *Palladium-Item* put it.[1] Perhaps for Clifford Dickman, then, this final chapter of life reveals his true character more fully than any other.

★   ★   ★

Time slowed down for Dickman when he ended his political career. Kesslers was on a roll, but because Dickman shared leadership duties with his sons, he found himself with more time on his hands than he'd enjoyed in decades. It was time to take on some new challenges.

He first reconnected with an old hobby that he'd been dearly missing: athletics. He had played some intermittent rounds of golf as mayor, especially in getting to know other state leaders in the Indiana Association of Cities and Towns. In the mid-1980s, he took up the great game in earnest, making his home course the hilly, ever-challenging Liberty Country Club, which is 10 miles south of Richmond. His golfing buddies included old friends, like his former fire chief Moon Mullin, and new ones he met on the links too. As for so many others, the game tested his patience—he once chucked a club so high up a tree that he needed a ladder to get it down. All the same, Dickman wasn't a bad golfer given his late introduction to the game; at his peak, he averaged bogey golf.

Dickman also revived his basketball game. In 1989, Richmond's Kiwanis Club began hosting the "Wayne County Basketball Sectional (The Way It Used to Be)," an old-timer basketball tourney for players who competed at least 25 years ago in Wayne County basketball.[2] The field was notable for including high schools that had long since closed up, including Boston, Economy, Williamsburg, and Dickman's own Webster Pirates.[3] Though he was nearly the oldest member of the Pirates squad, Dickman was captain and one of the team's top scorers. Webster shocked everyone when it won the tournament three years in a row, prompting the unlikely jest: "Break up the Webster Pirates!"[4]

Most of Dickman's retirement-era basketball career unfolded at the local senior center. Contrary to what one might expect, these weren't games of patty cake; they were intense battles. "I tell you, you don't get a layup. You get grabbed down and hacked," Dickman said about senior basketball. [5] "We beat each other to hell and back down there. It gets wild. It gets rough, but I love it. I'd rather do that than play golf because it's just fun to get beat up on and beat up on somebody else." [6] He said these words when he was on the cusp of 72; he would've said much the same at 22.

Dickman played his same style of ball, sticking to the high-percentage goals from the paint and eschewing long shots from the perimeter. Unsurprisingly, he was one of the culprits of the rough style of play. "I'll give you an illustration of what it's like," reported one of his teammates. "The last time we played ... I took my shoe off when I got home and there was blood on my sock. Cliff had smashed my toe. Of course, he didn't intend to, but that shows you how rough it can get." [7] After incidents like this, the players finally started calling their own fouls. Even Dickman agreed to the rule change, though he lamented that the foul-calling took some fun out of the game.

It wasn't just basketball and golf that satiated Dickman's delight for athletic competition. In 1992, he began participating in regional track-and-field meets. He tried his hand at the "weight pentathlon"—shot put, hammer throw, discus, javelin, and weight toss—plus the long jump and high jump. [8] He hadn't participated in any of these events since he'd been in the Army 40 years earlier. To his surprise, he fared well, qualifying for the White River Park State Games in Indianapolis on his first try. He put on a good show there too, winning the shot-put event for the 60–69 age group with a throw of 36 feet and

11 inches (about 13 feet less than his throws for the Army).[9] He went on to win the event at the statewide level 10 years in a row.

A few years later, Dickman's football coach from Earlham, Don Cumley, stopped in Richmond for a visit. Cumley was on his way to a national track meet in New York, and he encouraged his former player to consider trying for a national event himself. Realizing that his victories at the state level qualified him for the national competition, Dickman decided to give it a shot in 1997. He and Martha Jane journeyed to Tucson, Arizona for "the United States National Senior Sports Classic," which would later be shortened to the "Senior Olympics."[10] The trip was fun, but his performance was mediocre: he finished 13th out of 29 in shot put.[11]

The Tucson event lit a fire under Dickman. He'd had fun, but he wanted to do better. He built a circular stage with a toe board in his backyard and started practicing, just like he was a kid again. Between statewide and national meets, he traveled to Baton Rouge; Columbus; St. Louis; Pittsburgh; Grand Rapids; Maine; Charleston, West Virginia, Springfield, Illinois; Raleigh, North Carolina; Elizabethtown, Kentucky; and Hampton Roads, Virginia.[12] His top finish at a national event was 8th place, which was satisfactory but not quite his goal. The trips were great excuses for him and Martha Jane to get out and see the country: still steeped in their frugal ways, they didn't often travel outside Indiana and Ohio.

The Senior Olympics brought Dickman new plaques, medals, and ribbons year after year, but in 1992, his athletic achievements as a young man won special recognition: induction into the Earlham College Hall of Fame. It was no surprise for someone who "was perhaps the most well-rounded athlete in Earlham history."[13] His record of earning 16 varsity letters still has not been broken, and according to Dickman, it likely won't ever be, as the college changed its rules to allow an athlete to play only two sports per year.[14] Today, his legacy at Earlham is on display at the "Cliff Dickman Media Center," a two-story building that stands behind home plate at the college's baseball stadium.[15]

Dickman's post-retirement extracurriculars extended well beyond sports. He made a habit of reading history, and the intrigue of learning hit him like it never had before. As a student, he'd been too insecure in his intellectual ability to make conversation with his teachers and professors; in his old age, he waxed philosophical and thought up all kinds of topics he wished he could debate with his old instructors.

While some hobbies—like athletics and reading—suited Dickman well, others didn't. Perhaps inspired by his pilot-sons Bob and Dan, Cliff decided to take flying lessons. Aviation never really clicked with him. Student pilots are allowed to fly solo after 10 hours of instruction, but Dickman, having put in 20 hours, still hadn't gotten permission to solo from his instructor. Eventually, after some nudging from his student, the instructor reluctantly got out of the plane and let Dickman fly the pattern around the airport by himself. Watching nervously from the control tower, the instructor noticed that Dickman was too low on final approach, so he tried to radio his student, "Add power! Add power!" The message wasn't received; Dickman landed the wheels down in the grass and roughly bounced onto the runway. Not wanting to push his limited luck any further, that was his last flying lesson, though he eventually came to laugh about the incident: "I was just practicing a short-field landing!"

Construction, of course, had been a self-taught skill that Dickman had practiced since becoming a homeowner. His post-mayoral years allowed him the opportunity to perfect this craft. Having made significant improvements to his Southwest 4th and Northwest 7th Street houses, Dickman now turned to his and Martha Jane's home on South 23rd Street. The house, located in Richmond's historic Reeveston neighborhood, caught the Dickmans' eye while on the campaign trail in 1983. Not even a year later, the house went up for sale, and they called the owners and closed the deal that very day. The property, situated on a full acre, involved more yardwork than their previous two homes. It also required some home-improvement projects, which Dickman set to work on right away. Most notably (and without any help), he added wide front and back porches to the house.

The Reeveston house wasn't Cliff and Martha Jane's only property to manage. Inspired by their old neighbors Uncle Mutt and Aunt Greta, who owned a house on nearby Lake Lakengren, Cliff and Martha Jane purchased a vacant lot on the same lake in 1984. Dickman didn't have the expertise to build a house himself, but he did all the work that he could: constructing a deck off the house, tiling the floors, erecting a boat dock, building a 20-foot-high treehouse, crafting a bridge over a stream in the backyard, and installing an indoor firepole connecting the main level and the basement. By the late 1980s, the new Lakengren house (only about 15 miles from Richmond) was a favorite weekend retreat for the Dickmans.

It wasn't just their own children that loved the lake cottage; Cliff and Martha Jane had long since become grandparents. Their daughter Debbie and her husband, Marty Hanneman, had welcomed their son Jared into the family in 1976. Remarkably, Jared's birth came just a few years after Cliff and Martha Jane's youngest child, Cindy,

240

was born—making Cindy an aunt at the ripe old age of five. Cliff and Martha Jane became "Grandpa and Grandma" at 46 and 44, respectively. Over the course of the next 30 years, they came to have 27 grandkids—the last, Fred Mendenhall, was born in 2006.

Grandparenthood was a wonderful new world for Cliff and Martha Jane. As is commonly said, the job had all the perks of being a parent without the drawbacks. They played without having to discipline; attended athletic contests without having to drop off at practice; cooked favorite dinners without forcing anyone to eat their vegetables. And they were extremely fortunate—especially by today's standards—in having their kids and grandkids close by. When all the dust settled, Linda and Dave Major raised their kids outside Detroit, Ted and Kim Dickman raised theirs in Indianapolis, and the remaining six kids lived with their families in Wayne County. Most of the grandkids were reachable in minutes; the rest were only a morning's drive away.

For all their proximity, the eight kids and their spouses were, in many ways, on their own. Cliff and Martha Jane viewed their role as supporters, not a second set of parents. They gave advice only when asked, and they showed up at their kids' houses only when invited. Of course, the kids were eager to enlist their parents' help—whether it be babysitting help, an after-school pickup, or one of Cliff's specialty construction projects. Over the years, he put up a deck for Phil, built a treehouse with an attached swing set for Dan, tiled floors for Debbie and Bob, and installed a brick front porch for Linda.

The grandparents made plenty of special memories with their grandkids. They hosted summer bonfires in their driveway featuring Cliff's improvised hot-dog roaster: a rotisserie which he stripped out of a gas grill and mounted over the flames. The young ones loved visits to Lakengren, where they could slide down the firepole, climb the high treehouse, or dizzy themselves on a tire swing. The big family also enjoyed weekend tent-camping trips at Hueston Woods State Park in western Ohio.

The family also convened annually at the old Webster farm for a unique celebration: "Tractorfest." After all these years, Cliff's older brother Floyd continued to farm the land of his youth, and he was always glad to host a family party. Floyd maintained a collection of antique Farmall tractors, which had enough horsepower to pull a sizable wagon. With Cliff or Floyd in the driver's seat, the tractor towed the many Dickmans around the land where the two old men had spent their childhoods. Football games in the yard, explorations to the chicken coop, and a big barbecue rounded out the traditions of Tractorfest.

As is true in many American families, the greatest memories centered around Christmastime. In the early days of grandparenthood, Cliff and Martha Jane hosted the family gathering in their Reeveston house. Too cold to go outside, the house was overloaded with people and buzzing with energy. Babies cried, newly mobile kids raced after each other in their self-invented version of "tag," older cousins played Secret Santa and scratched off lottery tickets, and everyone helped themselves to a hearty plate of beef stew served over egg noodles—Martha Jane's beloved recipe. The patriarch and matriarch of the family, flooded with thank-you hugs from the youngsters and regaled with stories from their own kids, had not a second to themselves. And they couldn't have been happier about it.

Dickman continued to stay engaged with his Richmond home well into his later years. As a former mayor, his opinion on community issues carried extra clout. On occasion, he gathered with other former mayors to discuss the condition of the city and advise the current office-holder.[16] He opined to the *Palladium-Item* on local affairs like community morale, economic development, the need to vote, and the news media.[17] And he served as treasurer of Wayne County's fundraising committee for his old friend from Indiana politics, Senator Richard Lugar.[18]

Occasional engagement from the periphery wasn't quite the same, however, as his eight years at the center of the action. He missed being mayor, and what's more, he never quite shook the disappointment at losing his bid for a third mayoral term. He was a good sport about it, of course. In 2000, at a Kiwanis Club gathering of Richmond's six living mayors, Dickman—positioned between predecessor Byron Klute and successor Frank Walter-mann—jokingly grabbed both men in a headlock and said, "If people don't think time heals all wounds, I'm stuck here between two thorns!" But as is typical of his style of reflecting on the past, the early laugh gave way to something more profound: "Being mayor was the greatest job I ever had. I was so proud to be mayor."[19]

These may sound like the words of someone who thought he'd never be mayor again, but in truth, Dickman was at that very moment mulling a bid for another term. Just a week before the Kiwanis event, the current mayor, Dennis Andrews, unexpectedly announced his resignation to attend seminary.[20] Though it had been almost 17 years since Dickman held the title of mayor, he decided to throw his hat in the ring to replace Andrews. "I'm going to do it because I think I probably have the best qualifications," Dickman said confidently to the newspaper as he announced his candidacy.[21] Warding off any concerns about being the oldest candidate in the field (he was 70), he said, "Those people who say I'm too old to be mayor, they'd better try me first."[22]

The process for selecting Andrews's successor was unusual. Indiana law required that the precinct committeemen of the political party of the outgoing official select the replacement. Because Andrews was a Republican, the decision for his successor rested with the 31 Republicans chairing the city's precincts.[23] It was a lot of pressure for this small group of citizens, but the upside was that the selection process was brief and without the usual burdens of campaigning. In that sense, it was a low-stakes gamble for Dickman to get back into the mayor's office.

The field was comprised of six candidates. Each was well qualified for the job, and so the city was shocked when the precinct committeemen picked Andrews's successor on the first ballot. The winner was Shelley Miller, the city controller under Andrews and the first female mayor in Richmond's history. Eager to see Miller and the city succeed, Dickman wished her well, and he didn't regret his own failed bid either: "I'm not disappointed. I'm glad I did it."[24] It wasn't the final time Dickman entertained thoughts of running for mayor, nor was it the last time that someone would tease him with the prospect (he'd get that into his 80s).[25] But the 2000 mini-campaign was Dickman's last official bid for his all-time favorite job.

Dickman's political activity was far from over, however. In just a few short years, it took a new turn that is both humorous and somewhat inspiring. A local acquaintance, Victor Jose, planned to start a weekly group to talk politics. He was inviting Democrats, Republicans, and independents so as to create a true debate atmosphere. Would Richmond's former Republican mayor be interested in joining? Dickman agreed, but with one caveat. Jose and the other group members had all decided that they'd smoke cigars during the meetings; Dickman, never a smoker, said he would just drink scotch instead.

Thus began "The Problem-Solving Committee," though as Dickman says, "I don't think we've ever really solved anything." Instead, he colloquially (and affectionately) refers to it as the cigar group. The old guys, who still meet at the time of writing, don't pull any punches. They debate everything—war in the Middle East, Obamacare, taxes, the environment, abortion, guns. Controversial topics are the rule, not the exception, and Dickman is often the one who brings them to the fore. While he blusters most at his vocal opponents, his real annoyances arise when people don't hold opinions at all or are afraid to advocate for them. Ever the competitor, he prefers a good fight rather than victory by default.

Dickman can't help but wonder how two good people can disagree with each other at such a fundamental level. How, for instance, can one person see abortion as an evil, while another views its prohibition as an evil, but the two can still respect each other as good people, even as friends? It remains a mystery to him, but the cigar group is living proof that friendship can prevail amidst contradicting worldviews.

Perhaps one of the best models of civility and discourse we can find in politics today is, ironically, this loud, bickering, cigar-smoking group of geezers. No matter how many voices are raised or fingers pointed, the group always reconvenes the next week. For all their disagreements, they like each other too much, and they want to see each other again.

Clifford and Martha Jane's 60s and 70s stretched into their 80s and 90s, and life inevitably slowed down. Cliff

completed his final construction project at age 80: a ga-
zebo in his backyard equipped with rudimentary electric
and heating—a remarkable achievement for a person his
age and a favorite hangout of the cigar group. His maintenance responsibilities in the old Kesslers building slowly
thinned to zero. He kept up his involvement in Senior
Olympics until his early 80s, participating in his final
shot-put event at Baldwin Wallace University outside
Cleveland. He was winning more blue ribbons than ever
when he retired, usually thanks to the fact that he was
the only contestant in his age bracket. And most difficult
of all, he gave up the very game that had gotten him into
sports: basketball. Down at the Richmond Senior Center,
Cliff put up his last hook shot at age 85, keeping his
rough-and-tumble, toe-smashing style of play to the end.

"Getting old is hell," Dickman says with a wistful
smile. But for their age, he and Martha Jane have fared
remarkably well in health. Martha Jane has little more
to complain of than struggles with hearing. Cliff has a
pacemaker and still fights high blood pressure, just like
he did as a young man when the Marine recruiter told
him to "call the hearse." The most challenging day-to-day
impediment is Cliff's hands, which shake uncontrollably
whenever he uses them. At first, the ailment only im-
paired his ability to write; today, he can't pick up a fork
and relies on Martha Jane to feed him. Their dinnertime
isn't the vision of married life that they pictured more
than 65 years ago at St. Andrew's Church, but it is closer
to the sacrament's real meaning than most anything else
in the world.

Hard as it has been to come to grips with their own
old age, the far greater pain has been the loss of family
and friends from all chapters of life. Just a few years after
Martha Jane's parents and brother suddenly passed, Cliff
lost his mother Anna, who died at age 89 in her home on

the Webster farm.[26] The Dickmans' neighbors and great friends from Southwest 4th Street, Uncle Mutt and Aunt Greta, have passed on.[27] From Cliff's Earlham athletic days, he lost his basketball coach and lifelong friend, Howie Helfrich.[28] From the early days of running Kesslers, he said goodbye to his partner in business and fellow referee, Ray Mitrione.[29] From his time in political office, he's lost his fire chief and golf buddy, Moon Mullin; his city attorney, Robert Reinke; and his city controller, Don Meredith.[30] Webster classmates, friends from church, and good neighbors have passed on, as well—too many to count by name in these pages, but equally loved.

The toughest losses were family members. In the mid-2000s, Floyd fought a rough battle with bone cancer, but he kept his gruff humor and big smiles until the end. Faced with a prognosis of death in a matter of months, Floyd and his nephews went shopping for a special treat: new mudflaps for his pickup truck. The salesman, eager to sell his product and unaware of Floyd's condition, proudly told his customers that the mudflaps came with a "lifetime" warranty. "Hmph, well you must not think very damn much of your mudflaps!" Floyd retorted to the befuddlement of the salesman and howls of laughter from his nephews. In September 2006, death came for Floyd, the brother who had been like a father to Cliff.[31]

Along with Floyd, Cliff always enjoyed an especially close relationship with Kathleen, his oldest sister. Kath spent most of her life working in Cincinnati for Proctor & Gamble, and upon retiring, she decided to move home to Richmond. She and Cliff inherited the Webster farm from Floyd, and they oversaw its administration until her death in 2016 at age 96.[32] Like Floyd, Kath kept her sharp memory and quick wit until the very end.

Martha Jane too has lost her dearest friends in life: her two sisters. The oldest, Mary Maurer, died in 2010, followed by Hilda Herold in 2020.[33] Even for sisters, the three women shared a special bond. They lived in Richmond their entire lives, their kids grew up together, and indeed, Martha Jane and Hilda had both married Dickmans. Today, Martha Jane and Fr. John are the only Luermans left.

Knowing the pain of loss, Clifford and Martha Jane do what they can to support their friends in difficult stages of life. They're regular visitors to the nursing homes in Richmond—often beginning with someone they intended to visit, then roaming the hallways and stopping in rooms wherever they recognize a name placard, even when the name only rings a distant bell. The patients are eager for company, and that's what the Dickmans provide: a happy story to perk them up and a sounding board for folks who haven't had a conversation in a while. And as the couple walks out the door, Cliff always wishes the friend well and promises that they'll be back.

Of course, there isn't always a next visit. In the aftermath of death, they again make a point to show up at callings, funerals, and cemetery visits. Sad as it is to recognize, many of the great loves in Cliff and Martha Jane's life have now passed away, so they take walks around the cemetery to visit with them. "I hope I don't seem cocky by still being able to come visit you," he jokes to the gravestones and the people underneath them. They see their own plot in St. Andrew's Cemetery and the markers of the people who will surround them—Henry and Hedwig Luerman, Bob Luerman, Fr. John, Floyd, and Kath; Joseph and Anna Dickman are just around the corner. Their prayer is short and simple. "We'll see you again one day."

★ ★ ★

Whether because of their own age or the loss of those around them, the fragility of life is often on Cliff's mind, and he has become increasingly sentimental. It's a positive change, in many ways. He has started to reach out to people from long ago, even his old Webster High classmates. And he'll tell stories that he previously didn't share very often, like his days as a full-time athlete for the Army.

Dickman has also grown more willing to dispense his well-seasoned wisdom. In a speech to high school basketball players, he said, "If you take care of yourself and your body, you can have a great life."[34] To his son Ted on becoming chief of an accounting firm, he advised simply, "Be firm, and be fair." He reminds married couples that when it's hard to see eye-to-eye, "you've got to pull together. You can't have one horse pulling the whole wagon while one lags back." And to anyone, he'll say that as much as the country has changed in his lifetime, the core American dream that he knew as a young man is still alive today. Work hard, be fair and honest, and try to help the people around you, he prescribes. That's not a recipe for an easy existence, but it's the ticket to a great life.

Some combination of business sense and nostalgia keeps him hanging on to his childhood farm home in Webster, which passed into his hands after the deaths of Floyd and Kath. The farm is comprised of its original 154 acres which his parents purchased almost 90 years ago, plus an additional 26 acres that Cliff acquired in later years. Today, there aren't any livestock on the farm, nor is any Dickman responsible for the farming work. But with the help of a neighbor, the fields are still lined with rows of crops every summer—corn one year, soybeans the next. The people and the farming technology are different, but a drive down Flatley Road today gives the same picture it would have when the Dickmans arrived in 1935.

More than anything, Cliff Dickman's soft heart is all for his family: his kids, grandkids, and now great-grandkids, a milestone he and Martha Jane crossed in 2003. It has grown into a massive family—yet again, something far greater than the couple could have remotely imagined when they started out. Today, there are 103 members: two grandparents, eight kids and eight spouses, 27 grandkids and 15 spouses, and 43 great-grandkids, a number that is sure to be outdated as soon as this book goes to print.

Clifford and Martha Jane simply burst at the seams with pride in their family. It's not so much everyone's accomplishments that make them glow, though there is much to be proud of on that score. Today, their kids and grandkids are engaged in education, business, medicine, real estate, law, and the military; they are singers and pianists, college athletes and stage actors, mothers and fathers. But what really sweeps the grandparents off their feet is the thoughtful people their progeny have become: the type who call them on the phone, send them notes, visit whenever they can, and go on to marry and raise wonderful people themselves. No one is more thankful to be in the family than the couple who started it all; they know they've been overwhelmingly blessed.

Perhaps this gratitude is responsible for inspiring one of Clifford's newer practices: the prayer list. For his entire life, the general form of his nightly prayer routine has been the same: the Lord's Prayer, followed by his favorite hymn, "Morning Has Broken," and then a naming of people for whom he asks special blessings. But around 2010, he started something different. Instead of praying for groups ("our kids and grandkids"), he began saying the individual names of his 100+ family members, ancestors and descendants alike. He begins, "God bless Mom, Dad, Martha Jane's mom and dad, Martha Jane," and then he names his siblings, his wife's siblings, his kids and their spouses, grandkids and their spouses, and great-grand-kids. Living or deceased, born or unborn, he prays for each one of them from memory, and he won't turn in for the night until he says every name.

Funnily enough, the prayer list has become a surpris-ingly effective tool for Dickman to learn facts about his family's lives. For instance, according to his own prayer-list rules, if someone in the family begins a romantic re-lationship, he'll add the partner to the prayer list. And so, if he's fishing around for whether a grandchild is dating someone, he innocently asks, "Is there anyone I need to add to the prayer list?" It's hard not to be forthcoming. The prayer list also has fact-finding usefulness after a couple has gotten married, for they can very well expect to be asked the same question: "Anyone new for the prayer list?"

But the prayer list, more than anything, is simply ap-preciated—not only by family, but also by others around Richmond whom Dickman has added to the list of names over the years. Learning that they are on Cliff Dickman's prayer list, especially when they may not know of anyone else praying for them, is touching. He has evangelized through the practice too: some have been inspired to start prayer lists of their own. Dickman is glad to do it. The prayer is efficacious in its own right, and he also believes that his mind is kept sharp by the act of saying so many names and visualizing their faces every night. He won't break the habit, he says, until his mind won't let him go on anymore. "I have to keep doing it."

It's not only in nightly prayer that Cliff and Martha Jane see their family. For one, they've surprised all and become Instagram users, getting a virtual daily dose of their grandkids' lives no matter how far they live—from Kansas City in the west to Indianapolis in the middle to Charlotte and Washington, D.C. in the east. And their phone rings off the hook from family and friends: a caller can expect a busy tone more often than a ring tone.

Life in Richmond, of course, keeps them much busier. Their calendar is packed with the grandkids' sporting events, recitals, plays, and graduations. Even when the couple is at home, they're occupied. Someone is always visiting at Grandma and Grandpa's, or Mom and Dad's—whether they've come to do some yardwork or for a long afternoon chat. Grandma gives a hug and offers a sweet treat, invariably turning an initially hesitant "no" into a well-if-you-insist "yes." Grandpa goes for a bear-claw handshake and recounts a story from the old days. Surprisingly, the tale hasn't been heard before, yet unsurprisingly, it is endlessly entertaining. The visitors stay longer than intended, but they're glad they did. And when it finally comes time to go, the old couple walks out onto the back porch made by Clifford's own hands, watches the young family pile into the car, and keeps on waving good-bye until the car rounds the winding driveway and slips out of sight.

Every time Cliff and Martha Jane walk through St. Andrew's Cemetery to visit friends and family, they come to Floyd's tombstone. "Drive On," it says. That was Floyd's phrase, something he learned at age 19 when he lost his father and assumed responsibility for the ten people living off his family farm.

"Drive On" might as well be Clifford Dickman's motto too. Age may have limited his physical ability, but it hasn't limited his self-motivated duty to drive on with the business of life: persisting through rough days, giving his best to the people around him. He drives on in running the old Webster farm of his youth and in keeping alive the spirited debates of his cigar group. He drives on with his nightly prayer list, and he drives on being the best husband, father, grandfather, and great-grandfather that he can. Why? Because he doesn't know any other way. For it's not only the man that has made the record, but the record that has made the man. And if Clifford Dickman's life and times enable us to predict anything with certainty, it's that he will keep on driving until the job is done right, and to see what's in store for him next.

As each new morning breaks, Clifford and Martha Jane stand in awe of the years that have unfolded, and they are thankful for the gift of one more day. Each person that walks through their front door is still a treasure, and each challenge that awaits them remains an adventure. It is that final verse of Clifford's favorite hymn that manifests, more truly and eloquently than anything else, their daily prayer of unending gratitude:

Mine is the sunlight, mine is the morning,
Born of the one light Eden saw play.
Praise with elation, praise every morning,
God's re-creation of the new day! [35]

August 20, 2005
Clifford and Martha Jane celebrate their 50th wedding
anniversary.

AFTERWORD

After more than 65 years of marriage, some of Clifford and Martha Jane Dickman's traditions have ended, while new ones have been born. The tradition of gathering the entire family for Christmas, however, remains as sacrosanct as their first Christmas as a married couple in 1955.

And so, on the Saturday before Christmas, four generations of Dickmans gather to celebrate. Now too large of a get-together for anyone's house, the party is held in the old Kesslers building in downtown Richmond. The shelves may be empty and the hanger racks may not have any clothes, but in many ways, the store still feels like a second home. The one-time retail floor is filled with some of Cliff and Martha Jane's favorite relics from days past: a Baldwin electric organ, a bumper-pool table, and a pair of overstuffed recliners. And if home is where family is, then on this day, home is at Kesslers, for the room is jam-packed with children, grandchildren, and great-grand-children who have traveled from far and wide to be there.

Like any large family gathering, it's a scene of chaos, nostalgia, and joy. The tiny great-grandchildren marvel at Santa's sleigh in the display window, while their school-aged siblings chase each other up and down the

255

warehouse ramps and try to sneak onto the rickety elevator. The grandkids of the family, now in their 20s and 30s, reminisce with their cousins about the old days racing each other around like that, and they opt for an equally spirited game of bumper pool instead. The eight Dickman children split their time between teasing their siblings and holding their newborn grandchildren. Some things never change, while others change quite a lot.

Clifford and Martha Jane hold court in the center of the room. The little ones present them with their crayon-colored drawings, the young adults come up for a hug and a story, the older ones look on with amazement at the life and legacy of their own mom and dad. Yet at that moment, no one knows a deeper happiness than the couple who started it all. They've lived and grown with some of the people in the room for more than 60 years; others, they've met for the first time that very day. It doesn't matter. They are convinced that every effort, every prayer from the very beginning has been for each one gathered.

At last, someone announces that it's time to eat dinner. Everyone circles up, squeezed in shoulder-to-shoulder to make room for each of the 100-and-counting Dickmans. They go around one by one: announcing their big news for the year, offering thanksgiving for some blessing in their lives, or simply giving the group a little levity. Then, they all bow their heads and pray the grace: "Bless us, O Lord, and these thy gifts, which we are about to receive, from thy bounty, through Christ our Lord. Amen." *From thy bounty....*

All eyes turn to the patriarch and matriarch. Martha Jane takes her husband's forearm, squeezes, and gives him a knowing look. Clifford gazes slowly around the circle and thinks back to how it all began: a tenderloin sandwich with his one and only belle on a spring day in 1948.

He shakes his head at the bountiful circle that is his family, the greatest wonder that life has to offer. "I tell you," he says with a widening smile, "we have been so blessed."

ACKNOWLEDGEMENTS

This book wouldn't have been possible without the help of many dedicated family members, friends, and mentors. My first thanks go to my grandparents, Clifford and Martha Jane Dickman, who dedicated countless hours to sharing their stories with me. The whole range of human emotion was on display in these chats—triumph and defeat, happiness and sadness, humor and frustration. I will treasure these conversations for the rest of my life. The greatest hope I have for this book is that it does justice to these two individuals, who are the very models of life well lived.

I must also say a grateful word about my maternal grandparents, Richard and Mary Siebert (Pops and Grammie). Though not the subject of a book, this one could not have come about without them. You can't enjoy writing unless you enjoy reading, and my love for reading came from Pops; I like to believe he would have enjoyed this one about his great friend Clifford. Equally important in writing nonfiction is the ability to carry on an interview, press for more detail, and follow up when necessary; I can't help but think I learned those skills from Grammie.

My parents, Phil and Millie Dickman, were my biggest cheerleaders—as they usually are. From the first time I suggested the idea for this book in November 2019, they have been unequivocal supporters of it, and along the way, they provided much-needed encouragement, ideas, wisdom, and displays of interest. There are many reasons why I am proud to be a member of this family; I wouldn't have taken on this project otherwise. They are reasons #1 and #2.

THE MAN, THE RECORD

Thanks are owed to Cliff and Martha Jane's kids and their spouses, who are my aunts and uncles. They gave their own time for interviews, which were both entertaining and moving. My aunt, Debbie Hanneman, recorded a video interview of Cliff and Martha Jane in 2005 for their 50th wedding anniversary, which provided much helpful material for Chapter 7. I'm also grateful to my cousin, Emily Land, for assembling a Christmas video compilation of the Dickman grandchildren's favorite things about Grandma and Grandpa. My cousins' reflections provided much of the inspiration for the final chapter and the afterword.

There's an old saying that journalists write the first draft of history. I am now completely convinced this is true. This project flourished thanks to the diligent work of the *Palladium-Item*'s reporters over the second half of the twentieth century. I am beholden to them for so fastidiously documenting Richmond's history and Clifford Dickman's years as mayor.

Whatever writing skill I may have has been honed by professors, teachers, and peers. I am indebted to all of them for investing so much in me. More particularly for this project, I'm very grateful to my editor and friend Rebecca Devine, who brought tremendously helpful insights to the table and stripped my first draft of its excessive wordiness—all while moving into a new house and raising her two young daughters.

To anyone who knows me, it will come as no surprise that my wife Allyson Dickman was instrumental. Like my parents, she was a strong advocate for this project when I was first considering it, and for over two years, she has sacrificed nights and weekends for me to research, interview, write, and edit. Whenever I had doubts or spells of burnout, she pushed me forward. She weighed in on everything—from helping me organize the general direction of the book, to meticulously editing out my many typos, to composing the exact turn of phrase I needed to round out a sentence, to designing the cover. All this, while she was pregnant with and raising our son Arthur. As in life, Ally was my trusty partner in writing this book.

My final and greatest thanks go to Almighty God. As with any good endeavor, it would not have been possible without him.

Henry J. Dickman
March 26, 2022

NOTES

Introduction

[1] Wilson D. Miscamble, C.S.C., *American Priest: The Ambitious Life and Conflicted Legacy of Notre Dame's Father Ted Hesburgh* (New York: Image, 2019).

[2] Theodore Roosevelt, "The Strenuous Life" (speech, Chicago, Ill., Apr. 10, 1899), Voices of Democracy, https://voicesofdemocracy.umd.edu/roosevelt-strenuous-life-1899-speech-text/.

[3] Aristotle, W.D. Ross and Lesley Brown eds., *The Nicomachean Ethics* (Oxford: Oxford University Press, 2009), Book II, Ch. 6; Harvey C. Mansfield, *Manliness* (New Haven: Yale University Press, 2006).

Chapter 1: The Farm

[1] *Tebbe Family Tree, 1800–2016*, 1 (on file with author).

[2] Chris Flook, "One of Indiana's Oldest Towns, Let Oldenburg Charm You," Sep. 18, 2017, https://visitindiana.com/blog/index.php/2017/09/18/oldenburg-a-village-of-spires/.

[3] Clemens Dickman. *1910*; Census Place: *Ray, Franklin, Indiana*; Roll: *T624_350*; Page: *8B*; Enumeration District: *0048*; FHL microfilm: 1374363.

[4] *Tebbe Family Tree, 1800–2016*, 3–5 (on file with author).

[5] "Will Probated," *Palladium-Item*, May 22, 1953.

[6] Jim Cox, *Webster, Indiana* (Indianapolis: Dog Ear Publishing, 2012), 1–5.

[7] Dick Reynolds, "Congressional Quest Began With a Question," *Palladium-Item*, Dec. 6, 1981.

[8] Ibid.

[9] Ibid.

[10] "7 Killed One Day in State," *Franklin Evening Star*, Sep. 5, 1942; Obituary, "Joseph Henry Dickman," *Palladium-Item*, Sep. 8, 1942.

[11] Jim Cox, *Webster, Indiana* (Indianapolis: Dog Ear Publishing, 2012), 22–23.

[12] "Williamsburg's Second Half Rally Beats Webster 53–47," *Palladium-Item*, Feb. 27, 1948.

[13] See, e.g., "Webster Trips Economy Five," *Palladium-Item*, Feb. 14, 1946.

[14] Max Knight, "Father, Son Had Impressive Playing, Coaching Careers," *Palladium-Item*, Feb. 10, 1998.

15 "Average of 63 Points a Game Wins County Title for Giants," *Palladium-Item*, Feb. 26, 1947; "County Cage Tourney Opens Tonight With 2-Game Schedule," *Palladium-Item*, Jan. 16, 1947.

16 Max Knight, "Father, Son Had Impressive Playing, Coaching Careers," *Palladium-Item*, Feb. 10, 1998.

17 "Bulldogs Nip Pirates, 45–43," *Palladium-Item*, Nov. 2, 1947.

18 Dale Stevens, "Dickman Tourney's Top Scorer," *Palladium-Item*, Jan. 27, 1948; "Wayne County High School Basketball Schedules," *Palladium-Item*, Oct. 21, 1947.

19 Dale Stevens, "Fountain City Grabs Tourney; Webster Winner in Consolation," *Palladium-Item*, Jan. 25, 1948.

20 "Cambridge City, Williamsburg, Webster Win Final Loop Tilts," *Palladium-Item*, Feb. 22, 1948.

21 "Williamsburg's Second Half Rally Beats Webster 53–47," *Palladium-Item*, Feb. 27, 1948.

22 Jim Cox, *Webster, Indiana* (Indianapolis: Dog Ear Publishing, 2012), 22.

Chapter 2: Richmond

1 Thomas D. Hamm, *Earlham College: A History, 1847–1997* (Indianapolis: Indiana University Press, 1997), 1–2 (hereinafter *Earlham College*).

2 "History of Richmond & Wayne County, Indiana." Waynet. Accessed Apr. 19, 2020, https://www.waynet.org/facts/history.htm.

3 John Williams Buys, "Quakers in Indiana in the Nineteenth Century," Ph.D. dissertation (University of Florida, 1973), 8.

4 "Members of Indiana's 1816 Constitutional Convention." Indiana Historical Bureau. Accessed Mar. 15, 2021, https://www.in.gov/history/for-educators/download-issues-of-the-indiana-historian/indiana-statehood/members-of-indianas-1816-constitutional-convention/.

5 "History of Richmond & Wayne County, Indiana." Waynet. Accessed Apr. 19, 2020, https://www.waynet.org/facts/history.htm.

6 Mary Raddant Tomlan & Michael A. Tomlan, *Richmond, Indiana: Its Physical Development and Aesthetic Heritage to 1920* (Indianapolis: Indiana Historical Society Press, Indianapolis, 2003), 2, 15–16.

7 Ibid, 15–18.

8 Ibid, 36–37.

9 "Richmond Railroad Depot Historic District." Waynet. Accessed Apr. 19, 2020, https://www.waynet.org/nonprofit/depot.htm (last visited Apr. 19, 2020); "National Register of Historic Places Registration Form: Forest Hills Country Club," 18, Oct. 30, 2015, https://www.nps.gov/nr/feature/places/15000892.htm.

[10] Mary Raddant Tomlan & Michael A. Tomlan, *Richmond, Indiana: Its Physical Development and Aesthetic Heritage to 1920* (Indianapolis: Indiana Historical Society Press, Indianapolis, 2003), 19.

[11] "Gaar Mansion and Farm Museum." Waynet. Accessed Apr. 19, 2020, https://www.waynet.org/nonprofit/gaar_mansion.htm; "Gaar, Scott & Company." Morrisson-Reeves Library. Accessed Apr. 19, 2020, https://mrlinfo.org/history/business/gaarscott.htm.

[12] Mike Emery, "Retro Richmond: Once Known as the Lawn Mower Capital of the World," *Palladium-Item*, Sep. 24, 2018.

[13] "Wayne Works," Morrisson-Reeves Library. Accessed Apr. 19, 2020, https://mrlinfo.org/history/business/wayneworks.htm.

[14] "Hoosier Drill." Morrison-Reeves Library. Accessed Apr. 20, 2020, https://mrlinfo.org/history/business/hoosierdrill.htm.

[15] Mary Raddant Tomlan & Michael A. Tomlan, *Richmond, Indiana: Its Physical Development and Aesthetic Heritage to 1920* (Indianapolis: Indiana Historical Society Press, Indianapolis, 2003), 72–73.

[16] "Starr, Antique Piano Shop." Accessed Apr. 19, 2020, https://antique-pianoshop.com/online-museum/starr/.

[17] Thomas D. Hamm, *Earlham College: A History, 1847–1997* (Indianapolis: Indiana University Press, 1997), 1, 12.

[18] Ibid, xi, 1, 11–12, 32.

[19] "Levi Coffin." *Encyclopedia Britannica*, October 24, 2020. https://www.britannica.com/ biography/Levi-Coffin.

[20] George T. Blakey, "The Year Richmond, Indiana, Got Lost in the Census: 1850 as a Demographic Dilemma," *Indiana Magazine of History*, 36, no. 1 (1998): 43.

[21] James Clyde Sellman, "Social Movements and the Symbolism of Public Demonstrations: The 1874 Women's Crusade and German Resistance in Richmond, Indiana," *Journal of Social History*, 32, no. 3 (1999): 562–63.

[22] Ibid.

[23] This move engendered violence from the offended residents of Centerville. *See* "Hot Blood in Indiana," *New York Times*, Nov. 1, 1873.

[24] A. James Fuller, "Oliver P Morton and Civil War Politics in Indiana." Indiana Historical Bureau. Accessed Mar. 16, 2021, https://www.in.gov/history/about-indiana-history-and-trivia/annual-commemorations/civil-war-150th/hoosier-voices-now/oliver-p-morton-and-civil-war-politics-in-indiana/; "Oliver P. Morton." Morrisson-Reeves Library. Accessed Mar. 16, 2021, https://mrlinfo.org/history/biography/ mortonop.htm.

[25] "Oliver H. P. T. Morton." *Encyclopedia Britannica*, October 28, 2020. https://www.britannica.com/biography/Oliver-H-P-T-Morton; Michael W. McConnell, "Originalism and the Desegregation Decisions," 81 VA. L. REV. 947, 998, 1006 (1995); Steve Martin, "A Look Back at Richmond's Civil War Regiments," *Palladium-Item*, Jan.

11, 2015; Steve Martin, "Out of Our Past: Tales from the Civil War," *Palladium-Item*, Jan. 25, 2015.

[26] "Calvin Coolidge." Morrisson-Reeves Library. Accessed Mar. 16, 2021, https://mrlinfo.org/famous-visitors/calvin-coolidge.htm; "Dwight D. Eisenhower." Morrisson-Reeves Library. Accessed Mar. 16, 2021, https://mrlinfo.org/famous-visitors/Eisenhower.htm; "Franklin D. Roosevelt." Morrisson-Reeves Library. Accessed Mar. 16, 2021, https://mrlinfo.org/famous-visitors/Franklin-Roosevelt.htm; Steve Martin, "Out of Our Past: Truman Came to Richmond to Pick 'Madonna' Site, Returned as President," *Palladium-Item*, Sep. 11, 2020; "Ulysses S. Grant." Morrisson-Reeves Library. Accessed Mar. 16, 2021, https://mrlinfo.org/famous-visitors/Ulysses-Grant.htm; "William Howard Taft." Morrisson-Reeves Library. Accessed Mar. 16, 2021, https://mrlinfo.org/famous-visitors/WilliamHoward-Taft.htm; "Woodrow Wilson." Morrisson-Reeves Library. Accessed Mar. 16, 2021, https://mrlinfo.org/famous-visitors/Woodrow-Wilson.htm.

[27] Steve Martin, "Out of Our Past: President Benjamin Harrison Made Multiple Visits to Richmond," *Palladium-Item*, July 12, 2020.

[28] Steve Martin, "Out of Our Past: Teddy Roosevelt Paid at Least 6 Visits to Richmond – But Slept Through 1," *Palladium-Item*, July 31, 2020.

[29] Jill Weiss Simins, "The Lincoln Funeral Train in Indiana." Indiana History Blog. Accessed Mar. 25, 2021, https://blog.history.in.gov/the-lincoln-funeral-train-in-indiana/; Steve Martin, "Out of Our Past: Crowds Gathered to Mourn Where Lincoln's Funeral Train Stopped," *Palladium-Item*, Apr. 29, 2018.

[30] "Rutherford B. Hayes." Morrisson-Reeves Library. Accessed Mar. 16, 2021, https://mrlinfo.org/famous-visitors/Rutherford-Hayes.htm.

[31] Leonard S. Kenworthy, "Henry Clay at Richmond in 1842," *Indiana Magazine of History*, 30, no. 4 (1934): 353–59.

[32] "Frederick Douglass." Morrisson-Reeves Library. Accessed Mar. 16, 2021, https://mrlinfo.org/famous-visitors/Frederick_Douglass.htm.

[33] "Susan B. Anthony." Morrisson-Reeves Library. Accessed Mar. 16, 2021, https://mrlinfo.org/famous-visitors/susan-anthony.htm.

[34] Clifton J. Phillips, *Indiana in Transition: The Emergence of an Industrial Commonwealth, 1880–1920* (Indianapolis: Indiana Historical Bureau & Indiana Historical Society, 1968), 295.

[35] Mike Emery, "Retro Richmond: Once Known as the Lawn Mower Capital of the World," *Palladium-Item*, Sep. 24, 2018.

[36] Michael A. Banks, "War Wheels: Richmond, Indiana and World War II," *Traces of Indiana and Midwestern History*, 27, no. 2 (2014); "Wayne Works," Morrisson-Reeves Library. Accessed Apr. 19, 2020, https://mrlinfo.org/history/business/wayneworks.htm.

[37] "Hoosier Drill." Morrison-Reeves Library. Accessed Apr. 20, 2020, https://mrlinfo.org/history/business/hoosierdrill.htm.

38 "Richmond Baking Company." Morrisson-Reeves Library. Accessed Mar. 19, 2021, https://mrlinfo.org/history/business/richmondbaking.htm.

39 "About Wayne County." Accessed Apr. 20, 2020, https://visitrichmond.org/visitors/welcome/about-wayne-county; "Number of U.S. Million-aires and Value of $1 Million in Dollars of the Year 2002 for Selected Years 1848 to 1988." Accessed Apr. 20, 2020, https://liberalarts.oregonstate.edu/sites/liberalarts.oregonstate.edu/files/polisci/faculty-research/sahr/inflation-conversion/pdf/number-of-us-million-aires.pdf.

40 Leonard Joseph Moore, *Citizen Klansman: The Ku Klux Klan in Indiana, 1921–1928* (Chapel Hill: University of North Carolina Press, 1991), 111.

41 "Daniel Gray Reid." Morrisson-Reeves Library. Accessed Mar. 17, 2021, https://mrlinfo.org/history/biography/reiddg.htm; "Our History." *Reid Health.* Accessed Mar. 17, 2021, https://www.reidhealth.org/ about/our-history. The bulk of the contribution for Reid Hospital came from Daniel Reid, a Richmond native who moved to New York and made a fortune in the tin-plating industry. Richmond citizens nonetheless helped to finance the construction.

42 George T. Blakey, "The Year Richmond, Indiana, Got Lost in the Census: 1850 as a Demographic Dilemma," *Indiana Magazine of History*, 36, no. 1 (1998): 44; "Indiana City/Town Census Counts, 1900 to 2010." StatsIndiana. Accessed Mar. 16, 2021, https://www.stats.indiana.edu/ population/PopTotals/historic_counts_cities.asp.

43 "Indiana City/Town Census Counts, 1900 to 2010." StatsIndiana. Accessed Mar. 16, 2021, https://www.stats.indiana.edu/ population/PopTotals/historic_counts_cities.asp.

44 Leonard Joseph Moore, *Citizen Klansman: The Ku Klux Klan in Indiana, 1921–1928* (Chapel Hill: University of North Carolina Press, 1991), 108, 115–19.

45 "Starr Piano Company." Morrisson-Reeves Library. Accessed Apr. 19, 2020. https://mrlinfo.org/history/business/starrpiano_bus.htm. Many of these names appear on the Gennett Records Walk of Fame in the Gorge today.

46 "Gennett Records: The Little Studio That Could." Riverwalk Jazz. Accessed Mar. 16, 2021, https://riverwalkjazz.stanford.edu/?q= program/gennett-records-little-studio-could.

47 Ibid.

48 "William Jennings Bryan." Starr-Gennett Foundation. Accessed Mar. 16, 2021, http://www.starrgennett.org/william-jennings-bryan/.

49 "Hill's Floral Products." Morrisson-Reeves Library. Accessed Apr. 20, 2020, https://mrlinfo.org/history/business/hillfloral.htm.

[50] Leonard Joseph Moore, *Citizen Klansman: The Ku Klux Klan in Indiana, 1921–1928* (Chapel Hill: University of North Carolina Press, 1991), 112–13.

Chapter 3: Martha Jane

[1] J. Scott Keltie, *The Statesman's Year-Book* 1016 (1908).

[2] *Passenger and Crew Lists of Vessels Arriving at New York, New York, 1897–1957.* Microfilm Publication T715, 8892 rolls. NAI: 300346. Records of the Immigration and Naturalization Service; National Archives at Washington, D.C.

[3] Ibid.

[4] "Given Citizenship Papers," *Richmond Item*, Sep. 26, 1931.

[5] 1930; Census Place: *Richmond, Wayne, Indiana*; Page: *9B*; Enumeration District: *0034*; FHL microfilm: *2340372*.

[6] "The Perfect Circle Co." Waynet. Accessed Mar. 15, 2021, https://www.waynet.org/waynet/spotlight/2003/030521-perfectcircle.htm.

Chapter 4: Earlham

[1] Thomas D. Hamm, *Earlham College: A History, 1847–1997* (Indianapolis: Indiana University Press, 1997), 177.

[2] Ibid, 171–74.

[3] Ibid, 181.

[4] Ibid, 183.

[5] Ibid, 178.

[6] Ibid.

[7] Ibid, 182–83.

[8] Ibid, 226–27.

[9] Ibid, 186.

[10] Ibid.

[11] D. Elton Trueblood, *While It Is Day: An Autobiography*, (New York: Harper and Row, 1974), 52.

[12] *Earlham College*, 187–88.

[13] 141 *Cong. Rec.* S1872 (1995).

[14] Ibid, 196.

[15] Ibid, 218–19.

[16] Ibid, 213–14.

[17] Ibid, 221–24.

[18] Ibid, 217–21.

[19] "41 Candidates Turn Out for Quaker Eleven," *Palladium-Item*, Sep. 6, 1949.

[20] "Earlham Grid Practices in Full Swing, *Palladium-Item*, Sep. 7, 1949.

[21] Don Cumley to Clifford Dickman, undated.

22 Dale Stevens, "Crippled Quaker Gridders Face Rose Here Saturday Afternoon, *Palladium-Item*, Oct. 29, 1949.

23 "Cliff Dickman, Stan Huntsman Are Honored," *Palladium-Item*, Oct. 20, 1952; "Name Dickman Most Valuable, Honorary Quaker Grid Captain," *Palladium-Item*, Nov. 12, 1952.

24 Herb Wass, "Whites Drub Maroons 32–0 in Display of Earlham College Football Power," *Palladium-Item*, Sep. 14, 1952.

25 "Helfrich Loses Finger After Freak Injury," *Palladium-Item*, Nov. 24, 1949.

26 "Earlham Defeats Canterbury in 50–48 Game; Dickman High," *Palladium-Item*, Jan. 18, 1950.

27 Herb Wass, "Dickman, Moore Lead Earlham to 53–52 Win over Hanover," *Palladium-Item*, Feb. 21, 1951.

28 Herb Wass, "DePauw Noses Out Earlham 44 to 35, In Close Contest," *Palladium-Item*, Dec. 10, 1950.

29 Dick Shellenberger, "Shellouts," *Earlham Post*, Mar. 4, 1952.

30 "Earlham Honor Given Moore and Dickman, *Palladium-Item*, Mar. 18, 1953.

31 "15 Richmond Athletes Enter State AAU Meet," *Palladium-Item*, June 5, 1953; "Earlham Thinlies Defeat Hanover; Goens Stars, *Palladium-Item*, Apr. 19, 1953.

32 "Clifford Dickman," Earlham College, accessed Feb. 23, 2021, https://goearlham.com/honors/hall-of-fame/clifford-dickman/44/kiosk.

33 "Sports Roundup," *Palladium-Item*, May 31, 1953.

34 *Earlham College*, 203–05.

35 "Hill's Floral Products," *Morrisson-Reeves Library*, accessed Feb. 23, 2021, https://mrlinfo.org/history/business/hillfloral.htm.

36 "Earlham Students Plan Annual Geology Field Trip Apr. 3–10, *Palladium-Item*, Apr. 2, 1951.

37 "Oil Fields, Mines to Be Seen This Week by Earlham Class," *Palladium-Item*, Apr. 13, 1952.

38 *Earlham College*, 230.

39 Earlham College, *Sargasso 1953 Yearbook* (Richmond, IN: 1953), 156.

40 Dudley Clendinen, "East, A Senator from Carolina, A Suicide at 55," *New York Times*, June 30, 1986.

41 "Steve Marble, Jim Fowler, Naturalist Who Brought Animals to TV on 'Wild Kingdom,' Dies at 89," *Los Angeles Times*, May 9, 2019.

42 Earlham College, *Sargasso 1953 Yearbook* (Richmond, IN: 1953), 65. The yearbook mistakenly called him "Glubber" rather than "Glover." I have corrected the spelling error.

Chapter 5: The Army

1 "Engagements Are Announced," *Palladium-Item*, Aug. 30, 1953.

2 "In the Service," *Palladium-Item*, Dec. 14, 1953.

[3] Millett, A. R. "Korean War," Armistice, *Encyclopedia Britannica*, Sep. 10, 2020. https://www.britannica.com/event/Korean-War/Armistice.
[4] Jody Peacock, "Dickman Has Good 'Shot' for Gold Medal," *Palladium-Item*, June 4, 1993.
[5] Donald A. Carter, "Forging the Shield: The U.S. Army in Europe 1951–1962," (Center of Military History: Washington, D.C., 2015), 1, 15.
[6] Ibid, 58–63.
[7] Yvonne Lanhers, "St. Joan of Arc," *Encyclopedia Britannica*, May 26, 2001, https://www.britannica.com/biography/Saint-Joan-of-Arc.
[8] Obituary, "James D. Stone ('Jim')," *Herald Bulletin*, Jan. 1, 2021.

Chapter 6: Putting Down Roots

[1] "Dickman-Luerman Rites Read in Pretty Church Ceremony," *Palladium-Item*, Aug. 21, 1955.
[2] Ibid.
[3] Jim Cox, *Webster, Indiana* (Indianapolis: Dog Ear Publishing, 2012), 24.
[4] Obituary for "Whitey" Kessler, *Palladium-Item*, May 3, 1959.
[5] "'Whitey' Kessler Gets Gimbel Honor," *Richmond Item*, Mar. 16, 1924.
[6] "'Whitey' Kessler Announces the Opening of His Sports Shop," *Richmond Item*, Apr. 27, 1934.
[7] Dick Reynolds, "Congressional Quest Began with a Question," *Palladium-Item*, Dec. 6, 1981.
[8] Obituary, "Whitey" Kessler, *Palladium-Item*, May 3, 1959.
[9] Max Knight, "Former Referee Mitrione Maintains Positive Outlook Despite Illness," *Palladium-Item*, Apr. 21, 1997.
[10] "Dan Mitrione Loved His Work, His Family and His Home Town," *Palladium-Item*, Aug. 11, 1970; "Mitrione One of 58 Police Advisers in Latin America," *Palladium-Item*, Aug. 7, 1970.
[11] Former Local Police Chief's Body Found in Stolen Car," *Palladium-Item*, Aug. 10, 1970.
[12] Carlos Osorio & Marianna Enamoneta, "To Save Dan Mitrione Nixon Administration Urged Death Threats for Uruguayan Prisoners," National Security Archive, Aug. 11, 2010, https://nsarchive2.gwu.edu/NSAEBB/NSAEBB324/index.htm; "Sens. Hartke, Bayh Send Appeal for Release of Mitrione by Rebels," *Palladium-Item*, Aug. 9, 1970.
[13] "Mitrione's Family, Friends Pray for His Life, Rescue," *Palladium-Item*, Aug. 9, 1970.
[14] "Former Local Police Chief's Body Found in Stolen Car," *Palladium-Item*, Aug. 10, 1970.
[15] "'Callous Murder,' Nixon Says of Mitrione Death," *Palladium-Item*, Aug. 11, 1970.

16 "Mitrione Family Receives Messages from Across U.S.," *Palladium-Item*, Aug. 11, 1970.

17 "Addio Caro Amico for Dan Mitrione," *Palladium-Item*, Aug. 14, 1970.

18 "Frank Sinatra to Stage Benefit Here for Mitrione Children," *Palladium-Item*, Aug. 21, 1970.

19 Ed Kaeuper, "Mitrione Fund Still Helps Educate Family's Children," *Palladium-Item*, Dec. 7, 1980; Mary Agnes Starr & Don Fasnacht, "Sinatra, Lewis Perform to Aid Mitrione Children," *Palladium-Item*, Aug. 30, 1970.

Chapter 7: The Dickmans

1 Though the quote has not definitively been traced to Chesterton, many attribute it to him nonetheless. See, e.g., Jenni Simmons, "The Small Things," *Curator Magazine*, Apr. 10, 2009 (quoting Chesterton).

2 Martha Jane provided these descriptions in a video interview recorded by Debbie Hanneman for the couple's 50th wedding anniversary.

3 Obituary, "Margaretta K. Bradway," *Palladium-Item*, June 29, 1992.

4 Obituary, "Merle V. Bradway," *Palladium-Item*, Jan. 11, 1980.

5 Theodore Roosevelt, *Theodore Roosevelt: An Autobiography*. (New York: Charles Scribner's Sons, 1920), 7–8.

Chapter 8: Man of the Community

1 Arthur C. Brooks, "A Formula for Happiness," *New York Times*, Dec. 14, 2013; see also Charles Murray, *Coming Apart* (New York: Crown Forum, 2012), 259–67.

2 Neil Postman, *Amusing Ourselves to Death* (New York: Penguin Books, 1985).

3 See, e.g., Robert D. Putnam, *Bowling Alone: The Collapse and Revival of American Community* (New York: Simon & Schuster, 2000), 54–64.

4 Dick Reynolds, "Congressional Quest Began with a Question," *Palladium-Item*, Dec. 6, 1981.

5 "Mall Planners Are Selected," *Palladium-Item*, Jan. 18, 1970; Richard Holden, "Retailers Credit Promenade with Business Upturn," *Palladium-Item*, June 18, 1974.

6 "Church Groups: Parish Council (Holy Family)," *Palladium-Item*, Jan. 15, 1972.

7 Florence Lawson, "New Holy Family Church to Be Built," *Palladium-Item*, Aug. 16, 1977.

8 "Players on Sectional Teams Hear Miami's Net Coach," *Palladium-Item*, Feb. 19, 1965.

[9] W.R. Emslie, "Advisory Committee Is Named by Mayor," *Palladium-Item*, Mar. 26, 1964.

[10] Max Moss, "Jaycees Pick Cliff Dickman As 'Outstanding Young Man,'" *Palladium-Item*, Apr. 4, 1965.

[11] Jan Clark, "Flatley Comes Home to Richmond, 300 Honor Him at Testimonial," *Palladium-Item*, Feb. 20, 1972.

[12] "First Chamber of Commerce Board of 18 Is Elected," *Palladium-Item*, Dec. 19, 1965.

[13] Max Moss, "Jaycees Pick Cliff Dickman As 'Outstanding Young Man,'" *Palladium-Item*, Apr. 4, 1965.

[14] Advertisement, "Cliff Dickman: Republican Candidate for Wayne County Representative in the Indiana Legislature," *Palladium-Item*, Apr. 5, 1964; Max Knight, "Two Richmond Teams in Wayne Co. Finals," *Palladium-Item*, Aug. 9, 1956.

[15] "General Gifts Division Leaders in Townsend Center Fund Drive," *Palladium-Item*, Feb. 24, 1963.

[16] "Dickman Is Chairman of Multiple Sclerosis Drive," *Palladium-Item*, May 10, 1964.

[17] Ibid.

[18] Ibid.

[19] "Pick Dickman to Head OEO Head Start Advisory Group," *Palladium-Item*, Feb. 28, 1968.

[20] "United Fund Workers Honored," *Palladium-Item*, Jan. 28, 1970.

[21] "Mental Health Gathering Planned May 19 at Liberty," *Palladium-Item*, May 13, 1970.

[22] "County Junior Achievement Firm Rated Among Top 100 in Nation," *Palladium-Item*, June 10, 1970.

[23] "Commissioners Pick Dickman As Successor to Eggemeyer," *Palladium-Item*, Jan. 23, 1967.

[24] Max Moss, "Jaycees Pick Cliff Dickman As 'Outstanding Young Man,'" *Palladium-Item*, Apr. 4, 1965.

[25] Ibid.

[26] "Group Working to Promote Interest in Food Stamps," *Palladium-Item*, June 12, 1970.

[27] Max Knight, "Olympic Team Fund Drive Starts," *Palladium-Item*, Aug. 29, 1967.

[28] "Commissioners Pick Dickman As Successor to Eggemeyer," *Palladium-Item*, Jan. 23, 1967.

[29] "Group Will Study Applications for Civil Defense Director Post," *Palladium-Item*, Oct. 9, 1969.

[30] "Nursing Association Elects Officers, Considers Clinic," *Palladium-Item*, Dec. 4, 1969.

[31] "3 Local Men Named to Boy Scout Offices," *Palladium-Item*, June 15, 1975.

32 Max Knight, "Former Referee Mitrione Maintains Positive Outlook Despite Illness," *Palladium-Item*, Apr. 21, 1997.

33 Ibid.

34 Max Knight, "Dickman's Been Around Sports Block a Few Times," *Palladium-Item*, Feb. 3, 1997.

35 Linda C. Gugin & James E. St. Clair, *The Governors of Indiana* (Indianapolis: Indiana Historical Society, 2006), 338–39.

36 Advertisement, "Cliff Dickman, Republican for Wayne Representative," *Palladium-Item*, Apr. 26, 1964.

37 "More Expenses Are Filed for Primary Election," *Palladium-Item*, June 3, 1964.

38 "Close Legislative Race Won by Waltz," *Palladium-Item*, May 6, 1964; "GOP Representatives' Vote," *Palladium-Item*, May 6, 1964.

39 "Cloud and Waltz Winners in 4-Way Legislature Race," *Palladium-Item*, May 4, 1966.

40 "Commissioners Pick Dickman As Successor to Eggemeyer, *Palladium-Item*, Jan. 23, 1967.

41 Association of Indiana Counties, Here When You Need It: County Government, May 2009, https://www.indianacounties.org/egov/documents/1251296396_485260.pdf.

42 Fred S. Lord, "County Asked to Help Pay for '75 Landfill Operation," *Palladium-Item*, Aug. 6, 1974; Richard Holden, "County Weighs Landfill Near Present Location," *Palladium-Item*, Oct. 16, 1973.

43 "Commissioners Await Word from State Election Board on Voting Machines," *Palladium-Item*, Feb. 29, 1972; "State Election Board Gives OK for Votomatic Machines Here," *Palladium-Item*, Mar. 1, 1972.

44 Advertisement, "Why Oppose the Master Plan for Wayne County?," *Palladium-Item*, Mar. 14, 1967.

45 Fred S. Lord, "Public Balloting on Master Plan Urged; Commissioners Doubt Law Permits Voting," *Palladium-Item*, Apr. 12, 1967.

46 Richard Holden, "County Planning 8-Story Building," *Palladium-Item*, Jan. 23, 1974.

47 See, e.g., Clifford J. Dickman, "If Government Watches Its Step Press Should Watch Its 'Line,'" *Palladium-Item*, Mar. 3, 1979; C. David Mogollon & Samantha Shook, "Leaders Want More Positive News," *Palladium-Item*, June 8, 1992.

48 "Final Wayne Co. Returns," *Palladium-Item*, Nov. 6, 1974; "Wayne Co. Final Returns," *Palladium-Item*, Nov. 4, 1970.

49 "16 Perish in Double Explosion and Fires," *Palladium-Item*, Apr. 7, 1968.

50 Dickman was not alone in thinking the city had been bombed. See Ed White, "'Thought We Were Bombed,' Department Store Clerk Says," *Palladium-Item*, Apr. 7, 1968.

51 "Blast Cause Sought As Toll Rises," *Palladium-Item*, Apr. 8, 1968.

[52] Jason Truitt, "Richmond Remembers '68 Explosions," *Palladium-Item*, Apr. 5, 2018.

[53] "Victims on Casualty List," *Palladium-Item*, Apr. 9, 1968.

[54] See, e.g., "16 Killed, 100 Injured in Blast and Big Fire in Richmond, Ind.," *New York Times*, Apr. 7, 1968.

[55] "Robert F. Kennedy." Morrisson-Reeves Library. Accessed Mar. 25, 2021, https://mrlinfo.org/famous-visitors/Robert-Kennedy.htm.

[56] Pub. L. No. 90–481 (1968).

[57] Dick Reynolds, "Memorial for 41 Who Said Last Goodbyes," *Palladium-Item*, Nov. 3, 1978.

Chapter 9: "A Richmond Man for Richmond's Future"

[1] Indiana City/Town Census Counts, 1900–2010," STATS Indiana, accessed July 13, 2020, https://www.stats.indiana.edu/population/PopTotals/historic_ counts_cities.asp.

[2] "Dickman Announces Candidacy for Mayor," *Palladium-Item*, Feb. 17, 1975.

[3] Fred S. Lord, "GOP Sets Sights on City Hall," *Palladium-Item*, May 7, 1975; Fred S. Lord, "GOP Sets Sights on City Hall," *Palladium-Item*, May 7, 1975.

[4] Fred S. Lord, "GOP Sets Sights on City Hall," *Palladium-Item*, May 7, 1975.

[5] Tom Cool, "Short Term, Politics of Current Mayor in Contrast to Pattern of City's Past," *Palladium-Item*, Nov. 27, 1975.

[6] Fred S. Lord, "9 Republican Races; 6 for Democrats in City's Primary Balloting Tuesday," *Palladium-Item*, May 4, 1975.

[7] Jim Fleming, "Klute to Quit; Howell Named Successor," *Palladium-Item*, Jan. 15, 1975.

[8] "Candidate Howell Rejects 'Political Appointee' Label," *Palladium-Item*, Oct. 29, 1975.

[9] Fred S. Lord, "Chairmen of Both Major Parties Claim Victory Ahead in City Election," *Palladium-Item*, Nov. 2, 1975.

[10] "Republicans Seek Backers for Dickman," *Palladium-Item*, Aug. 10, 1975.

[11] "150 Attend GOP Event," *Palladium-Item*, Aug. 13, 1975.

[12] "300 Persons Attend Republican 'Speak Out,'" *Palladium-Item*, Aug. 26, 1975.

[13] John Schroeder, "Dickman Tells FOP He Wants Police, Fire Departments 'Out of Politics,'" *Palladium-Item*, Oct. 9, 1975.

[14] John Schroeder, "No Repeat of 'Minutemen,' Candidates Promise Firemen," *Palladium-Item*, Oct. 23, 1975.

15 Emmett Smelser, "Mayor Candidates List Goals, Priorities—If Elected," *Palladium-Item*, Oct. 19, 1975.

16 Tom Cool, "City Police Morale, Leadership Issues Discussed by Candidates for Mayor," *Palladium-Item*, Oct. 3, 1975.

17 Tom Cool, "Dickman Cites Low Morale, Pledges to Cut 2 Officials," *Palladium-Item*, Sep. 12, 1975.

18 "Dickman's Pledge to Kiwanians: Job-Producing Administration," *Palladium-Item*, Oct. 26, 1975.

19 "Candidate Howell Rejects 'Political Appointee' Label," *Palladium-Item*, Oct. 29, 1975.

20 "Dickman Tells Plans to Boost Employment," *Palladium-Item*, Oct. 10, 1975.

21 "Dickman's Pledge to Kiwanians: Job-Producing Administration," *Palladium-Item*, Oct. 26, 1975.

22 "Dickman Tells Plans to Boost Employment," *Palladium-Item*, Oct. 10, 1975.

23 John Schroeder, "Something Old and Something New As Mayor Candidates Trade Blows," *Palladium-Item*, Oct. 23, 1975.

24 Advertisement, "Cliff Dickman," *Palladium-Item*, Oct. 22, 1975. Emmett Smelser, "Mayor Candidates List Goals, Priorities—If Elected," *Palladium-Item*, Oct. 19, 1975.

25 "Dickman Tells Plans to Boost Employment," *Palladium-Item*, Oct. 10, 1975.

26 "City GOP Candidates Wind Up Campaigns," *Palladium-Item*, Nov. 2, 1975; Tom Cool, "Candidate Dickman Decries Practices of Other Party," *Palladium-Item*, Oct. 29, 1975.

27 Tom Cool, "City Police Morale, Leadership Issues Discussed by Candidates for Mayor," *Palladium-Item*, Oct. 3, 1975.

28 "Sign Something Special," *Palladium-Item*, Sep. 21, 1975.

29 See, e.g., "Dickman Criticizes City Costs," *Palladium-Item*, Oct. 31, 1975.

30 "Busy Schedule Ahead for Local GOP Team," *Palladium-Item*, Oct. 19, 1975.

31 "GOP Shows Set Sunday," *Palladium-Item*, Oct. 9, 1975.

32 John Schroeder, "Something Old and Something New as Mayor Candidates Trade Blows," *Palladium-Item*, Oct. 23, 1975; Richard Holden, "Mayoral Candidates Trade Barbs on Panel Before RHS Students," *Palladium-Item*, Oct. 29, 1975; Tom Cool, "Lions Club Hears Three Candidates Go Over Familiar Ground," *Palladium-Item*, Oct. 30, 1975; "Women Voters Hear Views of Candidates for Mayor," *Palladium-Item*, Sep. 10, 1975.

33 "Dickman Urges Heavy GOP Voter Turnout," *Palladium-Item*, Oct. 15, 1975.

34 Tom Cool, "City Police Morale, Leadership Issues Discussed by Candidates for Mayor," *Palladium-Item*, Oct. 3, 1975.

[35] "Candidate Howell Rejects 'Political Appointee' Label," *Palladium-Item*, Oct. 29, 1975.

[36] Advertisement, "We Endorse Dickman," *Palladium-Item*, Nov. 2, 1975.

[37] Richard Holden, "City Democrats Rally to Theme of 8 Years' Progress," *Palladium-Item*, Aug. 17, 1975.

[38] Ibid.

[39] "Governor Boosts Dickman," *Palladium-Item*, Nov. 3, 1975.

[40] John Schroeder, "Businessmen Told Dickman's Plan for Luring Industry," *Palladium-Item*, Oct. 24, 1975.

[41] D. Elton Trueblood, "Admires Dickman," *Palladium-Item*, Oct. 27, 1975.

[42] Richard Holden, "GOP Head Boosts Dickman, Party," *Palladium-Item*, Oct. 12, 1975.

[43] Advertisement, "To the Voters of Richmond," *Palladium-Item*, Nov. 2, 1975.

[44] Tom Cool, "'It Was Teamwork,' Says Dickman as Republicans Recapture City Hall," *Palladium-Item*, Nov. 5, 1975.

[45] Fred S. Lord, "Control of City Hall Goes to Republicans," *Palladium-Item*, Nov. 5, 1975.

[46] Thomas S. Milligan, "Party Rivals See Vote Heartening," *Palladium-Item*, Nov. 9, 1975.

[47] Editorial Board, "City Hall in New Hands," *Palladium-Item*, Nov. 6, 1975; Fred S. Lord, "Control of City Hall Goes to Republicans," *Palladium-Item*, Nov. 5, 1975.

[48] "City Election Losers Spent $1,830 More Than Winners," *Palladium-Item*, Dec. 21, 1975.

[49] Tom Cool, "'It Was Teamwork,' Says Dickman as Republicans Recapture City Hall," *Palladium-Item*, Nov. 5, 1975.

[50] Ibid.

[51] "Howell, After Defeat, to Tie Up Loose Ends," *Palladium-Item*, Nov. 5, 1975.

[52] "He Won; Ford's Glad," *Palladium-Item*, Nov. 14, 1975. Technically, the telegram said "you have my *ward* congratulations" (emphasis added). The quote has been corrected.

[53] Fred S. Lord & Tom Cool, "Dickman Makes Appointments; Eyes Goals for Administration," *Palladium-Item*, Nov. 9, 1975.

[54] Tom Cool, "New Fire Chief Appointed; Mayor-Elect Not Consulted," *Palladium-Item*, Nov. 12, 1975.

[55] Tom Cool, "Dickman Expects No More Appointments Until December," *Palladium-Item*, Nov. 19, 1975.

[56] Editorial Board, "The GOP Patron-Age," *Palladium-Item*, Dec. 21, 1975.

[57] Steve Truitt, "Dickman Names Incumbents, 3 Newcomers to City Posts," *Palladium-Item*, Dec. 19, 1975.

58 Richard Holden, "Controller, Sanitary District Head Appointed by Mayor-Elect Dickman," *Palladium-Item*, Dec. 7, 1975.

59 Tom Cool, "Paul Mullin Named Richmond Fire Chief," *Palladium-Item*, Dec. 29, 1975.

60 "New Names at City Hall," *Palladium-Item*, Jan. 1, 1976.

61 Bob Levin, "Liberty Bell Peals as '76 Arrives," *Palladium-Item*, Jan. 1, 1976; "New Year's Eve Celebration City's First Bicentennial Event," *Palladium-Item*, Dec. 31, 1975.

62 Tom Cool, "Better Richmond Dickman's Goal," *Palladium-Item*, Jan. 1, 1976.

63 Steve Martin, "Out of Our Past: Richmond Poet Made Term 'Hoosier' Respectable," *Palladium-Item*, Dec. 31, 2017; Tom Cool, "Short Term, Politics of Current Mayor in Contrast to Pattern of City's Past," *Palladium-Item*, Nov. 27, 1975.

64 "Some Additions to the Script," *Palladium-Item*, Jan. 4, 1976.

65 "Mayor Dickman's Inaugural Text," *Palladium-Item*, Jan. 2, 1976. I have corrected minor typos.

Chapter 10: "A Richmond Man for Richmond's Future"

1 Editorial Board, "Mayor's First 100 Days," *Palladium-Item*, Apr. 8, 1976.

2 Tom Cool, "One Day in the Life of Clifford J. Dickman: It's Routine, But Different," *Palladium-Item*, July 11, 1976.

3 Fred S. Lord, "She Manages the City's Manager," *Palladium-Item*, Feb. 14, 1981.

4 Bill Engle, "Trimble Retires from Public Eye," *Palladium-Item*, Dec. 27, 2000; "Sketches of Candidates in Nov. 4 Balloting," *Palladium-Item*, Oct. 28, 1975.

5 Tom Cool, "One Day in the Life of Clifford J. Dickman: It's Routine, But Different," *Palladium-Item*, July 11, 1976.

6 Clifford Dickman, "If Government Watches Its Step Press Should Watch Its 'Line,'" *Palladium-Item*, Mar. 3, 1979.

7 Fred S. Lord, "Dickman's Plans? Just Possibly It's 'Yes,'" *Palladium-Item*, Aug. 2, 1978.

8 Tom Cool, "Friends with Murray 27 Years, Gibbs Says; Not Told of Raids," *Palladium-Item*, May 2, 1976.

9 Tom Cool, "Surface Responsible for Leaving City Police in Dark on Raids," *Palladium-Item*, May 28, 1976.

10 Editorial Board, "Waiting for Explanation," *Palladium-Item*, May 23, 1976.

11 Ibid.

[12] Tom Cool, "Mayor Says Gibbs Resignation Might Not Be Taken If Offered," *Palladium-Item*, May 27, 1976.

[13] Tom Cool, "Louis Gibbs Resigns as Local Police Chief," *Palladium-Item*, June 15, 1976.

[14] Tom Cool, "Chris Picked to Serve as Next Police Chief," *Palladium-Item*, July 1, 1976.

[15] Editorial Board, "Speaking of Fire Dept. Hours," *Palladium-Item*, Apr. 7, 1976.

[16] Tom Cool, "Firefighters Return to 56-Hour Week with Wage Increase," *Palladium-Item*, Mar. 11, 1977.

[17] Tom Cool, "Police, Firemen Warn of 'Action' Unless City Resumes Wage Talks," *Palladium-Item*, Aug. 6, 1977.

[18] Associated Press, "Dayton Homes Burn in Strike by Firemen," *New York Times*, Aug. 10, 1977.

[19] Editorial Board, "Striking Firemen Forfeit Respect," *Palladium-Item*, Aug. 12, 1977.

[20] Richard Holden, "City Firemen Vote to Strike," *Palladium-Item*, Aug. 12, 1977.

[21] Ibid.

[22] Richard Holden, "Firemen Decide Against Strike, Apparently Accept City's Offer," *Palladium-Item*, Aug. 14, 1977.

[23] U.S. Bureau of Labor Statistics, "Consumer Price Index for All Urban Consumers," accessed Dec. 17, 2020, https://fred.stlouisfed.org/series/CPIAUCSL.

[24] Earl M. Ryan, "Property Tax Reform in Indiana: 1973 Through Public Question 1," Indiana Fiscal Policy Institute, Nov. 2010.

[25] Clifford Dickman, "Richmond's '79 Budget Squeeze Will Require Cost and Service Cuts," *Palladium-Item*, June 25, 1978.

[26] Fred S. Lord, "Council Considers Priorities," *Palladium-Item*, Jan. 17, 1982.

[27] Ibid.

[28] See, e.g., Richard Holden, "Federal Aid Bad in Principle, But Can't Be Turned Down: Dickman," *Palladium-Item*, Dec. 29, 1978.

[29] Clifford Dickman, "Bills in Legislature Important for Financing Hoosier Cities," *Palladium-Item*, Jan. 20, 1979.

[30] Clifford Dickman, "Richmond's '79 Budget Squeeze Will Require Cost and Service Cuts," *Palladium-Item*, June 25, 1978.

[31] Ed Kaeuper, "Trash Collectors? Public Views Vary," *Palladium-Item*, Sep. 19, 1976.

[32] "Merit Plan Supported by Police," *Palladium-Item*, Jan. 2, 1976.

[33] Tom Cool, "Grohsmeyer to Head Police Merit Group," *Palladium-Item*, Jan. 29, 1976.

[34] Tom Cool, "Local Policemen Soon May Face Eligibility Lists, Written Exams," *Palladium-Item*, June 30, 1976.

NOTES

35 Editorial Board, "Merit System for Police," *Palladium-Item*, May 11, 1977.

36 "Project Director Is Appointed to Push Local Civic Center," *Palladium-Item*, Aug. 31, 1976.

37 Tom Cool & Fred S. Lord, "Overflow Crowd on Hand for Civic Center Debate," *Palladium-Item*, Sep. 22, 1976.

38 Fred S. Lord, "Funds OK'd for Land Purchases," *Palladium-Item*, Oct. 5, 1976; Tom Cool, "Civic Center Idea Is Not Dead, According to Direct of Project," *Palladium-Item*, Dec. 26, 1976.

39 Tom Cool, "Civic Center Idea Is Not Dead, According to Direct of Project," *Palladium-Item*, Dec. 26, 1976.

40 For example, Avco Corp., which once was Richmond's largest employer with 4,000 on its payroll, steadily reduced its local workforce before shuttering the plant in 1974. "Avco Plant Is Closing," *Palladium-Item*, Jan. 3, 1974.

41 Bill Engle, "Civic Leader Dies at 95," *Palladium-Item*, June 14, 2002.

42 Phil Hall, "Richmond Industrial Leaders Elated over News of Chrysler," *Palladium-Item*, Oct. 10, 1978.

43 Editorial Board, "Relief from Doubt," *Palladium-Item*, Oct. 15, 1978; Editorial Board, "What Can It Mean?," *Palladium-Item*, Oct. 15, 1978.

44 Fred S. Lord, "Work to Start Soon on Industries Road," *Palladium-Item*, Oct. 18, 1978; Phil Hall, "City Told Timing Important in Chrysler Plans," *Palladium-Item*, Oct. 10, 1978.

45 Phil Hall, "Chrysler Corp. Officials Attend Ground-Breaking Ceremonies," *Palladium-Item*, Nov. 16, 1978.

46 Phil Hall, "Chrysler Won't Build Here," *Palladium-Item*, Jan. 4, 1979; Phil Hall, "Disappointment, Now Joy in Kokomo," *Palladium-Item*, Jan. 4, 1979.

47 Fred S. Lord, "Chrysler Decision Disappoints City and Industrial Officials," *Palladium-Item*, Jan. 4, 1979.

48 Editorial Board, "Just Disappointment," *Palladium-Item*, Jan. 7, 1979.

49 Fred S. Lord, "Chrysler Decision Disappoints City and Industrial Officials," *Palladium-Item*, Jan. 4, 1979.

50 "Dickman Praises German Decision," *Palladium-Item*, Nov. 22, 1979.

51 Fred S. Lord, "Jobless Rate Most Serious Problem," *Palladium-Item*, Apr. 14, 1979.

52 Editorial Board, "Mayor's First Year," *Palladium-Item*, Jan. 9, 1977.

53 Fred S. Lord, "Licensing Key Element in Parlor Ordinance," *Palladium-Item*, Nov. 6, 1977; Fred S. Lord, "Massage Parlor Agrees to Close Down in April," *Palladium-Item*, Sep. 27, 1978.

54 "100 Attend City Bus System Dedication," *Palladium-Item*, Jan. 31, 1979; Advertisement, "The Corta Buses ... Another First for Richmond," *Palladium-Item*, Oct. 10, 1979; Fred S. Lord, "Features of

Richmond's New Transit System Are Described," *Palladium-Item*, Feb. 1, 1979.

[55] Steven Rattner, "Gas Crisis Has Complicated Origins," *New York Times*, Jan. 30, 1977.

[56] Richard Holden, "City Faces Serious Oil Shortage," *Palladium-Item*, Feb. 2, 1977.

[57] Tom Cool, "Mayor Appeals to Stores to Cut Hours for Sake of Fuel Savings," *Palladium-Item*, Feb. 2, 1977.

[58] Richard Holden, "City Faces Serious Oil Shortage," *Palladium-Item*, Feb. 2, 1977.

[59] Dick Reynolds, "Businessmen to Meet," *Palladium-Item*, Feb. 2, 1977; Tom Cool, "Mayor Appeals to Stores to Cut Hours for Sake of Fuel Savings," *Palladium-Item*, Feb. 2, 1977.

[60] Dick Reynolds, "Local Stores Reduce Hours to Save Fuel," *Palladium-Item*, Feb. 3, 1977.

[61] Tom Cool, "Grocers in Discord over Cutting Hours," *Palladium-Item*, Feb. 4, 1977.

[62] "Conservation Efforts Going Well: Dickman," *Palladium-Item*, Feb. 6, 1977.

[63] "Energy Conservation Measures May Relax if Weatherman Right," *Palladium-Item*, Feb. 8, 1977.

[64] Tom Cool, "Mayor Declares Emergency Over," *Palladium-Item*, Feb. 10, 1977.

[65] "Picketer Wants Cleaner Streets," *Palladium-Item*, Jan. 22, 1978.

[66] Richard Holden & Tom Cool, "Richmond to Get Road Salt—Maybe," *Palladium-Item*, Jan. 24, 1978.

[67] Steve Truitt, "Drivers Fight the Ice; More Snow in Forecast," *Palladium-Item*, Jan. 25, 1978.

[68] Associated Press, "1978 Blizzard Left Richmond Area Paralyzed," *Palladium-Item*, Jan. 27, 2013; Jason Truitt, "40 Years Ago: Blizzard Brings Life to a Halt," *Palladium-Item*, Jan. 25, 2018.

[69] Steve Truitt & Karen Tucker, "Blizzard Brawls, Richmond Crawls," *Palladium-Item*, Jan. 26, 1978.

[70] Dick Reynolds, "Blizzard of '78 Still a Fresh Memory," *Palladium-Item*, Jan. 26, 1983.

[71] Ibid.

[72] "Blizzard-hit Area Feeble," *Palladium-Item*, Jan. 27, 1978.

[73] Associated Press & United Press International, "Indiana to Get Federal Help," *Palladium-Item*, Jan. 27, 1978.

[74] "U.S. to Aid in Snow Removal," *Palladium-Item*, Jan. 30, 1978.

[75] "City Alleys Cleared in Snow Removal Efforts," *Palladium-Item*, Feb. 1, 1978.

[76] Editorial Board, "Firm Steps Against the Snow," *Palladium-Item*, Feb. 5, 1978.

NOTES

[77] Tom Cool, "Democrats Quit Snow Task Force, *Palladium-Item*," Feb. 10, 1978.

[78] Editorial Board, "Snow Snafu Complete," *Palladium-Item*, Feb. 24, 1978.

[79] Editorial Board, "Solid Plans for Snow," *Palladium-Item*, Nov. 20, 1978; Fred S. Lord, "City's Snow Army Almost Ready," *Palladium-Item*, Nov. 13, 1978.

[80] Fred S. Lord, "Dickman's Plans? Just Possibly It's 'Yes,'" *Palladium-Item*, Aug. 2, 1978.

[81] Fred S. Lord, "Dickman to Seek 2nd Term," *Palladium-Item*, Jan. 12, 1979.

[82] Fred S. Lord & Steve Truitt, "City Voter Turnout Is Lowest Ever," *Palladium-Item*, May 9, 1979; "The Democrats; The Republican," *Palladium-Item*, May 6, 1979.

[83] Editorial Board, "Only One for Mayor?," *Palladium-Item*, June 7, 1979.

[84] Carolyn Beaver, "Democrats Pick Barber," *Palladium-Item*, June 24, 1979.

[85] Curt Smith, "Barber Questions Mayor's Efficiency," *Palladium-Item*, Oct. 6, 1979; Curt Smith, "Mayor Hasn't Lived Up to Promises: Barber," *Palladium-Item*, Aug. 17, 1979; Fred S. Lord, "Barber Collects Trash to Show City Problem," *Palladium-Item*, Sep. 6, 1979; Fred S. Lord, "Voter Apathy Beware: City Candidates Coming," *Palladium-Item*, Oct. 2, 1979; Mary Ferguson, "Democrats Offer Voters Choice in Deciding City Leadership," *Palladium-Item*, June 30, 1979; Otis W. Barber, "Democrat Sees 'Better Way,'" *Palladium-Item*, Oct. 20, 1979.

[86] See, e.g., Advertisement, "If You Care About Efficient, Experienced City Management ...," *Palladium-Item*, Oct. 3, 1979.

[87] Advertisement, "Help Us Continue Reversing Crime Rates," *Palladium-Item*, Oct. 7, 1979; Clifford Dickman, "Mayor Seeks New Vistas," *Palladium-Item*, Oct. 20, 1979; Curt Smith, "Barber Questions Mayor's Efficiency," *Palladium-Item*, Oct. 6, 1979; Fred S. Lord, "Dickman Says City Has Cut 87 Jobs," *Palladium-Item*, Oct. 20, 1979.

[88] Gene Policinski, "City Receives 'Achievement' Award," *Palladium-Item*, Sep. 20, 1979.

[89] Editorial Board, "We Can Take a Bow," *Palladium-Item*, Oct. 1, 1979.

[90] Richard Holden, "Democrats Open Campaign Office," *Palladium-Item*, Sep. 30, 1979.

[91] Richard Holden, "First Fortify, Then Ratify," *Palladium-Item*, Aug. 8, 1979.

[92] David W. Dennis, "Dennis Backs Dickman," *Palladium-Item*, Nov. 2, 1979.

[93] Fred S. Lord, "Orr Endorses GOP Slate in Richmond," *Palladium-Item*, Oct. 9, 1979.

[94] D. Elton Trueblood, "Dickman Courageous," *Palladium-Item*, Oct. 22, 1979.

[95] Editorial Board, "Dickman for Mayor," *Palladium-Item*, Oct. 28, 1979.

[96] Phil Hall, "Dickman Relieved; Barber to Run Again," *Palladium-Item*, Nov. 7, 1979.

[97] Karen Bertsch, "Democrat Says GOP Mayor Reason a New Way Is Needed," *Palladium-Item*, Oct. 27, 1979.

[98] Tom Cool, "Dickman Scorns Unions in Government and Women's Role in Unemployment," *Palladium-Item*, Jan. 14, 1977.

[99] Karen Bertsch, "Democrat Says GOP Mayor Reason a New Way Is Needed," *Palladium-Item*, Oct. 27, 1979.

[100] Tom Cool, "Dickman Scorns Unions in Government and Women's Role in Unemployment," *Palladium-Item*, Jan. 14, 1977 (emphasis added).

[101] See, e.g., Cindi Arbuckle, "City Conditions Candidate Topics," *Palladium-Item*, Oct. 17, 1979; "Group Hears Candidate," *Palladium-Item*, Oct. 12, 1975; "Women Voters Hear Views of Candidates for Mayor," *Palladium-Item*, Sep. 10, 1975.

[102] Richard Holden, "Public vs. Private: A Question of Who's in Charge," *Palladium-Item*, Apr. 16, 1980.

[103] Richard Holden, "Putting the 'Candid' in Candidate," *Palladium-Item*, Nov. 2, 1979.

[104] Fred S. Lord, "Democrat Barber Wants a Chance," *Palladium-Item*, Oct. 28, 1979; Otis W. Barber, "Democrat Sees 'Better Way,'" *Palladium-Item*, Oct. 20, 1979.

[105] Clifford Dickman, "Mayor Seeks New Vistas," *Palladium-Item*, Oct. 20, 1979; Fred S. Lord, "Dickman Wants to Finish Projects," *Palladium-Item*, Oct. 28, 1979.

[106] Fred S. Lord, "His Administration Better Than Others: Dickman," *Palladium-Item*, Oct. 10, 1979.

[107] Fred S. Lord, "Dickman Wins Second Term," *Palladium-Item*, Nov. 7, 1979.

[108] "Republicans Now Have 7–2 Edge," *Palladium-Item*, Nov. 2, 1979.

[109] Steve Koger, "The Challenger Congratulates the Incumbent," Photograph, *Palladium-Item*, Nov. 7, 1979.

[110] Phil Hall, "Dickman Relieved; Barber to Run Again," *Palladium-Item*, Nov. 7, 1979.

[111] Editorial Board, "To the Winners...," *Palladium-Item*, Nov. 11, 1979.

Chapter 11: A New Decade

[1] Richard Holden, "Officials Pledge City Best of Ability," *Palladium-Item*, Jan. 2, 1980.

2 Carolyn Beaver, "Sanitary District to Get $29 Million," *Palladium-Item*, Oct. 3, 1979.

3 Clifford Dickman, "Mayor Previews City Action and Challenges for the 1980s," *Palladium-Item*, Dec. 23, 1979.

4 Center for Urban Policy & the Environment, "Annexation in Indiana: Issues and Options," Nov. 1998.

5 Editorial Board, "Expanding Richmond," *Palladium-Item*, Nov. 11, 1980.

6 Ibid.; Editorial Board, "Annexation—Again," *Palladium-Item*, Jan. 13, 1980.

7 Clifford Dickman, Letter to the Editor Reply, *Palladium-Item*, July 17, 1977.

8 Fred S. Lord, "Annexation Effort May Start in March," *Palladium-Item*, Jan. 13, 1980.

9 Richard Holden, "Dickman Sees Bigger City, Fee Hikes," *Palladium-Item*, Nov. 7, 1979.

10 "Annexation Foes to March Friday," *Palladium-Item*, Nov. 12, 1980; Cindi Arbuckle, "It's Time to Move on Annexation: Dickman," *Palladium-Item*, Jan. 10, 1980; Fred S. Lord, "Annexation Effort May Start in March," *Palladium-Item*, Jan. 13, 1980.

11 Carolyn Beaver, "Center Township Tells City: Keep Out!," *Palladium-Item*, Jan. 16, 1980; Kathy Barks, "Anti-Annexation Flyers Coming Out," *Palladium-Item*, Jan. 22, 1980.

12 Fred S. Lord, "Commission Ties on Annexation," *Palladium-Item*, Aug. 27, 1980; Fred S. Lord, "Planners Okay Annexation," *Palladium-Item*, Oct. 29, 1980.

13 "Annexation Foes to March Friday," *Palladium-Item*, Nov. 12, 1980; Steve Koger, "Brian Hughes ... and Steve Martin Hold Protest Signs During Meeting," Photograph, *Palladium-Item*, Nov. 18, 1980.

14 "Dickman at Atlanta Conference," *Palladium-Item*, Dec. 2, 1980.

15 Fred S. Lord, "Council Rejects Annexation," *Palladium-Item*, Dec. 2, 1980.

16 Fred S. Lord, "No Move to Annex for Now," *Palladium-Item*, Dec. 20, 1980.

17 Editorial Board, "We Can 'Make Do,'" *Palladium-Item*, Mar. 30, 1980; Fred S. Lord, "Balancing Act Means Fund Cut," *Palladium-Item*, Mar. 21, 1980; Fred S. Lord, "Cooperation Needed to Stretch City Dollars," *Palladium-Item*, Feb. 1, 1981.

18 Cathy Mong, "City, County Gain in New Census Figures," *Palladium-Item*, Nov. 23, 1980.

19 "Recalculation of 1980 Census Could Bring City More Money," *Palladium-Item*, June 7, 1981.

20 Board of Governors of the Federal Reserve System, "Bank Prime Loan Rate," accessed Mar. 20, 2022, https://fred.stlouisfed.org/series/MPRIME.

[21] Associated Press, "Indicators Agree: It's a Recession," *Palladium-Item*, Apr. 17, 1980.

[22] Editorial Board, "Coming Out of It?" *Palladium-Item*, June 8, 1980.

[23] Editorial Board, "More Are Working," *Palladium-Item*, Aug. 4, 1980.

[24] Fred S. Lord, "Dickman Hopes Projects Will Spur North Richmond," *Palladium-Item*, Aug. 15, 1980.

[25] Fred S. Lord, "Hospital or Prison?," *Palladium-Item*, Mar. 26, 1981.

[26] Gail Baruch, "Gorge Nears Opening Despite Delays," *Palladium-Item*, June 6, 1980.

[27] Fred S. Lord, "South L Street Plan Approved," *Palladium-Item*, Oct. 21, 1980; Fred S. Lord, "South L St. Project Faces Stiff Opposition," *Palladium-Item*, Sep. 14, 1980.

[28] Kyle Kreiger & Tim Roberts, "PRC Reopens; 26 Protesters Arrested," *Palladium-Item*, June 16, 1982; Tim Roberts, "Strikers Block Entrance at PRC," *Palladium-Item*, June 15, 1982.

[29] Kyle Kreiger, "Mayor Seeks Middle Path on PRC," *Palladium-Item*, June 16, 1982.

[30] Kyle Krieger, "Strikers Hang in Effigy Manager of PRC Plant," *Palladium-Item*, Sep. 28, 1982.

[31] "Mayor Had Special Protection in Parade," *Palladium-Item*, June 29, 1982.

[32] Samuel B. Stone, "Home Rule in the Midwest," Ind. Univ. Pub. Pol'y Inst., July 2010, 2.

[33] Fred S. Lord, "Dickman Wants Help for Cities' Money Woes," *Palladium-Item*, Sep. 20, 1982; Fred S. Lord, "Mayors Asked to Support Reagan Economic Plans," *Palladium-Item*, May 29, 1981; "Mayor's on a Committee," *Palladium-Item*, Nov. 28, 1976.

[34] Cathy Mong, "Dickman Replaces Hudnut As Head of State GOP Mayors," *Palladium-Item*, Dec. 13, 1980.

[35] "Dickman on Orr Committee," *Palladium-Item*, Feb. 3, 1980.

[36] Kathy Barks Hoffman, "Quayle Styles Self As Bureaucracy Killer," *Palladium-Item*, Oct. 7, 1980.

[37] Dick Reynolds, "Dickman Gets 'Good Feeling' from Meeting at White House," *Palladium-Item*, May 24, 1983; "Mayor to Attend Meeting," *Palladium-Item*, Nov. 25, 1982.

[38] Richard Holden, "Richmond Welcomes Disney Music," *Palladium-Item*, Apr. 17, 1981.

[39] Richard Holden, "In Case of Nuclear Attack...," *Palladium-Item*, Mar. 6, 1979.

[40] See, e.g., "Army Reserve Marks 200th Birthday at Ball," *Palladium-Item*, Apr. 12, 1976.

[41] "Scouts Will Be Seated in Government Posts," *Palladium-Item*, Feb. 5, 1980; "Constitution Week Set," *Palladium-Item*, Sep. 15, 1979; "Richmond Chamber of Commerce Will Sponsor Free Enterprise Week," *Palladium-Item*, June 22, 1977; "'Kiss Your Baby Week' To

Begin," *Palladium-Item*, Apr. 15, 1976; "Mayor Proclaims May 1–7 'Be Kind to Animals Week,'" *Palladium-Item*, Apr. 29, 1977; "Officials Honored in Conjunction with Weights, Measures," *Palladium-Item*, Mar. 6, 1978.

[42] See, e.g., Kyle Krieger, "Young Runners Shine on a Very Gloomy Day," *Palladium-Item*, Oct. 21, 1983 (Wilma Rudolph got the key on this occasion); "21st Optimist Season Open in Ceremonies," *Palladium-Item*, May 23, 1976.

[43] Cathy Mong, "Mayor Welcomes New Earlhamites," *Palladium-Item*, Sep. 7, 1980.

[44] Jan Clark, "Ewbank Leaves Everlasting Mark in Richmond," *Palladium-Item*, Nov. 19, 1998.

[45] Dick Reynolds, "'It's Amazing How He Can Touch People,'" *Palladium-Item*, May 20, 1980.

[46] University of Notre Dame, "2021 Media Guide, Notre Dame Football," 87.

[47] Steve Pionski, "Devine: Never Coached Man Like Vagas," *Palladium-Item*, May 20, 1980.

[48] Ibid.

[49] Andrew Glass, "Members of Investigative Delegation Shot in Guyana, Nov. 18, 1978," *Politico*, Nov. 18, 2010.

[50] Richard Reynolds, "Only a Week Ago Unbelievable Turn of Events Began to Unfold," *Palladium-Item*, Nov. 26, 1978.

[51] Jason Truitt, "Retro Richmond: Remembering the Rose Festival," *Palladium-Item*, Sep. 16, 2018; "Rose Festival Schedule," *Palladium-Item*, June 25, 1981.

[52] Jon Berry, "Official Ceremonies, Arts Center Dedication Open Rose Festival," *Palladium-Item*, June 23, 1976.

[53] "The Parade Lineup," *Palladium-Item*, June 21, 1981.

[54] Dick Reynolds, "Georgians Confirm Plans for Trip," *Palladium-Item*, May 13, 1981.

[55] Dick Reynolds, "Richmond Not on Top 40 Hit List of Pop Singer Barry Manilow," *Palladium-Item*, Apr. 18, 1982.

[56] Dick Reynolds, "Manilow Declines Invitation," *Palladium-Item*, Apr. 22, 1982.

[57] Tsitsi Dzamwari, "'We've Got to Get Rid of this Color Thing,' says Rev. King," *Palladium-Item*, Apr. 3, 1978.

[58] Tsitsi Dzamwari, "250 Marchers Remember King," *Palladium-Item*, Apr. 3, 1978.

[59] Tsitsi Dzamwari, "Rev. King: 'I Know the Danger of Hate,'" *Palladium-Item*, Apr. 3, 1978.

[60] Kyle Kreiger, "Richmond Mayor's Pay More Than Many Others," *Palladium-Item*, Aug. 1, 1982.

[61] Fred S. Lord, "City Officials Fight Two-Front Inflation," *Palladium-Item*, May 4, 1980.

62 "The Republican," *Palladium-Item*, May 6, 1979.
63 "A Question for Passerby?" *Palladium-Item*, Aug. 29, 1977.
64 Editorial Board, "Does This End It?" *Palladium-Item*, Sep. 1, 1977.
65 Dick Reynolds, "Congressional Quest Began With a Question," *Palladium-Item*, Dec. 6, 1981.
66 Clifford Dickman, "Balanced U.S. Budget Takes Priority Over Funds for Cities," *Palladium-Item*, Mar. 29, 1980.
67 Jeff Stinson, "Dickman Says Cities Should Take Share of Cuts," *Palladium-Item*, Sep. 23, 1981.
68 Emmett Smelser, "Dickman Wants More Power for Cities," *Palladium-Item*, Oct. 9, 1983 (internal quotation marks omitted).
69 Henry Olsen, *The Working Class Republican: Ronald Reagan and the Return of Blue-Collar Conservatism* (New York: Broadside Books, 2017).
70 Fred S. Lord & Tim Roberts, "'New Federalism' Reaction Is Mixed," *Palladium-Item*, Jan. 27, 1982.
71 Jeff Stinson, "Dickman Says Cities Should Take Share of Cuts," *Palladium-Item*, Sep. 23, 1981.
72 Editorial Board, "Cities Should Pay Their Own Way," *Palladium-Item*, Sep. 25, 1981.
73 Jeffrey Stinson, "Dickman to Assembly: Cities in Cash Pinch," *Palladium-Item*, Feb. 4, 1981.
74 Camilla Warrick, "Let's Pitch In, Dickman Urges," *Palladium-Item*, Jan. 31, 1982; Fred S. Lord, "Cities, Citizens Must Become More Self-Reliant," *Palladium-Item*, Jan. 9, 1982; Fred S. Lord, "City to Collect Tree Limbs March 1–5," *Palladium-Item*, Feb. 18, 1982; Richard Holden, "Public Vs. Private: A Question of Who's in Charge," *Palladium-Item*, Apr. 16, 1980.
75 Carl Bargmann to Clifford Dickman, undated.

Chapter 12: Congress and Chemscam

1 Linda Bloom, "'I Like My Job Very Well': Mayor," *Palladium-Item*, Jan. 30, 1980.
2 Fred Lord, "Dickman May Run in New 2nd District," *Palladium-Item*, July 17, 1981.
3 John Straw, Joan Dutour, Kirk Overstreet, Jr., Sean Reilly, Jeffery Rhoades (compilers), "Congressman Philip R. Sharp Papers, 1970–1994," Archives and Special Collections Ball State University, 2002, https://lib.bsu.edu/archives/findingaids/MSS156.pdf.
4 Richard Holden, "Sharp to Represent District," *Palladium-Item*, Nov. 6, 1974.
5 David E. Rosenbaum, "Wiggins for Impeachment; Others in GOP Join Him," *New York Times*, Aug. 6, 1974; Jon Berry, "Area Politicians

Express Sadness at Resignation, Hope for Future," *Palladium-Item*, Aug. 9, 1974.

[6] Fred S. Lord, "It's Official: Dickman Running for Congress," *Palladium-Item*, Dec. 8, 1981.

[7] Ibid.; Jim Callaway, "On the Road," Photograph, *Palladium-Item*, Dec. 8, 1981; Larry Lough, "New 2nd District Gets Another Anti-Sharp Campaigner," *Muncie Star*, Dec. 9, 1981.

[8] Greg Goldsmith, "2 Announce Candidacies," *Muncie Evening Press*, Dec. 8, 1981.

[9] Larry Lough, "New 2nd District Gets Another Anti-Sharp Campaigner," *Muncie Star Press*, Dec. 9, 1981.

[10] Jeffrey Stinson, "All Three GOP Rivals Focus on Beating Sharp," *Palladium-Item*, Apr. 18, 1982.

[11] See, e.g., "Dickman to Emcee Dinner," *Palladium-Item*, Mar. 17, 1982; Kit Curless, "Mutz Sees Renewal of American Dream," *Palladium-Item*, Apr. 2, 1982.

[12] "Muncie Man to Run for 2nd District Seat," *Palladium-Item*, Nov. 4, 1981.

[13] Jeffrey Stinson, "All Three GOP Rivals Focus on Beating Sharp," *Palladium-Item*, Apr. 18, 1982.

[14] Fred S. Lord, "VanNatta Cites His Experience," *Palladium-Item*, Jan. 1, 1982.

[15] Fred S. Lord, "County Chairmen Predict Close Race," *Palladium-Item*, Apr. 4, 1982. The race had a fourth candidate, Chester Coomer, but he was not a serious contender.

[16] Jeffrey Stinson, "All Three GOP Rivals Focus on Beating Sharp," *Palladium-Item*, Apr. 18, 1982.

[17] Fred S. Lord, "Congressional Candidates Agree—Economy Is Key Issue," *Palladium-Item*, Apr. 4, 1982.

[18] Editorial Board, "Interesting Primary Ahead for Congress," *Palladium-Item*, Feb. 14, 1982.

[19] "Dickman Says Sharp Abuses Franking Right," *Palladium-Item*, Mar. 31, 1982; "Dickman, Sharp At Odds Over Meetings in District," *Palladium-Item*, Apr. 15, 1982.

[20] "Dickman, Sharp At Odds Over Meetings in District," *Palladium-Item*, Apr. 15, 1982.

[21] Obituary, "Henry J. Luerman Dies; Mayor's Father-in-Law," *Palladium-Item*, Jan. 19, 1982.

[22] Obituary, "Hedwig F. Luerman," *Palladium-Item*, Feb. 8, 1982.

[23] Obituary, "Robert A. Luerman," *Palladium-Item*, Feb. 24, 1982.

[24] Obituary, "Jerome A. Dickman," *Palladium-Item*, Dec. 22, 1982.

[25] Jeffrey Stinson, "All Three GOP Rivals Focus on Beating Sharp," *Palladium-Item*, Apr. 18, 1982.

[26] Fred S. Lord, "Dickman Blames Lack of Funds for Loss," *Palladium-Item*, May 9, 1982.

285

[27] Jeffrey Stinson, "Dickman 'Jilted' by Hudnut?" *Palladium-Item*, Apr. 22, 1982.

[28] Ibid.

[29] "Reaganomics Loom over Congress Races," *Indianapolis Star*, May 3, 1982.

[30] Fred S. Lord, "Early Survey Shows Light Turnout of Area Voters," *Palladium-Item*, May 4, 1982.

[31] Fred S. Lord, "VanNatta to Face Sharp for Area Congress Seat," *Palladium-Item*, May 5, 1982.

[32] "Official Results of Primary Election Listed," *Palladium-Item*, May 15, 1982.

[33] "2nd District Votes," *Palladium-Item*, May 5, 1982.

[34] "Delaware County Ballot," *Muncie Star Press*, May 6, 1982.

[35] Fred S. Lord, "VanNatta to Face Sharp for Area Congress Seat," *Palladium-Item*, May 5, 1982.

[36] Fred S. Lord, "Dickman Blames Lack of Funds for Loss," *Palladium-Item*, May 9, 1982.

[37] Kyle Kreiger, "Sharp Hopes for New Spirit of Cooperation," *Palladium-Item*, Nov. 3, 1982.

[38] Brian Francisco, "Sharp Defeats MacKenzie to Win 6th Term," *Muncie Star Press*, Nov. 7, 1984.

[39] Diane Goudy, "Sharp Victory Has Bit of Suspense," *Palladium-Item*, Nov. 9, 1988.

[40] David Penticuff, "McIntosh Wins 2nd District Seat," *Muncie Evening Press*, Nov. 9, 1994.

[41] Patrick T. Morrison, Myrta J. Pulliam, Eric C. Rodenberg, & Ernest A. Wilkinson, "Chemical Sales Bribery Sweeps Indiana," *Indianapolis Star*, Aug. 1, 1982.

[42] "Details of Cities' Excess Purchases Revealed in Probe," *Indianapolis Star*, Aug. 2, 1982; Fred S. Lord, "Local Units Reviewed in Chemicals Probe," *Palladium-Item*, Aug. 2, 1982.

[43] Fred S. Lord, "Dickman Calls for Chemical Cost Disclosure," *Palladium-Item*, Aug. 3, 1982.

[44] "Grand Jury Convenes," *Palladium-Item*, Dec. 7, 1982.

[45] Fred S. Lord, "Grand Jury Subpoenas City Records, Mayor Says," *Palladium-Item*, Dec. 21, 1982; Tim Roberts, "Grand Jury Subpoenas Wayne Co. Records," *Palladium-Item*, Dec. 20, 1982.

[46] Fred S. Lord, "Grand Jury Subpoenas City Records, Mayor Says," *Palladium-Item*, Dec. 21, 1982.

[47] Editorial Board, "Hiring of Sanitary Lawyer Backfires," *Palladium-Item*, Jan. 30, 1983.

[48] Tim Roberts, "Cambridge City Official Is Target of Grand Jury," *Palladium-Item*, Jan. 25, 1983; Tim Roberts, "Mayor Bans Use of Lawyer," *Palladium-Item*, Jan. 20, 1983.

NOTES

49 Tim Roberts, "Grand Jury Studies City's Scrap Sales," *Palladium-Item*, Jan. 7, 1983.

50 Tim Roberts, "Jury Probe Extended to Asphalt Purchases," *Palladium-Item*, Jan. 12, 1983.

51 Tim Roberts, "Jury Targets Transportation Head," *Palladium-Item*, Jan. 22, 1983.

52 Tim Roberts, "Jerry Haynes: The Man Behind the Charges," *Palladium-Item*, Mar. 13, 1983.

53 Tim Roberts, "Jury Targets Transportation Head," *Palladium-Item*, Jan. 22, 1983.

54 Tim Roberts, "No System Can Prevent Dishonesty, Mayor Says," *Palladium-Item*, Feb. 27, 1983.

55 "Jury Hears Transportation Head," *Palladium-Item*, Jan. 28, 1983; "Salesman Spends Only Short Time with Jury," *Palladium-Item*, Jan. 31, 1983; Tim Roberts, "Chemical Case Indictments May Be Near," *Palladium-Item*, Feb. 1, 1983; Tim Roberts, "Salesmen Testify for Grand Jury," *Palladium-Item*, Jan. 26, 1983.

56 Kyle Kreiger & Tim Roberts, "Suspended Haynes Declines Comment," *Palladium-Item*, Feb. 4, 1983; Tim Roberts, "Haynes, Carson Are Arraigned," *Palladium-Item*, Feb. 5, 1983; Tim Roberts, "Haynes Faces 172 Counts, Zook 26," *Palladium-Item*, Feb. 4, 1983.

57 Kathy Barks Hoffman, "Dickman Didn't Ask Haynes About Bribes," *Palladium-Item*, Feb. 4, 1983.

58 Tim Roberts, "Haynes, Carson Are Arraigned," *Palladium-Item*, Feb. 5, 1983.

59 "Kickback Counts Listed," *Palladium-Item*, Feb. 5, 1983.

60 Fred S. Lord, "City Councilmen Saddened by Indictments Against Haynes," *Palladium-Item*, Feb. 4, 1983.

61 Bill Thornbro, "Candidates Cite Jobs as Top Priority," *Palladium-Item*, Aug. 18, 1983.

62 Tim Roberts, "No System Can Prevent Dishonesty, Mayor Says," *Palladium-Item*, Feb. 27, 1983.

63 Tim Roberts, "Scavenging by Sanitary District Workers Studied," *Palladium-Item*, Mar. 27, 1983.

64 Editorial Board, "City Has Problem with Scrap Fund," *Palladium-Item*, Jan. 23, 1983.

65 Tim Roberts, "Scavenging by Sanitary District Workers Studied," *Palladium-Item*, Mar. 27, 1983.

66 Tim Roberts, "Goodknight Faces 3 Indictments," *Palladium-Item*, Apr. 18, 1983.

67 Editorial Board, "'Minor' Charges Face Goodknight," *Palladium-Item*, Apr. 23, 1983; Tim Roberts, "Goodknight Will Remain," *Palladium-Item*, Apr. 19, 1983.

68 Tim Roberts, "Landfill Salvage Funds Spent for Varied Uses," *Palladium-Item*, Apr. 18, 1983.

[69] Emmett Smelser, "Grand Jury Quarries Both Boulders and Pebbles," *Palladium-Item*, May 29, 1983.
[70] Tim Roberts, "Mayor Can Only Watch, Hope During Inquiry," *Palladium-Item*, Jan. 23, 1983.
[71] Fred S. Lord, "Councilman Carter to Run for Mayor," *Palladium-Item*, Dec. 15, 1982.
[72] Tim Roberts, "No System Can Prevent Dishonesty, Mayor Says," *Palladium-Item*, Feb. 27, 1983.
[73] Kathy Barks Hoffman, "Dickman to Seek 3rd Term," *Palladium-Item*, Feb. 28, 1983.
[74] Editorial Board, "Indictments Leave City Hall in Limbo," *Palladium-Item*, Feb. 6, 1983.
[75] Editorial Board, "Dickman Shows His Loyalty Again," *Palladium-Item*, Apr. 24, 1983.
[76] Tim Roberts, "City Democrats Working on Platform," *Palladium-Item*, Apr. 23, 1983.
[77] "Carter Cites Need for Leadership from City," *Palladium-Item*, Apr. 21, 1983.
[78] Kathy Barks Hoffman, "Buying for City a Complex Routine," *Palladium-Item*, Feb. 7, 1983.
[79] Kathy Barks Hoffman, "Chemscam 'Too Spread Out' to Detect," *Palladium-Item*, Feb. 20, 1983; Tim Roberts, "No System Can Prevent Dishonesty, Mayor Says," *Palladium-Item*, Feb. 27, 1983.
[80] Tim Roberts, "Republican Foes Dickman, Carter Trade Salvos," *Palladium-Item*, Apr. 28, 1983.
[81] Ibid.
[82] Bill Thornbro, "Candidates Play 'Beat the Clock,'" *Palladium-Item*, Apr. 25, 1983.
[83] Tim Roberts, "Republican Foes Dickman, Carter Trade Salvos," *Palladium-Item*, Apr. 28, 1983.
[84] Tim Roberts, "Record Turnout in Tight Races," *Palladium-Item*, May 4, 1983.
[85] "Jim Carter Concedes Vote Loss," *Palladium-Item*, June 18, 1983.
[86] Tim Roberts, "Carter Undecided on Challenge to Recount," *Palladium-Item*, June 16, 1983.
[87] Robert D. Orr to Clifford Dickman, May 12, 1983.
[88] Tim Roberts, "Record Turnout in Tight Races," *Palladium-Item*, May 4, 1983.
[89] Fred S. Lord, "2 More Are in Race for Mayor," *Palladium-Item*, Mar. 2, 1983; Tom Cool, "Short Term, Politics of Current mayor in Contrast to Pattern of City's Past," *Palladium-Item*, Nov. 27, 1975.
[90] Fred S. Lord, "2 More Are in Race for Mayor," *Palladium-Item*, Mar. 2, 1983.
[91] Tim Roberts, "Record Turnout in Tight Races," *Palladium-Item*, May 4, 1983.

NOTES

[92] Tim Roberts & Kathy Barks Hoffman, "Dickman, Meredith to Testify," *Palladium-Item*, May 7, 1983.

[93] Tim Roberts, "Grand Jury Again Indicts Sanitary District Head," *Palladium-Item*, May 20, 1983.

[94] Emmett Smelser, "Dickman Says He's Pressured to Suspend Goodknight," *Palladium-Item*, May 27, 1983.

[95] "Goodknight Decision Is Due on Tuesday," *Palladium-Item*, May 26, 1983.

[96] Tim Roberts, "Goodknight Suspended," *Palladium-Item*, June 1, 1983.

[97] Editorial Board, "Suspension Right in Santiary Case," June 1, 1983; Emmett Smelser, "Grand Jury Quarries Both Boulders and Pebbles," *Palladium-Item*, May 29, 1983.

[98] Bill Thornbro, "Waltermann Says Richmond Is Looking for 'New Directions,'" *Palladium-Item*, Sep. 25, 1983.

[99] Bill Thornbro, "Candidates Cite Jobs as Top Priority," *Palladium-Item*, Aug. 18, 1983; Emmett Smelser, "First Mayoral Debate Failed to Draw Distinctions," *Palladium-Item*, Aug. 21, 1983; Kathy Barks Hoffman, "Candidates Agree on Many Issues," *Palladium-Item*, Oct. 27, 1983; "The Mayor's Race," *Palladium-Item*, Oct. 16, 1983.

[100] Bill Thornbro, "Candidates Cite Jobs as Top Priority," *Palladium-Item*, Aug. 18, 1983.

[101] Tim Roberts, "Dickman Calls Democrat Policy 'Pie in the Sky,'" *Palladium-Item*, Nov. 3, 1983.

[102] Bill Thornbro, "Labor Endorses City Democrats," *Palladium-Item*, Oct. 4, 1983.

[103] Bill Thornbro, "Reagan Is 'A Shameful Blot,' Says Union Official at Local Rally," *Palladium-Item*, Sep. 6, 1983.

[104] Associated Press, "Dickman Defeat Seen by Top State Democrat," *Palladium-Item*, Sep. 26, 1983.

[105] "Lugar Endorses Dickman," *Palladium-Item*, Nov. 3, 1983.

[106] Tim Roberts, "Sewage Treatment Plant Tour Impresses Quayle," *Palladium-Item*, Aug. 31, 1983.

[107] Dan D. Theobald, "Strong Leader," *Palladium-Item*, Oct. 27, 1983.

[108] Editorial Board, "City Hall Challenge Requires Experience," *Palladium-Item*, Oct. 30, 1983.

[109] Dale Perry, "The Men Who Would Be Mayor: Third Time Out, Dickman Still Loves a Challenge," *Palladium-Item*, Oct. 30, 1983.

[110] Tim Roberts & Kathy Barks Hoffman, "It's Waltermann with 70 Percent," *Palladium-Item*, Nov. 9, 1983.

[111] Associated Press, "Democrats Tighten Grip on Indiana's Cities," *Palladium-Item*, Nov. 9, 1983.

[112] Kathy Barks Hoffman & Tim Roberts, "Dickman Attributes Loss to Chemscam," *Palladium-Item*, Nov. 9, 1983.

[113] "Clifford Dickman," *Palladium-Item*, Jan. 15, 1983.

[114] Tim Roberts, "Haynes Pleads Guilty in Chemscam," *Palladium-Item*, Mar. 27, 1984; Tim Roberts, "Jerry Haynes Is Sent to Jail," *Palladium-Item*, May 17, 1984.

[115] Tim Roberts & Dave Holthouse, "Haynes Gets Little Sympathy," *Palladium-Item*, May 18, 1984.

[116] Tim Roberts, "Judge Dismisses Goodknight Cases," *Palladium-Item*, Dec. 7, 1983.

[117] Tim Roberts & Susan Loughmiller, "Goodknight Is Returned to Job," *Palladium-Item*, Dec. 13, 1983.

[118] Tim Roberts, "Jury Witnesses Say Reputations Have Been Hurt," *Palladium-Item*, Feb. 19, 1984.

[119] Eric C. Rodenberg, "Judge Praises Defense," *Palladium-Item*, Mar. 9, 1990.

[120] Eric Co. Rodenberg, "Texas Prison Camp Welcomes New Inmate: Gerald Surface," *Palladium-Item*, May 19, 1990.

[121] "Cooperation Wins Enterprise Zone," *Palladium-Item*, Dec. 6, 1983.

[122] Tim Roberts, "City Officials Want to Make Zone a Success," *Palladium-Item*, Dec. 6, 1983.

[123] Tim Roberts, "Waltermann Fires 11 Workers," *Palladium-Item*, Jan. 1, 1984.

[124] Kyle Kreiger, "Mayors to Race in Cars Sunday," *Palladium-Item*, June 16, 1984; Norma Carnes, "Mayor Gets Honor—Or a 'Roast'?", *Palladium-Item*, Jan. 22, 1986.

[125] Dale Perry, "The Men Who Would Be Mayor: Third Time Out, Dickman Still Loves a Challenge," *Palladium-Item*, Oct. 30, 1983.

[126] Tim Roberts, "'What a Pleasure It Has Been ...,'" *Palladium-Item*, Dec. 20, 1983.

Chapter 13: A Family Enterprise

[1] "Kesslers Sports Shop," *Palladium-Item*, Jan. 26, 2005. "Sales" refers to revenues, not profits.

[2] Susan Loughmiller, "Kessler's to Open 2nd Store," *Palladium-Item*, July 29, 1984.

[3] Mark Braykovich, "Businesses Quietly Grow Outside City," *Palladium-Item*, Feb. 23, 1986.

[4] "Sanburn Changing Owners," *Kokomo Tribune*, Apr. 18, 1989.

[5] "Largest Team Dealers in America: Kesslers Sport Shop," *Sporting Goods Dealer* (November–December 2002), 14.

[6] C. David Mogollon, "Kesslers Moving to Bigger Store," *Palladium-Item*, Feb. 25, 1990.

[7] "Business Spotlight, Kesslers Sport Shop Inc.," *Palladium-Item*, Oct. 2, 1995.

[8] Larry Price, "Awards Nothing New for Local Businessman," *Palladium-Item*, May 19, 1995.

9 NSGA, Sporting Goods Industry Hall of Fame Inductees, 2021, https://www.nsga.org/globalassets/hall-of-fame/6.20nsga_2021_hof_pasthofinductees-web_final2.pdf.

10 Larry Price, "Awards Nothing New for Local Businessman," *Palladium-Item*, May 19, 1995.

11 Ibid.

12 Max Knight, "Dickman's Been Around Sports Block a Few Times," *Palladium-Item*, Feb. 3, 1997.

13 Ibid.

14 "Bob Dickman and Ronny Flowers Elected to NSGA Hall of Fame," *SGB Media*, Aug. 27, 2018, https://sgbonline.com/nsga-appoints-bob-dickman-and-ronny-flowers-to-hall-of-fame/.

15 Julie Pitts, email to author, July 14, 2021; NSGA, Sporting Goods Industry Hall of Fame Inductees, 2021, https://www.nsga.org/globalassets/hall-of-fame/6.20nsga_2021_hof_pasthofinductees-web_final2.pdf. The other father–son pair is William and Willard Voit, best known for Voit volleyballs, soccer balls, and basketballs.

16 "Largest Team Dealers in America: Kesslers Sport Shop," *Sporting Goods Dealer* (November–December 2002), 14.

17 Bernhardt Dotson, "Changing Hands," *Palladium-Item*, Dec. 21, 2003.

18 "Largest Team Dealers in America: Kesslers Sport Shop," *Sporting Goods Dealer* (November–December 2002), 14.

19 Ibid.; "Success Has Benefitted Richmond," *Palladium-Item*, Dec. 21, 2003; "Kesslers Sports Shop," *Palladium-Item*, Jan. 26, 2005.

20 "Success Has Benefitted Richmond," *Palladium-Item*, Dec. 21, 2003.

21 Bernhardt Dotson, "Changing Hands," *Palladium-Item*, Dec. 21, 2003.

I'm grateful to Bob, Ted, Phil, and Dan Dickman for much of the information in this chapter.

Chapter 14: "Drive On"

1 Vernon Redd, "Richmond Athlete Defies Father Time," *Palladium-Item*, Sep. 22, 2001.

2 Jan Clark, "Attendance Concerns Surround Old-Timers Draw," *Palladium-Item*, Sep. 18, 1994.

3 "Tournament Rosters for the 12 'Oldtimers' Teams," *Palladium-Item*, Nov. 10, 1992.

4 Dick Reynolds, "Webster Goes After 4th Straight," *Palladium-Item*, Nov. 7, 1993.

5 Vernon Redd, "Area 9 Plays Host to Old-School Hoops," *Palladium-Item*, Sep. 17, 2001.

6 Vernon Redd, "Richmond Athlete Defies Father Time," *Palladium-Item*, Sep. 22, 2001.

7 Ibid.

[8] "Richmond Athlete Scores High at Senior Track Meet," *Palladium-Item*, Aug. 21, 2002; Vernon Redd, "Richmond Athlete Defies Father Time," *Palladium-Item*, Sep. 22, 2001.

[9] Jody Peacock, "Dickman Has Good 'Shot' for Gold Medal," *Palladium-Item*, June 4, 1993.

[10] Max Knight, "Pair of Senior Athletes Going to National Event," *Palladium-Item*, May 20, 1997.

[11] Max Knight, "Richmond Men Have Fun at Senior Sports Event," *Palladium-Item*, June 6, 1997.

[12] "Dickman Takes 3 Seconds, 3 Thirds at Masters Meet," *Palladium-Item*, May 13, 2001; "Local Man Competes at Kentucky Senior Games," *Palladium-Item*, Sep. 25, 2002; "Local Man Competes in National Senior Games," *Palladium-Item*, June 11, 2003; "Richmond Man Competes," *Palladium-Item*, Sep. 26, 2009; "Richmond Men Win 11 Firsts," *Palladium-Item*, May 24, 2011; "Sports Briefs," *Palladium-Item*, June 14, 2005; "Sports Briefs," *Palladium-Item*, June 30, 2004; Vernon Redd, "Richmond Athlete Defies Father Time," *Palladium-Item*, Sep. 22, 2001.

[13] "1992 Earlham College Athletic Hall of Fame Inductees," *Palladium-Item*, Oct. 23, 1992.

[14] Max Knight, "Dickman's Been Around Sports Block a Few Times," *Palladium-Item*, Feb. 3, 1997.

[15] "Earlham Baseball Camps," Earlham College, accessed July 16, 2021, https://www.earlhambaseballcamps.com/sadler-stadium.cfm.

[16] Larry Price, "Mayors Past and Present Meet, Agree to Lobby for Civic Hall Funds," *Palladium-Item*, May 7, 1992.

[17] Bill Engle, "Early Voting Gets Off to Slow Start in Richmond," *Palladium-Item*, Oct. 27, 2015; C. David Mogollon & Samantha Shook, "Leaders Want More Positive News," *Palladium-Item*, June 8, 1992; Samantha Shook, "Former Mayor: 'We Mostly Need More Confidence in Ourselves,'" *Palladium-Item*, May 31, 1992.

[18] Advertisement for Dick Lugar, United States Senator, *Palladium-Item*, May 4, 2012.

[19] Bill Engle, "Mayors Flash Back to Time in Office," *Palladium-Item*, Sep. 2, 2000.

[20] Bill Engle, "Andrews Resigns," *Palladium-Item*, Aug. 23, 2000.

[21] Bill Engle & Don Fasnacht, "Dickman Announces Candidacy," *Palladium-Item*, Sep. 20, 2000.

[22] Tara Tamaribuchi, "Bridge to a New Era: Candidates Share Visions for Richmond's Future," *Palladium-Item*, Sep. 24, 2000.

[23] Don Fasnacht, "Replacement Rules Emerged from Chaos," *Palladium-Item*, Sep. 3, 2000.

[24] Bill Engle, "Quick Decision Surprises Other Candidates," *Palladium-Item*, Sep. 26, 2000.

NOTES

[25] Micah Sommer, "Area Honors Its Own," *Palladium-Item*, Jan. 29, 2011.

[26] Obituary, "Anna E. Dickman," *Palladium-Item*, Sep. 3, 1985.

[27] Obituary, "Margaretta K. Bradway," *Palladium-Item*, June 29, 1992 (also acknowledging her husband Merle's death in 1980).

[28] Joan Giangrasse Kates, "Howard Helfrich, Teacher and Coach at Glenbrook North, Dies," *Chicago Tribune*, Aug. 5, 2015.

[29] Obituary, "Evelyn F. Mitrione," *Palladium-Item*, Mar. 31, 2011 (acknowledging her husband Ray's death in 1997).

[30] Obituary, "Donald E. Meredith," *Palladium-Item*, Jan. 22, 2001; Obituary, "Paul M. 'Moon' Mullin," *Palladium-Item*, May 20, 2012; Obituary, "Robert L. Reinke," *Palladium-Item*, Jan. 30, 2021.

[31] Obituary, "Floyd J. Dickman," *Palladium-Item*, Oct. 1, 2006.

[32] Obituary, "Kathleen D. Rogers," *Palladium-Item*, Feb. 21, 2016.

[33] Obituary, "Hilda Luerman Dickman Herold," *Palladium-Item*, Dec. 22, 2020; Obituary, "Mary E. Maurer," *Palladium-Item*, Apr. 3, 2010.

[34] Jan Clark, "Former Mayor Offers Advice to Prep Athletes," Feb. 24, 2002.

[35] Eleanor Farjeon, "Morning Has Broken," in *The Songbook of the Salvation Army* (1986), #35.

INDEX

Perfect Circle Co., 40, 266
Pike, Byron, 114
Plank, Kevin, 222
Powell, Colin, 223
PRC Recording Co., 170, 171,
    193, 207
Puckett, James, 136
Quayle, Dan, 172, 207
Quinn, William Paul, 24
Reagan, Ronald, 182, 186
Reinke, Robert, 124, 132, 133,
    134, 247
Riddell, John, 222
Roberts, Charles, 135
Rogers, Kathleen
    née Dickman, 2, 10, 82, 247,
    248, 249
Rohe, Don, 76
Roosevelt, Franklin, 25
Roosevelt, Theodore, xi, 26, 104
Root, E. Merrill, 49
Ryan, Leo, 176
Ryder, Tim, 135
Sandala, Susann
    née Dickman, 2, 14, 61
Seegers, Heinrich and Mary
    Elizabeth, 34
Sharp, Philip, 129, 130, 159,
    179, 185, 186, 188, 189, 191,
    192, 193
Siebert, Mary
    née Kline, 259
Siebert, Richard, 259
Sinatra, Frank, 89
Smith, John, 19, 20, 27
Smith, Mary Louise, 130, 132
Spalding, A.G., 222
Specuzza, Anthony, 76
Starr Piano Company, 22, 29,
    37

Stephens, Carolyn
    née Dickman, 93, 100, 227
Stephens, James, 104
Stephenson, D.C., 28
Stone, Jim, 69
Surface, Gerald, 142, 194, 195,
    204, 205, 210, 211
Taft, William Howard, 25
Tebbe Family, 2
Thornburg, Philip, 77
Trimble, Jo Ellen, 132, 139,
    140, 162, 209
Trueblood, D. Elton, 47, 48, 49,
    59, 130, 159
Truman, Harry, 25
Van Dyke, George, 55
Van Sickle, Wayne, 111
VanNatta, Ralph, 187, 188,
    191, 193
Vivian, Arthur, 148
Volcker, Paul, 169
Waller, Fats, 29
Wallin, Franklin, 174
Waltermann, Frank, 204, 206–
    12, 243
Waltermann, Joseph, 204
Waltz, Ralph, 112, 113, 271
Wambo, Herman, 114
Wayne Works, 22, 27
Webster Pirates, 15, 16, 17, 236
Weigel, Dana, 136
Welk, Lawrence, 29
Welsh, Matthew, 112
Williams, Marion, 179
Willis, Ralph, 135
Wilson, Woodrow, 25
Wittman, Joann
    née Dickman, 2, 14
Zaleski, Ray, 112, 124, 175